It is important for this book to reach the widest possible audience. People need to know Randy's story because it will save lives. However, this is not a book for the squeamish or faint-hearted. It contains scenes and events that are raw beyond civilized imagination.

This story has great importance on two levels. Even a cursory reading will reveal a heartfelt first-person's account of the horrors caused by drinking and driving. That, in itself, is enough to make any thoughtful reader take stock of his or her own attitudes and actions, and do whatever is necessary to avoid the kinds of life-destroying behavior described in this story.

More fundamentally, this book reminds us that there are very real and powerful forces seeking to take each of us down. Although these forces may have different forms for different people, humans are equally defenseless against all of them unless God intervenes. That divine intervention is the pivotal happening in Randy Wiens' life, and it is the central theme of his book, spelled out through all the ups and downs of his relationships, his various careers, and his determined search for inner peace.

There are heartbreaking events and relationships, and people who are simply evil through and through. It has been necessary to describe all these unsparingly so that we can better appreciate this true story's miraculous outcome. Readers who persevere to the end will be rewarded as they see how God has enabled Randy Wiens to truly become His work in progress.

Richard Kirkman
Retired Teacher, Professional Artist

NOW I KNOW WHO I AM

A WORK IN PROGRESS

RANDY WIENS

"... From the first sentence, Randy takes the reader on a roller coaster ride of gripping revelations that keep the reader spellbound until the last word is read ... a gut-wrenching story that amazingly is true ..."
—Beth Allen, M.A. CCC-sp
Speech/Language Pathologist

A WORK IN PROGRESS

WINEPRESS **WP** PUBLISHING

Packaged by WinePress Publishing, PO Box 428, Enumclaw, WA 98022. The views expressed or implied in this work do not necessarily reflect those of WinePress Publishing. The author(s) is ultimately responsible for the design, content and editorial accuracy of this work.

Unless otherwise noted, all Scriptures are taken from the Holy Bible, New International Version, Copyright © 1973, 1978, 1984 by the International Bible Society. Used by permission of Zondervan Publishing House. The "niv" and "New International Version" trademarks are registered in the United States Patent and Trademark Office by International Bible Society.

Scripture references marked kjv are taken from the King James Version of the Bible.

Scripture references marked nasb are taken from the New American Standard Bible, © 1960, 1963, 1968, 1971, 1972, 1973, 1975, 1977 by The Lockman Foundation. Used by permission.

ISBN 1-57921-734-6
Library of Congress Catalog Card Number: 2003116119

Dedication

To Sheryl, my wife for twenty-two years. Thank you for your courage and perseverance. You never failed to model the values and virtues of following the right path. I'm listening now. My hope is to inspire others as you have inspired me.

To our children, Ranger, Kodi, and Logan. Your love and forgiveness have humbled me. I am truly blessed to have you in my life.

To all the members of Sheryl's family. I am so grateful for all of you. Thank you for your mercy, grace, and forgiveness.

Contents

Acknowledgments

I would like to thank the following people for all of your time, hard work, graciousness, patience, kindness, help, and support in my life. I am eternally grateful to all of you. I am also thankful to all of you who helped to make this project a reality.

I believe it takes a village of people to raise, and to help, the individual person survive physically and emotionally in his or her life. The following list of people is a large part of my village:

Sheryl, Ranger, Kodi, Logan
Connie
Darryl
Mom
Dad
Hank and Babe
Larry, Ron, and Marg
Craig and Monica
Ken and Vivian
Butch
Brenda
Don and Kenra
Karyn, Matt, and Tana
Tom and Cindy
Steve
Carol
Philip and Beth
Lloyd
Richard
Dr. Bill
Pastor Dan
Athena Dean and all the people at Winepress Publishing

I want to fit everyone above at the top of my village list, but there is not enough room.

I also want to say that there are many other people who have inspired, helped and supported me in my life. To all of you, thank you from the bottom of my heart.

Important Notes

This is a true story. However, it is written from my perspective only. The details and experiences I share may not coincide with some of the readers' memory or point of view regarding the same experiences.

I wrote this book in order to figure out who I was as a person. It was not written to hurt anyone. Now that it is finished, I believe my story can help others. I pray others can learn from my mistakes.

Finally, some of the names in the book have been changed out of respect for the people involved and to protect their privacy.

Letter to My Father

Dad,

I cherish the relationship we have today. When we talk or visit, my eyes well up in respect and love for you. Seeing and talking to you triggers overwhelming emotions of how hard you have worked in your life and how passionate you have always been to do your best.

Now, I understand your reasons for cutting me loose on life as a young boy. Your culture embodied your male children as stoic symbols and representations of your family name. Because of that deeply entrenched philosophy, you raised me tough and strong and independent just like you were raised. In turn, you demanded more from me than the average dad.

For many years, I was confused and angry regarding your fathering methods, but now I understand what your intentions really were at the time. You meant to mold me into a strong young Wiens who was capable of making it in the real world no matter how difficult it was. You need to know now that you succeeded in your mission.

Dad, I pray for your good health every day. I pray we will have many more years of love and friendship.

May God bless you Dad. I love you.

Your son, Randy

Letter to My Mother

Mom,

When Connie and Darryl notified me of your death, I didn't cry. I waited until I hung up the phone, drove to a secluded hilltop, and walked to a monstrous lonely pine tree and sat at its base. There, I could sense your presence. I could let the floodgates open.

My dearest Mom, we had come far over the last several years. We were both lost for so long, but God's great mercy and grace allowed us to find ourselves. He taught us about forgiveness, and because of that gift, we were spared a life of isolation and emotional torment. Together, we learned that family and others come first.

I've learned so much from you Mom. And I miss everything about you. I crave your hugs and kisses and endless words of encouragement and support. I miss your moose steak, mashed potatoes, and homemade bread. When I close my eyes, I imagine I'm sitting at your kitchen table. I'm completely at peace; I imagine it's the next thing to heaven. Even though those aspects were missing in my earlier life, you made up for all of it a hundredfold. That's why God took you. You were ready to be with Him.

Mom, I love you.

Your son, Randy

CHAPTER 1

The Accident

I killed my wife. I didn't mean to do it. But I killed her just the same. I could soften the reality by saying I was only just responsible for her death, or that I only just caused her death. I could even believe my loved ones and friends when they say it was all just a terrible accident. But those wouldn't be the facts. I know I killed Sheryl, my loyal, and faithful, and loving wife of twenty-two years. And I'll have to live with that fact until I die.

It all began forty-five minutes after we packed and left the motel. I leaned forward a little to place my empty Bud Light bottle in the cup holder just above the CD player on the dashboard. As I leaned back in my driver's seat, Sheryl disconnected her seatbelt and leaned over the console between the bucket seats. She kissed me tenderly on the cheek. As she sat back down, she looked at me intently as if she was deep in thought. I didn't want to make eye contact with Sheryl under the extreme emotional circumstances, but I could feel her penetrating stare. The tension hung in the air so thickly; it was like molasses in winter.

"I finally understand, honey!" Sheryl blurted, with her voice cracking slightly.

"Whaddaya mean?" I responded quietly and glanced towards her, but I still avoided her eyes. I was too emotional to look at her.

"I finally understand. It's over like you said," she said sadly.

Before I could reply again, we had entered the second half of an upside down S-turn. Simultaneously, my mind seemed to halt abruptly in mid-thought as my eyes became tunnel-focused on the two high-beam headlights crossing the centerline towards us. Without thinking, I swerved hard to the right to avoid a head-on collision.

The fifty-five miles per hour country road we had been traveling on was paved as flat as a squished Canadian penny on a remote wilderness railroad track. The road poured into the first half of the S and then banked about ten degrees to the right. It tilted steeper to the left on the latter half. The steepness of the bank, and a deep gully running parallel to the road, created a cliff-like, forty-foot drop immediately off the right shoulder in the direction I swerved. But somehow, I corrected appropriately before our vehicle became airborne or slid or rolled down the steep embankment. I was able to control our GMC Z71 4x4 enough to ride the three-foot wide dirt shoulder about ninety-two feet. Unfortunately though, I made a bad mistake. When I tried to pull the truck back onto the road, I turned the steering wheel too sharply to handle the three-inch lip of pavement. The truck spun out of control counter-clockwise. It continued its slide about a half turn. Then, it slid sideways across both paved lanes, still at about fifty miles per hour. The 4x4 slid off the opposite side of the highway's shoulder into and across a shallow eight-foot wide ditch. As the truck's right tires caught the backside of the ditch, the momentum hurled the truck instantaneously into a violent series of rolls.

I don't know exactly when, or on which one of the truck's revolutions Sheryl was ejected, because I either lost consciousness or blacked out in the turbulent rush and confusion of the accident. My theory is that when the truck flipped onto its right side the first time, the passenger window disintegrated on its initial impact with the rocky ground. As the truck continued its clockwise roll, the powerfully propelled truck's spin caused a vicious whipping action like a tornado of steel annihilating everything in its path. Without realizing it, I probably grasped the steering wheel tightly out of sheer instinct or unconscious reaction. But, Sheryl had nothing to hold her from catapulting out of the broken window. She didn't have a seatbelt on in a vehicle for the first time in all of the twenty-two years I had known her. I had never worn one.

The airtime Sheryl's body encountered must have been several seconds, because the cops said later in their report that the truck rolled at least three or four times. Unfortunately, the total distance the truck traveled in all of its rolls was exactly equal to the distance her body flew and landed brutally onto the hard ground. When the truck finally came to rest on its roof, Sheryl was completely under the truck's massive weight. At that precise instant, my wife began the slow, barbaric, and gruesome process of being crushed to death.

At the same time Sheryl was thrown helplessly into flight, I must have intuitively gripped the steering wheel with unusual strength conjured up by an adrenaline rush. That was the only explanation I could think of as to why I wasn't thrown out too. Even so, the force of the truck's roll must have ripped the steering wheel from my hands at some point. It proceeded to toss me about the cab somewhat mercifully until the truck finally stopped rolling and came to rest in an inverted position. When I came to my senses and realized what had just actually happened, I was sitting upright on the ceiling below Sheryl's inverted seat; for all intensive purposes, unscathed. I instinctively jerked my head to the right searching for her. But all I saw was a black nothing. Instantly, a complete horror engulfed my cognitive processes. I desperately groped the upside-down back seat area and the rest of the cab in vain. Where was she, I thought? Was she hurt? Dead? Was she lying mangled somewhere out there in the eerie darkness surrounding me?

Blaming myself, a ghostly feeling engulfed me. I felt myself shudder involuntarily with a new and ferocious fear. I felt like a gut-shot polar bear trying desperately to protect her vulnerable cub. As I glanced to my left to begin my search for Sheryl, I noticed her door was wide open in my capsized world. It was beckoning me like a cool drink on a hot day. The spine-tingling ambience was grossly intensified when I stood up straight into a complete void of darkness facing away from Sheryl's side of the truck. The lights in my universe seemed like they had mysteriously turned off forever.

Suddenly, it seemed like my mind and body were switched on from the off position like the power lever being thrown to illuminate Candlestick Park for a Giants game. All my senses kicked into overdrive. And because of that new and keen awareness, I heard my truck still idling almost noiselessly even though it had just gone through the ultimate torture test. I seemed to be thinking clearly at that point. Or maybe it was instinct taking over. But whatever was driving my actions initiated my headlong dive into the truck. First, I slammed the automatic gearshift into park. Then, I ripped the keys out of the steering console to minimize the fire danger. Gas fumes were burning in my nose, and that wasn't good. Plus, I still didn't know where Sheryl was or what happened to her in the pandemonium. I was still a little dazed and confused. However, I calculate that only a few seconds actually elapsed from the time I realized she wasn't in the truck, I tore the keys from the ignition, and I jumped back into the dark.

"Sheryl! Sheryl! Where are you!?" I screamed at the top of my lungs. Then, there was nothing. No response! No noise from anywhere. "Sheryl . . . Sheryl!" I screamed again.

The agonizing wait seemed like an eternity. I cringed at the noiseless night. An utter sense of despair engulfed my body and mind as I realized I was standing in thick, knee-high weeds damp from the wintry early morning dew. Horrified, I stood, abandoned from the world and all its pleasures and conveniences. All I could do was beg through the complete void of darkness for my wife to somehow signal me, or call out to me that she was okay.

Suddenly, out of the night's relentless scorn, I heard it!

"I'm under here." Sheryl's voice, although frail and muffled, was unmistakable as it penetrated the darkness.

Instantly, Sheryl's voice seemed to re-ignite my senses. I had a burst of hope surge through me like a tidal wave. My mind raced in elation as I desperately tried to distinguish exactly where it was coming from. But, that seemed impossible. The winter cloud cover had completely blackened the sky. No light illuminated anything—anywhere. It seemed that when I turned the truck off, I obliterated every light in the universe at the same time. Like an inexperienced blind man without his cane or Seeing Eye dog in the middle of a four-lane freeway, I wheeled around toward the truck and Sheryl's glorious sound. She was beckoning me from below me somewhere!

I quickly dropped to all fours. The wet weeds brushed my face as I became dog-like. I groped frantically in my four-legged frenzy toward Sheryl's voice. The cement-like rock and clay mixture beneath the weeds were hard and malicious in their attack on my knees and hands. But the pain was reticent, as my brain didn't recognize anything but its determination to get to Sheryl as fast as I could.

"I'm under here," she said again in a garbled voice that seemed to echo eerily through the darkness from a distance. Immediately, a sense of relief engulfed me as I groped the ground in the blackness searching for Sheryl's precise location. She was talking! "She must be okay!" I thought.

"Sheryl, keep talking. I can't see you!" I yelled.

"I'm under the truck," she responded. But this time her voice sounded more impaired for some reason.

I crawled as fast as I could toward Sheryl's voice and viciously banged my head on the elevated truck bed in my haste. I felt a sharp pain briefly on my upper forehead, but I ignored it. I ducked under the bed. I continued to grope the ground in my desperation to feel my wife's flesh on my fingertips. Although I eagerly anticipated finding her right away at that point, a few seconds later, the reality monster slashed at my brain like a twelve-foot buzz saw. When I submerged beneath the truck, I fumbled around for a landmark of some kind. Just then, I located the back of the cab and the edge of the rear window. I followed them into the blackness. Exactly at the middle of our extended cab and sliding back window, I heard Sheryl's groaning by my left hand.

"Oh, no!" I blurted softly to myself. The truck was completely on top of Sheryl! She was buried under the roof with the entire upended truck over and around her body like a tomb of steel and cloth and plastic.

"Sheryl. I found you. Are you okay?" I said somehow with a sudden surprised calmness this time. It seemed that, although my mind was flooded with uncontrollable fear and frustration, I was able to speak to Sheryl without panicking.

"Sheryl! Don't try to talk. Save your strength. I'm gonna dig you out!"

"Get me outta here. I don't wanna die here!" she spat at me sternly through the darkness in her tough athletic coach's voice. I could tell right away that she was mad at me. I had heard that disgruntled tone many times before. But this time I thought her anger was a godsend. I knew that when she became angry and indignant for any reason, her fire usually aided her greatly in accomplishing whatever she endeavored to do. In my mind at the time, this included surviving the slow, crushing, life-and-death struggle wracking her body and mind under the truck.

In my entire life, I had never met a woman tougher than Sheryl. She had exhibited her extraordinary mental and physical toughness countless times over the years in our household and at all of the basketball, soccer, water polo, and softball games I watched her play throughout our married life. However, this time her austere tone signaled she was in great peril.

"Hold on. I'm at your head. I'll get you out. You need to save your breath!" I commanded her firmly.

I fully understood Sheryl's dire predicament. The new strength in her voice puzzled me somewhat though, because her previous responses had all been labored as if her breathing was handicapped. As I began to scratch and claw the rock and clay with my hands like a moose mad from thirst, I thought maybe Sheryl's position wasn't as bad as I first assumed. Maybe by some sort of miracle, the truck's weight wasn't slowly crushing her the way I imagined it. After all, I couldn't see my hand in front of my face. At best, I knew I was only guessing. So I just made the ground fly as fast as my finger-flesh and nails could manage. But as the rocks, dirt, and weeds flew behind me, it only took a short time to realize my bare hands would never be able to free Sheryl. My soft, sit-be-hind-a-teacher's-desk hands were scoured raw very rapidly. My nails began to bleed. They became supersensitive in their extreme pain, which ultimately hindered my ability to move the dirt and rock from around Sheryl as fast as I knew they needed to be for her to have a chance. At the same time, I could feel warm blood trickle down my forehead over the bridge of my nose and into my eyes from the whack I took from the bed of the truck. But I forgot about the dent in my head in less than a second. My concentration was on exposing Sheryl's head so she could at least breathe. I figured if she could breathe adequately, then she would be okay until help arrived.

Seconds later, I heard the glorious sound of a vehicle's engine approaching from the direction we were traveling to a few minutes earlier.

"Sheryl! Hold on. A car's comin'. I'm gonna flag 'im down for help! Save your strength!" I almost yelled at her as I crawled out from under the truck to run.

By the time our truck had stopped rolling though, it had ended up about eighty feet off the road. When I scrambled from under the truck, I began to run blindly through the darkness toward the sound of the vehicle coming toward us. In my surprise, I noticed I had misjudged the actual distance the truck ended up from the road. My gross miscalculation made the time much longer than I anticipated in reaching the road. Besides that, I couldn't see the thick, knee-high weeds and brush in my path inhibiting my speed. But I was so repulsed for causing the predicament to begin with, I just plowed a trail as fast as my legs would carry me anyway. No matter what happened, I knew it was do or die. I felt I had to get to that car before it passed us by. Sheryl's life depended on it. I thought it was the only chance to reach help at that time of night, and to get my wife out alive!

When I broke through the last of the weeds and reached the shoulder of the road, the car was on me like a steel blanket. It flew by so close that I could have kicked its rear right tire. Horrified and mad at myself at the same time, I realized I was too late. I flailed at the air madly like a doped-up druggie on a hallucinogen trying to flag him down. But no dice! The car kept going. It even accelerated a little as it exited the S-turn into the long straight stretch moving away from us. Mortified by the injustice, I turned my anger on the driver for not stopping; I felt I probably could have beaten him to death in my rage if I ever had the chance.

However, I knew my reaction was totally deranged. My thoughts were not rational. So, I began theorizing that maybe the driver didn't see me in time because of the dungeon-like blackness. Or maybe the driver was a woman and she did see me, but she thought I was some lunatic or psycho with other criminal intentions. Or maybe it was simply my fault for not being fast enough to get to the road in time. Whatever the reason was, I knew I was absolutely alone in my desperation to save Sheryl.

Somehow, I knew I had to get her out of there. All I could think about was Sheryl under the truck slowly being crushed to death. Morbid thoughts began to creep into my brain, and a renewed sense of horror and disgust with myself blasted my psyche as I sprinted back to her. I was in a state of helplessness I couldn't remember ever experiencing before that moment in my entire life. I condemned myself completely for everything. At the same time, I imagined that maybe Sheryl was mangled or crippled under the unforgiving hulk of metal on top of her body. And because of the possible shock of the accident and her current circumstances, she couldn't physically feel her serious injuries. I wondered if any help would come in time. I wondered if the driver in the car that passed me was too scared to stop at 1 A.M. At the same time, I wondered if she might have called 911 on a cell phone she had with her anyway. I could only hope.

Most of all, I didn't know what I was going to do. Perplexed beyond my wildest imagination, my body and mind seemed to spin in a wild flurry of thoughts. I was alone. I was helpless. I had no control over my wife living or dying.

The distance back to Sheryl seemed shorter this time. My eyes were beginning to focus in spite of nature's seemingly dark plot against me. I could now see the topsy-turvy truck faintly silhouetted against the terrain in the background. So as I approached the truck, I was able to perceive a much clearer picture of the situation. The upended rear of the truck faced directly towards the road. I could see the bed of the truck was elevated off the ground a few feet and above the weeds about a foot. And when I pulled up from my weed-hobbled sprint, I knew exactly where Sheryl was this time.

When I plunged headlong under the truck directly to the sliding window area, I immediately resumed my frantic digging around Sheryl's head area. My thoughts re-focused on her immediate care, and I felt that exposing her head was the most practical course of action at that point.

"Sheryl! How are you? Can you hear me?" I tried to speak calmly, as I continued to rip the rocks and dirt from their cement-like home. I was a little winded in my haste from the road, and somehow, Sheryl perceived the distress in my voice and that no help was imminent.

"Can you lift it off?" she said in a wraithlike monotone again.

Even as she said the words, I knew lifting the truck off her was ludicrous. However, without hesitation, I jumped out from under the truck again. I knew the futility in digging Sheryl out too. It was almost to the point where I wanted to just start running as fast as I could to Snelling, a little country town about two miles away where I could phone for help myself. But I came to my senses just as quickly. There was no way I could leave my wife.

As I stood up, I wished that maybe some miracle would allow me to heft the massive weight through a sudden adrenaline surge enabling me superhuman strength. Strangely, I remembered a story I had heard years ago about a farmer lifting a full wagonload of one hundred pound spud sacks off a little girl trapped under it. The girl was the farmer's child. She had fallen off the wagon when a rattlesnake spooked the team of horses pulling it. The two geldings bolted into a shallow ravine. Out of control, two of the wagon's wheels shattered in a thundering crash. One of the horses had busted a leg, and the girl was trapped beneath the wagon from her mid-torso down. As one might hope though, the story ended happily. The farmer simply hastened up to the side of the tipped wagon. He took a mighty hold with his massive hands and arms. And with his legs squatted perfectly for a maximum power lift, he clean and jerked the wagon off his child in a single attempt. The girl was safe and uninjured.

Unfortunately though, I didn't have the luxury of living in the fantasyland like the story depicted. In my world at that precise moment, my wife was at death's door. And I was like a minuscule mouse trying to compete with a rhino in a head-butting contest. When I tried to lift the truck off her, I couldn't even budge the foreboding weight, let alone lift it. It simply wasn't going to happen. And I was powerless to do anything about it. I was totally out of control of the situation, and no matter what I did or didn't do, that fact wasn't going to change.

However, at that instant, I thought that maybe a miracle might happen after all. I heard another car coming, and this time, I had a head start. I was already standing up when I heard the vehicle's engine coming toward me. So I saved several seconds by not having to crawl out from under the truck and get up before I started running. I could also see quite clearly by then, so I made a bee-line to a point on the shoulder of the road ahead of the car coming enough to ensure the driver would see me this time. Just to make sure the driver saw me, when I got to the road ahead of the car like I planned, I stepped out onto the road several feet so the car would have to see me and stop. Or, he would have had to swerve or move to his left to avoid hitting me.

When the car swerved around me and then drove on without stopping, I was stupefied. I was unable to comprehend how not one person, but two different people, could bypass someone in obvious distress in the middle of the night without helping him. In horror and thoroughly distraught emotionally, I sprinted back to Sheryl once again. I wondered if my hideous nightmare would ever end. All I could do was continue to dig and try to expose her head so she could breathe easier.

"Sheryl! Hold on. Help is on the way!" I managed to spit out in my angst, as I reached Sheryl again, more winded this time.

But this time she only groaned. And once again, my heart sunk into the abyss. I knew she was weakening rapidly. She was battling like a valiant warrior, but she was losing her fight to the death. The only thing I could do was to keep digging.

Finally, I reached Sheryl's head. But I couldn't see her face. I felt her hair and the top of her head lightly. I searched for her mouth and nose. Instinctively, I knew I had to make it easier for her to breathe. Her labored responses had told me so. But unluckily, I couldn't find her face. It was mashed up against the bottom of the truck's roof. Her breathing was extremely hindered by that time too. It only came in sporadic grunts. Consequently, I didn't try to talk to her anymore, because I knew every breath of oxygen might be the one she needed to stay alive. All I could do was dig! My mind screamed Sheryl's agony.! Somehow, I had to help her!

Frantically, I concentrated all my efforts on the area under Sheryl's head. I tore at the clayed and rocky ground. I picked at the rocks hindering my progress. I threw the ones that came loose out of the way. Finally, I began to make some meaningful progress. I managed to expand the concave under Sheryl's head, and when I did, I cupped her head with one hand while I continued to dig with the other to prevent her neck from moving too abruptly. It wasn't long before I was able to lower her head a little so she could breathe more easily. But I never stopped digging for an instant. When one set of fingers got too sensitive, I traded hands. I would cup Sheryl's head with the sore hand and dig with the other.

Sometimes during the transition, the thought of holding my dying wife's head in my hand as her body was being slowly crushed to death overwhelmed me. I tried to be tough, but to no avail. I tried to be strong, but a fresh panic gripped my soul with renewed vigor every time I realized that I had violated my wife with extreme prejudice. It was unintentional, but my drinking, my stupidity, and my disrespect for the law had produced the same despicable result.

Unexpectedly, it came screaming out of the night. It pierced my ears and other senses. The unmistakable whine of the first emergency vehicle's siren was coming. Closer and closer it came as each valuable second ticked off Sheryl's death clock. It came from a distance and direction I couldn't identify yet. But it was coming. Apparently, one of the vehicles that drove by me on the highway must have had a cellular phone after all and reported the accident.

"Sheryl. They're comin'. Hold on. You'll be outta there in a minute," I whispered to Sheryl, as I laid her head gently into the hole and dove out from under the truck again.

Astounded once again by Sheryl's awesome toughness, I heard a strong and convincing groan that she was still with me. I almost jumped for joy as I made my third mad dash to the highway to signal the fast approaching fire truck. When it pulled up beside me on the shoulder, I yelled at the lone fireman through the open passenger window. I ordered him to radio for an ambulance and a tow truck, because I was sure that lifting the truck vertically was the only common sense way to prevent more damage on Sheryl's already-beaten body. He made the call quickly as instructed. Then he hustled after me back to my wife. On the way, I told him Sheryl had been under the weight of the truck for a long time and her breathing was becoming hard and overwrought. The instant he shined his huge flashlight onto the ground and followed the path to Sheryl's head where I told him to, he immediately made another call on his portable radio for a helicopter to come in.

It seemed like only a minute had passed before a convoy of law enforcement officers and emergency personnel arrived on the accident scene in a roar of decelerating engines. Some screeched to a halt on the pavement, and others braked hard onto the shoulder and threw up fog-like dust storms silhouetted in the fire truck's bright spotlights. Within seconds, cops and ambulance technicians ran around in every direction like ants repairing a colony hill.

Several of them ran directly toward the fireman, the truck, and me illuminated brightly in the myriad of emergency spotlights that had suddenly turned the darkness into light. One fireman carried a Jaws of Life contraption directly to the rear corner of the cab. Another carried an armload of two-by-sixes about three feet long as supporters for the jaws. When he dropped them beside where I was standing, I dropped to my knees before the boards could stop bouncing against each other. Furiously, I gathered three of them and readied them for the Jaws of Life fireman. I knew what to do, and I was so overwhelmed with worry about getting Sheryl out of danger, I felt I had to help somehow. I had been totally helpless until then. I had to take advantage of the opportunity.

At that instant, I felt a peculiarly aggressive hand on my right shoulder. Immediately, I was totally perturbed because I couldn't figure out what was so important that someone had to slow me down. I was trying to do my part like everyone else to get Sheryl out from under the truck. The intruder was slowing my efforts to do just that.

I wasn't surprised though when it turned out to be a California Highway Patrol officer. And when I corkscrewed toward him abruptly, he jabbed a quick step backwards. Obviously, he retreated into a defensive mode. He didn't know who I was, what my state of mind was, or if I was violent or dangerous or not. It also probably startled him a little when my six foot, four inch, two-hundred-twenty-pound frame towered over him when I stood up.

Under the tense circumstances, he didn't really know for sure what my next actions would be. So he just started talking to me calmly. Meanwhile, he stopped and stood his ground awaiting my next move.

"Sir. Please step over here out of the way so the emergency people can do their jobs," the cop requested sternly but politely.

His much larger partner moved from behind him to his side and directly in front of me as I stood up. I glanced back at my job for a second, but I could plainly see that the Jaws of Life firemen knew what they were doing too. However, instead of turning back to the cops, I plunged under the truck again to the shoulder of an emergency medical woman trying to check Sheryl's pulse from her left carotid artery.

"How is she?" I blurted to the woman as I hit the ground.

"Please go with the officers for now, sir. We're doing all we can for your wife," the lady said matter-of-factly.

Just then, the CHP officer instructed me to step to the side of my truck out of the way again. This time I obliged. When I stood up, I took a few steps away from the truck with my back to Sheryl and all the commotion encompassing the entire truck area. The larger cop told me to follow them over to a small clearing about twenty-five feet perpendicular to the truck and a little to the rear of Sheryl's open door. They wanted to ask me some questions regarding the accident. When we reached a rocky but flat area clear of weeds, they both tried to position their bodies so I would face them away from the rescue to take my attention off Sheryl. I'm sure they would've led me completely away from everything if the spotlights around the immediate area reached that far. However, the cops couldn't control the lighting situation or the weeds. So they began their interrogation anyway.

"Are you hurt?" the smaller cop said concernedly as he took the lead in the questioning. As a matter of fact, both cops were empathetic, sincere, and totally respectful in everything they asked and said to me the whole time during the conversation. I supposed the partners had experienced many accident scenes in their training and experience like I did when I was a police officer eighteen years earlier, especially when there was someone seriously hurt or killed in a melee like this one turned out to be. Besides that, I knew most cops were human beings who owned a conscience too. A few were selfish and totally uncaring. But these cops were two of the good guys. Of course, this accident scene reeked of potential tragedy like countless others they had undoubtedly experienced. But they did their job anyway, and they were respectful doing it.

"No. I don't think so," I said anxiously.

I glanced back at Sheryl at the same time to try to deduce why it seemed to be taking so long to get her out of there. I noticed just then that a tow truck had backed up to the inverted rear of my truck, and when the driver set the truck's air brakes with a powerful burst blasting above the commotion all around us all, it caught my attention.

"Your head is bleeding. And your hands look like they're pretty messed up. Do you need medical attention?" the cop said calmly, as I turned back towards him. But I only turned about halfway this time so I could keep an eye on the rescuers' progress and still try to be respectful and cooperative regarding his inquiries.

"No! I'm fine," I said apprehensively, wishing they would let me get back closer to Sheryl. I didn't want to be rude, but I felt they could ask their questions after she was safe.

"What happened?" the cop said directly, with his partner taking a step closer to me from his position behind. It seemed both officers were studying my face and body language rather intently. Evidently, they were forming the basis for their report. I figured the accident scene was their investigative responsibility. Also quite possibly, they knew they might have to testify in court if litigation ensued for some reason.

Basically, I realized they were just doing their jobs. And part of that job was to isolate and separate the people involved in the accident. I knew from my police experience that was mandatory department procedure. It was necessary to minimize further perturbation regarding the flying emotions that seem to naturally accompany accident scenes, especially with injuries or death at the scene. That included the cops', the rescue team's, and the people's emotions involved in the accident. Because I understood the officers' motives, I answered their questions quickly so I could get back to Sheryl.

"My wife and I were coming back from Sonora, and a car came across the centerline towards us right on that corner," I said hurriedly, pointing behind the officers at the S turn. "I had to swerve hard to avoid a head-on crash. When I tried to get control, my front tire caught the shoulder lip. We slid and rolled and ended up here."

"Are you sure it was a car?" the officer inquired.

"Yes. I'm positive," I responded immediately.

"Can you describe what the car looked like?"

"No. I was too busy trying to miss him," I said a little sarcastically this time. I felt he should have already figured that out. But then I realized he was probably trying to cover all the bases and keep me preoccupied at the same time.

"I noticed a hole under your truck. How long you been diggin'?" the cop continued.

"I don't know. It was close to 1 A.M. when I looked a few minutes before the accident. What time is it now?" I asked the cop inquisitively. I was in a mental fog, and I tried to piece the puzzle together in my mind somehow. I needed to know how long Sheryl was under the truck.

"It's one fifty-five," he said, looking at his wristwatch illuminated clearly by his partner's powerful flashlight. I stared at the watch for a few seconds trying to comprehend the time. It seemed to me that it had been hours since I first saw those headlights coming at us on the corner causing me to swerve.

"Who was drivin'?" the cop asked in his usual calm tone.

"I was," I retorted instantly, knowing exactly where the cop was going with his questions.

"Have you been drinking?" he asked, with a little more enthusiasm in his voice this time. He also stared directly into my eyes. It was obvious he was trying to decipher whether I would try to lie to him to escape responsibility like many drunk drivers tried to do.

"Yes," I responded without hesitation. I stared right back at his eyeballs so there was no doubt about my intentions. I had known from the time I crawled out of the rolled truck after I couldn't find Sheryl that I was going to jail sometime that night. But until that precise moment, I really had not dwelled on the prospect. My concern had been to save my wife.

However, right then, I knew I was in for it good. Whether the cops could smell the alcohol on my breath or not made no difference. It was mandatory law enforcement policy to obtain a blood test for alcohol content from the driver of any vehicle involved in an accident, especially when there was an injury or death involved. And even before the blood test, I knew these cops would ask me more questions about my drinking and driving and instruct me to perform roadside sobriety tests. Without a doubt, they would end up handcuffing me too. When they had safely hooked me up, they would put me in the back seat of their patrol car. After more questions to clarify details for their report, they would take me to the Merced County jail managed by the Merced County Sheriff's Office, the same police agency I had worked for during the first few years I was married to Sheryl.

"How much have you had to drink?" the cop said, continuing his query in a business-as-usual type manner.

"I don't know. I didn't count 'em," I said honestly.

"Were you drinking in the vehicle?" the other officer said this time.

The question caught me a little off guard though, only because it was the first time the larger cop had spoken to me. As he said it, the first cop admonished the larger officer with a reprimanding but brief glance. Apparently, the first cop had his own program for questioning me, and he didn't want any intrusion by his partner.

"Yes. I was drinking. I was drinking in my truck. And I was driving," I said peacefully, but sternly, as both cops got the message immediately that I was being totally honest under the circumstances, and I just wanted Sheryl taken care of.

Right then, I glanced back toward the open passenger door, and pointed toward the remainder of a broken six-pack of Bud Light beer bottles I noticed lying on some flattened weeds. I told the cops briefly that they were mine. At the same instant, I reached into my right pants pocket, grabbed a hold of my keys, and held them out to the first cop politely. I guessed I had put them in my pocket without thinking when I ripped them out of the ignition. Just then, as the first cop accepted my offer of the keys, I decided I was tired of the grilling.

"Now that we all know I'm going to jail, let's take care of my wife," I said a little more aggressively this time.

Simultaneously, as I was finishing the sentence, I turned and walked quickly back to the rescue efforts. Obviously, both cops had ascertained all the information they needed for the time being. Otherwise they would have tackled me, locked me up right there, and chucked me in the back seat of their patrol car. It was also apparent that they had some empathy. They seemed to respect my forthrightness in answering their volatile questions, and my honesty earned me the right to get back to Sheryl. Further, because I took responsibility without confrontation, maybe they felt I showed some integrity. Consequently, contrary to their training to keep the scene and its perpetrators under close control, they let me go back by Sheryl. Like me, they awaited my wife's disentombing.

I forgot about the cops altogether as soon as I turned and observed the hydraulic winch on the back of the tow truck lifting my truck bed straight up in the air a few feet. As the tow truck driver maneuvered the hydraulic winch lever masterfully, there were three EMT personnel still hunkered under my truck's bed. They were ready to attend to Sheryl's medical needs as soon as there was enough room under the truck and it was safe. They also knew, like I did, that a human body being compressed under a massive weight for any length of time was imminently perilous, let alone being gradually squashed like a bug for an hour straight.

In other words, they knew that most of Sheryl's body parts and inner organs had been violently compacted from the truck's initial blow. Thus, they hovered, ready to dive under the truck to maximize her waning chances of survival. The horrible weight slowly crushing her was like a monster seeking to destroy her body like Grendal's mother tried to vanquish Beowulf. The weight was tenacious and unforgiving, and in its relentlessness, it slowly tried its best to snuff out Sheryl's last breath and our children's mother. It slowly and methodically sucked Sheryl's fight and life from her. And as the time under the weight increased, her life-giving blood was slowly squished out of her organs to the point of their utter collapse and failure.

Slowly, but finally, the tow-truck's hydraulic apparatus lifted the hideous weight off Sheryl's body. Tormented, I could only stand there, helpless and scared to death. I stared apprehensively at Sheryl's body as it slowly became exposed on her bed of clay and rock. She was lying motionless, although from her position, I still couldn't see her face clearly. The top half of her body was rotated a little onto her left side. Luckily, the hole I dug enabled her face to turn sideways enough so the inverted roof of the truck didn't smash her face and cut off her breathing entirely. As more of the truck was removed, it appeared her legs were together and slightly bent. And both of her arms were positioned like they had been carrying something. In my desperation, I was optimistic the weight on Sheryl might have been cushioned somewhat by the position of her arms and body. In so doing, it shielded the initial blow and alleviated some of the horrible load on her. To me, that was a possible explanation why her breathing started off strong then got weaker as the weight became too mighty. I thought maybe that was the miracle I had wished for earlier, because just then, I heard a deep throaty groan escape Sheryl's lips. "Thank you Lord", I thought. She was going to be okay after all! Sheryl was still alive!

My mind reeled in trepidation as the medical crew went to work. They secured Sheryl's neck, felt for another pulse, and checked her blood pressure. Two firemen had a stretcher board ready for transporting her to the ambulance. It was backed up through the weeds within about 15 feet of the tow truck. Seconds later, the two firemen and two of the medical people hoisted Sheryl carefully onto the flat board. They strapped her down with Velcro straps, and gingerly, they stepped in unison out from under the overhanging truck and tow truck.

I quickly moved closer to Sheryl, so I could see her face clearly for the first time since we were in the truck together before the accident. She looked like she was sleeping, but her face was all scrunched up like she was having a frightening dream. Her face looked wrought with pain, and her brows were sunk in a deep frown from the gross physical stress she had endured for so long. Amazingly, her outside body parts seemed intact with no protruding bones, and she didn't appear to be mangled or disfigured in any way. It was definitely encouraging to see Sheryl's body intact, and right then and there, I prayed to God to help her be safe and not be seriously hurt. I also prayed to God that, if he was planning to plant anyone that night, I begged him to plant me instead of my wife.

Standing in total despair, I sadly reflected on Sheryl's mind-boggling toughness. She had never screamed her agony even once. She never cried out for God or for mercy. She only endured her torture like a great beast of burden overwhelmed by the payload of a hundred.

As I continued the minute inspection of Sheryl's body, another full rush of anguish engulfed my cognitive senses. Amidst all the action there was dead silence. No one was saying a word. All I could do was to watch helplessly as my wife was hauled off on a stretcher. All I could do was beat myself senseless because of what I caused. It seemed that, only a few minutes earlier, Sheryl and I were driving home. Whatever the outcome, Sheryl was on her way to the helicopter landing a mile down the road, the only appropriate landing area near the accident scene. The cops had told me when she was extricated that she would be flown to the hospital. But for me, I was going to jail.

Chapter 2

Sane or Asylum?

I turned away from the departing ambulance. For a few seconds, I just stood silently looking directly at the two CHP officers. Evidently, my body language indicated aggressiveness to the cops. In other words, I might have second thoughts about being arrested peacefully, because as soon as I swiveled in their direction and looked at them without moving, they separated. They halted about ten feet from each other, both in a subtle defensive stance. It appeared they had formulated a plan in preparation for anything I might do if I did happen to resist. If I ran or became hostile, they were ready. They knew I had been through an incredibly traumatic and emotional experience. Plus, I towered over them both and outweighed them by thirty or forty pounds. It was obvious they didn't want to take anything for granted. Whatever I did or didn't do though, I knew, and they knew, they were taking me to jail.

The two cops didn't perceive or comprehend the gross sickness I felt in my gut as I stood in the darkness in the middle of nowhere with their blinding flashlights in my eyes. When I faced the cops, I wasn't thinking about them at all. It may have seemed I was staring at them, which caused them concern about my change of heart regarding my cooperation during the arrest. But at that second, my mind was screaming in agony from the million daggers stabbing it. I didn't know whether Sheryl would live, die, or be crippled for the rest of her life because of my utter ignorance and stupidity to drink and drive. My mind raced back to her courageous battle under the truck for so long and my helplessness in getting her out. The agony she must have suffered for so long made me cringe as my head shook a few times on its own slowly before plunging to my upper chest. In the past, I had always been Sheryl's knight in shining armor with the ability to slay any dragon if I had to, or even if I just wanted to. But not this time. I had let her down disgustingly so, like a backstabbing ingrate who cared nothing for anyone but himself.

I finished my personal pity party for the time being and started to walk towards the two cops. My body and mind were greatly strained. But I knew my arrest was imminent anyway. All I wanted was to get it over with, so I could get to the jail. Sheryl's condition was haunting me; I needed to know. As I approached the officers, they were obviously poised for anything I brought their way. I looked at the larger cop intently as I got within about six feet of him, while his partner stood about twelve feet to my right.

"You don't have to worry. I'm not gonna give you any trouble," I stated matter-of-factly to both cops. "Do you want me in the car now?"

The cops both looked at me cautiously, then at each other for a split second. Again, the interrogator took the lead.

"Mr. Wiens, we are sorry for what happened to your wife, but we have to do our jobs," he said apologetically.

"I know," I said calmly. "Do you haveta tie me up?"

"Yes. It's department policy, but we need you to perform some road-side sobriety tests before we go anywhere," he explained candidly.

I didn't argue or balk at all. I knew it had to be done. Even if I had any intentions of combating the cops or resisting their tests, I knew any exhibition of uncooperative behavior was a judge's paradise. In a nutshell, it would foster further fodder for him frying me faster later. Also, the cops would probably make it rougher on me at the jail by telling the jail guards I was a hostile combatant who resisted arrest. For their safety, the guards would in turn, not allow me any phone calls or relay any news regarding Sheryl's condition. Therefore, I didn't take any chances.

I performed all the standard tests given to DUI suspects without further delay. The slighter investigating cop instructed me to stand straight up with my feet together and my hands by my side. He told me to tilt my head back, keep my eyes closed, and then touch my right forefinger to the tip of my nose. When I completed the task correctly, the cop told me to stand on one foot while I held my other foot six inches off the ground. I was instructed to balance on one foot until I was told to put my foot down. However, I was unable to comply. My usually superb dexterity was impeded somewhat due to my alcohol consumption. I touched my hanging toe to the ground a few times to maintain balance, and as soon as I did, the larger cop started writing a note about my failure in his notebook illuminated by his flashlight.

Failing that test, I was then instructed to walk heel to toe fifteen paces without stopping. The test was simple. But apparently, I only stepped off fourteen paces according to the officers' calculations. I thought I had counted the full fifteen, but when I mentioned it to the cops, they both looked at each other like, yeah, they got me now! This time, the larger cop horned in and told me I was mistaken. At the same time he made another note for his support evidence later. He also said I had one more test to execute—the Breathalyzer!

Similar to the ones I had experience with as a cop years earlier, the CHP officers wanted me to blow into a portable Breathalyzer machine to check my blood alcohol content. I knew the test was only a field examination to justify arresting me initially. Without it, the cops would have a weak case for probable cause. The previous tests of dexterity and control didn't mean much without the breath test, because on the uneven rocky ground in the dark with bright flashlights as the only illumination, physical tests wouldn't hold water in court. Even the fact that I admitted to drinking and driving carried no weight without the field BAC (breath alcohol content) test to sustain the other examinations.

I obeyed like an obedient hound. I clamped my lips tightly around the three-inch long, one half-inch wide, plastic nozzle protruding from a larger cylindrical contraption about the size of a hand-held video recorder. I blew hard and long as instructed. When the tester told me I could stop blowing, he also said I had to repeat the same process one more time to confirm the first test. He didn't want any confusion or conflicting results. The test was too serious not to be accurate. Before I complied though, I hesitated for a minute.

"What did it read?" I said inquisitively. Although I knew there was a remote chance that I wasn't over the legal limit, I needed to know for sure. My future hung in the balance like a cliff climber holding on to a minuscule ledge with his fingertips a thousand feet up.

"The first reading was .12," the cop said calmly. He was trying his best not to further antagonize me, or the potentially volatile situation. He knew the ultimate importance of the test results and how they would either hang or exonerate me.

As soon as the cop spit the number out to me, the words seemed to smolder in my brain while the cop reset the machine. While I waited and hoped, Sheryl's unknown condition nauseated me. I also knew my tribulations were only in the baby stages. Although the breath test was only a preliminary examination, it was enough to arrest me. And the blood test later would undoubtedly confirm the field breath tests. The DMV would suspend my driver's license forthwith. My insurance company would feast on my dramatically increased premiums because of my blatant disrespect of the privilege to drive. The DUI would stay tattooed on my record for seven years.

While I blew again, I was still hopeful Sheryl might not be seriously hurt. Even though she was a fifty-six-year-old woman, she had maintained an extraordinary fitness level. And to everyone who knew her, she could still compete with any athletic twenty-five-year-old, man or woman. Her competitive spirit and tenacity in the heat of battle was incomparable. And I imagined, and prayed to God again, that Sheryl's fortitude would keep her safe and undamaged.

In my consternation, I pondered the pending arrest and booking procedure. Inevitably, I knew I was headed for one of the local hospitals. First, a nurse would extract blood samples and expedite delivery of them to a California State criminal laboratory to test for alcohol content. A short time later, the results would be returned to the arresting agency as evidence. Depending on results, I would be fried or cleared. If the results of the two different tests didn't match, I would have a strong defense for lack of probable cause to arrest me in the first place. If the tests turned out to be close in their readings, I knew I would be convicted without a doubt.

After the blood draw, I would be booked into the same jail I had worked at several years before. I wondered if there were some cops still working at the jail with whom I worked and how embarrassing and humiliating the meeting would be when I got there. I had earned respect from my law enforcement peers and administrators because of my solid character and job performance as a cop myself. And I cringed at the thought of facing them all under these circumstances. Reputation was big in my life, and I was definitely not looking forward to the stares and subjective conversations behind my back based on their speculation only. In other words, I hated gossip, especially when I was its subject.

However, I knew it was natural for the guards and jail personnel to yap and to cultivate rumor and scandal whenever there was an opportunity, just to break the monotony of the job if nothing else. That was simply the nature of the beast I had created in my stupidity.

Suddenly, a tornado-like rush of disgust overwhelmed me. How could I still be thinking of myself, I thought. Sheryl was just brutalized because of my horrendous conduct, and I was worried about me—again! Thoughts of reprehensible selfishness wracked my thought process, and again, my eyes hit the ground. My head drooped, then it shook slowly back and forth again in utter shame, as if I had no idea what life was all about. It sure wasn't about me. At that moment, it was about Sheryl and our kids. I wondered if I had ruined it all for everyone.

Just then, I completed the second breath test. Without further articulation, I rotated around so I faced away from the cops and placed my hands behind me. Not hesitating, the smaller cop hooked me up quickly and smoothly with his notably experienced technique. Considerately, he double-locked the cuffs so they wouldn't tighten during the twenty-five minute ride and cause me more pain. However, he didn't realize something. There was no amount of physical pain he could subject me to that could thwart the guilt and anguish torturing my soul.

The trip to the hospital and jail was uneventful, except that I asked the officers if they would please let me know right away if they heard any news at all about Sheryl's condition. Naturally, my six foot four inch, two-hundred-twenty-pound frame was crammed into the sardine can-like patrol car. My entire body was abnormally contorted with the handcuffs bound behind me. I tried to move slightly from time to time to alleviate some of the discomfort. But I couldn't. I was tied up. I was helpless and not in control of anything; just like Sheryl had been.

The grim truth was violent and unnerving. Visions of Sheryl under the truck grew into an inescapable raging internal fire searing my heart, mind, and body. In my mind's eye, the hulk of a truck we had ridden together in countless times was on top of her, slowly snuffing her life out. Her dreadful groans pounded my ears, and combined with my inability to help her, I didn't know what my mind would make me do if she turned out to be seriously hurt. I began to wonder if the nightmare would ever end.

Everything at the hospital, including the blood draws, went according to the old procedure I was well acquainted with. There were no new surprises. When we finally arrived at the jail for the booking procedure, blasts of emotional dread seemed to pierce every cell in my skull. I felt scatterbrained. I couldn't think straight no matter how hard I tried. And by that time, every inch of my body exuded pain.

"What's your name?" an unfamiliar correctional officer asked bluntly.

"Randy Wiens," I responded, totally dispirited.

"Address?" the cop continued callously, as if he hadn't heard about the details of the accident and Sheryl's situation. To him, it seemed I was just another detestable miscreant that deserved the worst possible punishment available. I was just another piece of meat he had to sink his teeth into.

As the jail cop continued his questioning regarding my personal information, I proceeded to dictate everything he asked for as politely as I could under the circumstances. But just then, it all turned ugly when he asked me where I worked. When I told him I was an eighth-grade English and Social Studies teacher, he jerked his head up at me from his computer like a bull elk suddenly sensing imminent danger in the middle of grazing. It appeared he was grossly insulted by something I said or did. It didn't make sense either. I was confused as to what I did to set him off like that.

"You're a teacher, and you're out there driving drunk?" he spat sarcastically.

The implication of his sardonic comment made my guts churn even more than they already had been, if that was possible. Completely on edge from the ordeal I had just experienced, I felt like I was going to snap! I had no idea why the cop was riding me so hard, and I wished I could discuss his disrespect and verbal abuse in a back alley somewhere. Just the two of us. Better yet, I wished right then I could play hockey against him. Why? Because in hockey, I would be praised and rewarded if I viciously smashed his face in. The more blood I pounded out of the enemy the better. The stands would be more filled the next game—to see Randy Wiens, the wrecking ball.

However, I held my tongue hoping he would lay off. I had enough to worry about besides this prima donna with a badge. So I simply continued reciting my Social Security, driver's license, and emergency contact numbers instinctively upon the jail cop's demands. When it came time for him to take my picture and fingerprint me, I ignored his glare and his gruff attitude without even thinking about him. I was mad at myself and too worried about Sheryl.

In the meantime, the two CHP cops who arrested me stood over by the entrance to the booking area conversing. But they kept a close eye on me at the same time. I was their responsibility until the booking procedure was completed. When the jail cop told them he was finished with me, I arbitrarily turned away from the booking counter. I didn't know where exactly I would be taken next. Not thinking clearly, I had forgotten my copies of the booking paperwork on the counter in front of the correctional officer. So I halted in mid-stride towards the cops. Before I could turn around to retrieve the papers though, I heard the jail cop's voice from behind me ordering me to go back and get them.

"Hey, Wiens. You forgot something" he yapped sarcastically.

I turned around, and without making eye contact, I stepped back to the counter. I grabbed the papers aggressively. Trying to keep from blowing entirely, I turned back around to the two CHP cops as quickly as I could to avoid further confrontation with the jail cop. Obviously, the guard was taking my arrest personally. And I had a pretty good idea his condemning attitude would continue once the arresting officers hit the road again.

As the two CHP officers led me to the drunk tank, the jail cop snorted cynically to them to make sure I knew what I was being charged with. Now this comment from the guard, combined with its biting tone, disturbed me. Until that moment, I had assumed I was being booked for a DUI because I was drinking and driving and had gotten into an accident. Apparently though, that was further from the truth than I could have ever imagined.

Just as we all finally reached the drunk-tank door, the smaller CHP cop opened the door for me with a large key that had been clanging against many other jail keys on the ring he was tossed arbitrarily by the jail guard. Cooperatively, like I had behaved all night, I stepped inside the cement, box-like room. The stench in there almost knocked me over as I stepped through the door. It seemed like I was a matador being ravaged by a wounded bull. Someone must have puked in there earlier for sure. But the putrid stench of excrement definitely won the smelling contest hands down. Although, the reeking pong did take my mind off the guard's blurb about the charges for a few seconds before I began to quiz the CHP cop about them.

When I took a few steps directly towards a heavy-duty wooden bench bolted on the side of one of the concrete walls, I searched for a clean spot to sit down. When I found one, I sat on the bench gingerly, partly because I was leery of the filth, and partly because my back ached miserably. I was becoming as stiff as a board from the accident. By then, I wished I had accepted the cop's offer for medical attention at the accident scene.

Instead of whining to the cops about my ailments though, I decided I wanted some answers and information about Sheryl. Also, I had a distinct fear that I was being charged with something worse than I had initially anticipated. As I glanced towards the main investigating cop, he stepped into the rankness. He stood by the open door with his partner directly behind him watching me. From their fidgety body language, I perceived that neither of the officers wanted any part of the stinky dungeon they had just deposited me in. At the same time, I sensed they had something else on their mind. Otherwise, they would have simply slammed the heavy rubber room door signifying the completion of their job on my arrest. Then, they would proceed on their hunt for other perpetrators and malefactors on their beat.

"Have you heard anything about my wife's condition yet?" I asked the cops earnestly, before either of the cops could speak. I looked square into their eyes, trying to catch the slightest hint that Sheryl was going to be okay.

"Mr. Wiens," the cop said hesitantly. Simultaneously, as he began to address me, his eyes dropped towards the floor slightly as if he was embarrassed about something. I had assumed something strange was looming since the jail cop's sarcasm and castigating tone. But I sure wasn't prepared for the monsters coming to get me.

A long second later, the lead CHP officer abruptly jerked his head up as if he had suddenly found the courage to say what was on his mind. He stared directly into my eyes like he had done before. They were blistering in their penetrating gawk when his lips began to move.

"I'm very sorry to tell you, Mr. Wiens, but your wife died in the ambulance on the way to the chopper. The medical crew couldn't save her. You've been charged with gross vehicular manslaughter," he blurted as fast as he could.

I didn't assimilate what he said at first, even though I had been staring at him intently, awaiting his response to my probing question. Clearly though, the cop saw an instant and threatening transformation in my eyes. They changed from inquisitiveness to pure insanity, as my mind finally comprehended what it had just heard. His eyes averted from mine to try to minimize his harsh revelation to me. And then he began his hasty escape out of the drunk tank. Obviously, he wanted no part of the rage he sensed I might confront him with in my dementia.

"My wife is dead?" I stammered, as the cop reached the opening to the door. "My wife is dead!?" I repeated, much louder this time, to make sure the cop heard me. I finally understood the instant the cop turned his head toward me slightly and nodded briefly.

In the next seconds, the cop stepped out of the rubber room. And I fell into a raging emotional hell. I began to sob neurotically, completely out of control of any cognitive process. It was like a harrowing dream. It seemed that my mind had been cast maliciously into a blender on grind. In my brain, the monster had finally caught me. With a massive claw, it tore at my chest and upper torso, unmercifully ripping and clawing at my heart and its lifeblood. With another claw, it slashed at my facial flesh while its omnipotent jaws engulfed my head. It was quite clear that it was starving for vindication because I murdered its young one. No matter what the consequences, it wasn't going to stop until I realized I wasn't in control of anything in this world after all, after I had paid in full for all my sins, or I was dead one of the three. The ensuing time in the tank seemed like an eternity of sobbing uncontrollably. In my mind's eye, Sheryl was being slowly crushed to death, over and over again. Her agonizing pain screamed through my body, and I prayed to God that he would allow me to trade places with my wife instantly. No questions asked. I just wanted to be dead instead of her. How were my kids going to get through life without their mother, dead at their father's murderous hands, I thought? What would happen to them when I went to prison? I knew for sure that is where I was headed now. What would they do with both parents gone in the blink of an eye? How would they survive?

The visions became too excruciating to endure in my head. My unrelenting attack on my own brain seemed to suffocate me. My breathing came in short gasps like I had just skated all out for a two-minute shift in a championship hockey game I was playing in. My chest was heavy, and I realized in my panic I was losing it. I stood up and began to pace the room, still trying to comprehend the cop's news. As I walked back and forth, I put my hands on my hips to open my airway. That didn't work, so I sat down again and put my folded hands between my legs, rested my elbows on my knees, and leaned forward a little. Shortly, my breathing improved. It was still slightly labored, but I was able to control it somewhat. Strangely, my panic and loss of breath reminded me of Sheryl again. She too had gasped for air under the truck I put her under. The thought was grisly. I had just put my own wife under—not just under the truck—under the ground, six dirty, filthy feet under.

From time to time, I would rise out of my gross self-depredation and briefly regain a little control of my wild emotions. Seconds later, I would bash myself again. I was a vile and a despicable man. I had caused my wife's death. I had erased her from my kids' lives and the world altogether. How would I face anyone ever again as long as I lived, I thought?

Although I wasn't a religious person, it seemed that God was the only one who could save me from my own madness. I was completely broken as a man and as a human being. No other human could help or save me. I dropped to my knees and began to pray, for the first time I could remember, over the wooden drunk tank bench. The filth no longer mattered. I believed I wasn't fit for anything clean ever again.

"Father in heaven, you know I've denied you all these years. But, God, I need you now. I've never asked you for help before, but I'm begging you now. Please forgive me for what I've done and what I've caused. Please God, please forgive me. I need your help . . . I can't do this without you!"

My severe crying jags and my praying seemed to alternate automatically without me thinking about it. They were like someone was picking teams for a pick-up hockey game on a frozen remote lake ice in Canada. Second captain, first pick; first captain, second pick. My mind picked the teams in its cruise control mode entirely on its own. I had no control. As I prayed for my forgiveness, I would inevitably conjure up another vision of my dead wife and destitute kids. My sobbing would return again as uncontrollable rushes of guilt and remorse, because of what I had done. Minutes later, I would gain a little control, and once again, I would begin to pray again.

A short time later, a guard noticed that my sobbing and praying had subsided, at least for the time being. I was sitting on the wooden bench when she opened the tank door. She asked me if I wanted to make some phone calls.

Usually, it was strict jail policy to only permit inmates a single phone call upon completion of the booking process. However, in my case, the matron was the first of many sheriff's department personnel who did their best to be sympathetic to my situation and needs. Unlike the detestable ogre who booked me into the jail initially, several sheriff's officers, from guards all the way up to administrators, tried to help me any way they could. Some officers allowed me to place phone calls when they were available from their normal duties. Some asked me if they could call anyone for me, like family, or an attorney, for example.

When I was able to get out of the drunk tank to make my first phone call, I felt completely desolate. I was ravaged emotionally and psychologically. Even though I had just prayed to God for help and guidance, I was still totally confused at the best course of action. Emotions rampaged inside my brain, and in a daze I didn't know who to call first or what to say. I wanted to call Ranger, our twenty-one-year old son. He was our oldest, but he was on a church mission in Hawaii. And I didn't know how to contact him from the jail. His number was at my apartment. I thought about calling Kodi, our eighteen-year-old daughter. She and Carlie, my granddaughter, were living at our house with Sheryl, and I knew I had to notify them of the accident right away. I didn't want anyone but me to tell her. It was the same with Logan, our fifteen-year-old son. All three were home alone waiting for mom—and gamma—to come home. I knew that they all knew I would be going back to my apartment. But the thought would never have occurred to them that their mother was dead and their dad was in jail responsible for their mother's death.

As much as I ached to call and talk to my kids, I thought I had better rethink that plan. I knew they were home alone, and because of that, I knew without a doubt that telling them the horrific news was totally the wrong thing to do. I had to call another family member, and the only others living locally were Sheryl's brother and mother. I thought one of them could go to the house personally and somehow break the news to my children. Whatever their reaction would be then, at least they would have a family member around to pick up their pieces.

However, after reflecting on the prospect of calling Sheryl's mother first, I developed the daunting fear that she might have a heart attack, and I didn't want to be responsible for Sheryl's mother's death too. She had recently lost her husband of fifty-some-odd years, and I knew she would be especially vulnerable and sensitive to the news of her oldest daughter's death.

After standing by the phone in the hallway by a long row of jail drunk tanks for several minutes totally confused, I decided to call Sheryl's brother who also lived in town. He was a well-respected professional who seemed to always have a level head. But in my scatterbrained emotional state, I couldn't remember his telephone number, a number I had called a thousand times over the twenty-two years I had known him. I knew he had three or four lines to his house, several of them for his kids, but his direct line completely escaped me.

I stood without dialing for several more minutes fighting myself through a cloud of guilt and remorse. I tried to remember his number. But mostly I contemplated what I would say to him. Would I simply blurt out that I was driving drunk and I killed his sister in a wreck? Could I tell him Sheryl was slowly and brutally crushed to death under our truck when we crashed? I didn't know what to do or what to say.

During my confused state, the matron saw from her position from behind the booking counter that I wasn't talking. I was just leaning against the cement wall by the phone completely distraught. She walked over to where I stood and offered me some encouragement. And somehow our short exchange gave me the strength I needed to settle down a little emotionally. When I did, I was able to piece the number together in what was left of my brain. Then, I dialed it slowly.

It was about six in the morning when the telephone rang at Sheryl's brother's house. The incessant ringing sound in my ear seemed like a cavalcade of deafening shells exploding around and through me. It was like I was a defenseless soldier being bombarded mercilessly by a German Tiger tank. It was also a holiday. Around the third ring, I began to hope no one would be home. I wanted to be spared the agony of having to tell a family member that Sheryl was dead because of me. I didn't want to cause him, any of his family, or anyone else, the imminent onslaught of pain they would experience as they heard the news. As the phone continued to ring, I hoped desperately that my in-laws were traveling out of town like they often did. When their answering machine didn't kick on, I was relieved somewhat. I felt I had dodged another monster's emotional bullet. However, I knew the face-to-face meeting with Sheryl's entire family was inevitable at some point.

I hung up before the sixth ring, and without thinking, my fingers seemed to dial my friend Mark's number like I was supposed to from the beginning. Mark was a friend with whom I had formed a close bond a few years before the accident. Our families were very close as well, especially their son and Logan, my son. They were best friends. They played baseball, basketball, and soccer together on many all-star teams. Mark and I took a liking to each other during the countless games and road trips we shared watching our boys.

Naturally, it seemed that calling my friend initially was the most practical course of action under the circumstances. Somehow, I knew he would be able to take care of the ugly business of calling my kids and informing them of their mother's death, how she died, and who caused it. Besides, I had no choice. I couldn't get ahold of Sheryl's brother. I couldn't call her mother. I definitely couldn't call my kids. And I didn't know any other family phone numbers from memory.

I dialed my friend's number instinctively, and he answered on the second ring.

"Hello," he said, sleepily.

"Mark." I said, with my voice cracking slightly. "This is Randy."

"Hey. What's goin' on?" he said, in his usual greeting, but with an uneasy tone. I had never called him before so early in the morning. Plus, the tone in my voice sounded troubled. So naturally, he assumed something was wrong.

"Sorry to wake you," I said, hesitating a few seconds before I could spark the courage to spit out the horrible news.

"What's wrong?" Mark said concernedly. I could hear him shuffle in the background as if he had sensed real trouble and felt he had to sit up in his bed so he could attend to my needs more intently.

"Mark. I'm in jail. Sheryl and I were coming back from Sonora last night. A car came across the line on a corner. I swerved and rolled. Sheryl was killed." I spat out in a sudden outburst of emotion and guilt.

"Sheryl was killed?" Mark stammered. Dumbfounded, Mark yelled over to his wife. She had been sleeping like Mark, and she was rudely awakened by the urgency in his voice.

"Tammy . . . Tammy! Randy and Sheryl were in a car wreck and Sheryl was killed." I heard Mark yell to Tammy and back on the phone to me.

"Mark. I'm so sorry to have to put you guys through this, but I desperately need your help." I somehow said a little more calmly this time. At the same time, I was trying to find the courage to tell him I was booked for gross vehicular manslaughter because I had been drinking and driving.

"Mark. I was drinking," I blurted.

"Oh no!!" Mark gasped, and then complete silence gripped the phone line. Heart struck, Mark had handed the phone to Tammy, now awake from the bedlam.

"What do you want us to do, Randy? We are here for you," Tammy said calmly in her usual businesslike manner.

Immediately, upon Tammy's offer of support and help, I broke down again emotionally. I was so relieved that my friends didn't discard me, or refer me to someone else, that I began to cry again in complete humility and appreciation for their graciousness. Without hesitating, they had assumed the arduous task of contacting my kids and Sheryl's family, as well as providing me with anything else I needed.

"Tammy. I'm sooo sorry! Please tell my kids what happened. But, please. Please try your best to break the news to them as easily as possible," I sobbed at Tammy, pleading with her to take care of my kids.

"We'll take care of everything, Randy. Don't worry. Where are you, and are you hurt at all?" Tammy asked me. Her tone was inquisitive but soothing, and it allowed me slight but much-needed relief from the unmerciful emotional monsters plaguing my every brain cell.

"I'm at the county jail. I'm okay physically." I told her sadly. "Please call Sheryl's brother too. I tried calling him earlier, but there was no answer."

"Don't worry. We'll take care of all that. The biggest thing for you now is to get a hold of yourself. We'll get through this together." Tammy said calmly and encouragingly.

"Thank you!" I cried again, not being able to control the flow of tears. I had no idea the human body was capable of producing so many tears. "I'll try callin' again later, but I don't know when. I'm at the mercy of the jail guards," I told Tammy through a torrent of sobs.

CHAPTER 3

Bail or Bondage

The ensuing four days were a hellish rogue nightmare. They became an endurance marathon for pure cognitive survival. My mind simply couldn't block out the gruesome events encompassing Sheryl's death. I tried to find relief in sleep, but my eyes couldn't capture its merciful blessing. It seemed the instant my eyes might finally close and offer a slight reprieve from the relentless pounding pressure behind them, I would see Sheryl's face and body being slowly crushed to death over and over again in my mind's eye. The hideous nature of the entire experience painted a mental family portrait of Sheryl, Ranger, Kodi, and Logan brought to ruination because of me; the villainous husband and father.

Shift change occurred in the jail an hour after I finished talking to my friends. I was immediately relieved to notice that a few of my old sheriff's department counterparts were still working in the jail after all the years. Many others had been promoted out of the jail to patrol or other divisions of the sheriff's department. But there were still a few who remained who were willing to help a fallen comrade. Of course, all of them remaining in the jail had long tenure, which in turn, provided them with strictly day shifts and no more graveyards and weekends away from their families. That was lucky for me.

Having help inside was a miracle. Several of my old buddies told me that if I needed more phone calls to let them know right away. They offered me food and coffee regularly. They offered to make calls for me. Or they just offered an ear if I just wanted to talk. I was eternally grateful for their graciousness and encouraging intentions, but I couldn't seem to hold my head up. I felt so depressed and low and worthless at that point; I couldn't look anyone in the face. I was permitted to make another phone call a short time later though. I was confident that my friends would have taken care of my kids and called Sheryl's brother and mother by that time. But I still felt I needed to talk to one of them out of respect for Sheryl and her family.

When I called again, I was a little stronger emotionally this time. My friends' encouragement and awesome attitude to help me had relieved a little of the overall mental anguish that had been crushing on my mind slowly—similar to Sheryl's body when she was under the truck only a few hours earlier still alive.

Sheryl's brother picked up on the first ring this time. To make a long story short, it was the most difficult phone call I ever had to make. When I hung up, I felt like my own guilt was whipping me unmercifully with its steely barbed chains. And a renewed sense of anguish and remorse engulfed my brain again. My heart was broken for Sheryl, our children, and all of Sheryl's family and friends. I knew I had caused the destruction of a dear member of the human race. And Sheryl didn't deserve any of it. My stubborn arrogance had destroyed her. The worst thing was that I couldn't do anything about it. I could only face the music and bear whatever monsters came my way. Invariably, I knew they would come after me out of their loyalty and love for Sheryl. For some, it would be strictly a personal attack on me. For others, it would be a massive and an overwhelming assault against the common concept of the murderous drinking drivers running rampant in all of human society. All I could do was to take my medicine like a man. Like I was brought up to do.

Disclaimer to the readers of this book:

It is very important for you to understand that no part of this book is intended to hurt, judge, or attack anyone for any reason. Because of the experiences in my life, I developed a generally defective mindset regarding life, love, and relationships. And until sometime after the accident, I had no idea how unreasonable, selfish, and arrogant I was in them. Furthermore, I didn't engage in life, willing to play by society's rules. Others, including my family and loved ones at times, were secondary priorities. Some of my thoughts and opinions of others were poisoned and grossly twisted. Most importantly, I reveal how I thought until after the accident, how lost I really was spiritually and emotionally, and how wrong I was about so many things. No one caused my problems. No one forced, manipulated, or coerced me to make the bad decisions I made. I blamed others at times, but that was only displaced anger I never knew how to cope with before the accident. So please don't take anything I say personally. If you do find yourself thinking that I am judging you or attacking you, please understand that I wasn't sane back then. I wasn't whole. I was tainted. My mind wasn't right. That sickness caused me to lash out at others and blame them for the monsters in my life instead of taking responsibility for my own inadequacies. That is how I thought then. It isn't how I think now.

In my mind back then, I knew a few of Sheryl's family and friends would undoubtedly campaign for my death penalty. Even though some of them didn't know me very well, they would want to hang me. Literally. There was no doubt in my mind that vigilantism would suddenly be acceptable in their society and culture. I imagined they would all enjoy the great spectacle in watching my body squirm frantically and my feet and legs thrash at the air beneath me until I dangled limp, desperately sucking my last life-giving particle of oxygen. Sheryl was just too awesome as a daughter, person, and a friend for some of them not to try to vindicate her tragic loss somehow, someway. And if my physical demise wasn't in their power to bring about, I knew for sure they wouldn't accept less than the harshest punishment they could make a judge believe I deserved.

Before too long though, those distasteful thoughts vanished. I figured my own bashing was a thousand times more malicious than anything anyone else could ever bring to the table anyway. As my mind dove back into the fiery pit, I envisioned my kids' initial reaction to the news of their mother's death. I couldn't shake the shame and the mental anguish I imagined my children would have to endure because of me. The thoughts made my skin crawl. It was impossible to keep from fidgeting, or my mind from racing back and forth and through all of the ugly and gruesome events that had occurred during the previous few hours.

After I hung up the phone with Sheryl's brother, a jail guard I didn't know told me I had to go back to my stinky concrete tank. I cooperated fully and returned peacefully. I swallowed several slugs of water from the filthy water fountain beside the drunk tank's toilet. Then I sat down to try to gather my faculties. A short second later, I realized there was still one more phone call I had to make. Out of respect for Karyn, I felt I had to be the one to tell her what happened. I definitely didn't want her to hear about it from anyone else but me.

Leading up to the accident about six months earlier, Sheryl and I decided to finally get a divorce. We had been married for twenty-two years. The reasons we didn't get along were vast and deep, although only one main reason stood out in my stupid mind as the culprit. For most of our marriage, I believed wrongly that Sheryl's religion had buried us as a married couple from the outset of our wedding vows. In other words, I blamed religion for a lot of my unhappiness and emotional woes. I believed I didn't need spirituality in my life, and I wasn't about to allow anyone to shove it down my throat. So, I denied religion altogether and didn't believe in any of its spiritual blessings.

It is a morbidly sad fact that I was so hardheaded and narrow-minded back then. I realize now that I was the culprit in our family dysfunction, not religion or anything else. I denied God and claimed to the world that only weaklings needed Him. But I was the one who was really weak. The arrogance in my egotistical mindset at the time is disgusting and vile to me now. But back then, everything was everyone else's problem and fault and not mine. It was natural Sheryl and I had all the problems we did. I'm surprised she stuck with me for twenty-two years.

We finally decided to call it quits in May of 2000. From my perspective, our relationship had disintegrated and died completely. In my mind, I didn't want to try any more. I gave up. I didn't see any sense at all in continuing to beat my head against the stone wall Sheryl and I had built between us for more than two decades.

So when I went to Canada alone after my teaching job was over for the summer vacation, we began to make plans for a new future. I moved out on my return as planned; we had lived in the same house together for twenty out of our twenty-two years. The apartment I found was only a few blocks away though, so it was convenient to see my children regularly. I was also still close to the school I taught at, and my dog, Rascal, was able to share quality time with Sheryl and the kids and with me.

A short time after I physically moved out of my house, I met Karyn. She was with a friend of hers sitting in the pool hall where I was drinking and playing pool. There were only four or five patrons in the entire establishment that afternoon. So eye contact with Karyn was inevitable. Within minutes we were talking and joking. And as we strutted our stuff, we both realized immediately we had tripped onto something special. However, Karyn put the brakes on anything physical due to the fact I wasn't divorced yet and I wasn't a Christian.

About religion and living a Christian life, I told Karyn that my life had been controlled by religion for over twenty years. Consequently, I didn't have the emotional or psychological strength to enter into another religious battle with her. I also told her that I was probably the wrong man for her if she thought she would or could possibly convert me. I explained to Karyn that personally, I had believed in a higher power all my life. And it was quite simple to me. I believed in my heart, mind, body, and soul that there had to be a higher power of some form. Whether that higher power was a man, woman, or an it, I believed for sure there was someone or something out there much greater than the human being. I was totally convinced that no human had the supreme omnipotence to create the human body, nature, the earth, the universe, or anything in it.

I continued spewing my religious philosophy to Karyn; that my simple and tenuous religious views had caused supreme havoc throughout my married life. When Sheryl quizzed me about what I believed in regarding religion, our discussions would always end up in an argument. Why? Because Sheryl's religious beliefs could never be compromised. For me, spirituality was infinitely simpler. And I didn't feel I needed to adhere to, what I thought to be at the time, her man-made version of it.

The night I explained my religious beliefs to Karyn, and the serious problems I felt religion had caused in my long marriage, I almost ended our relationship before it began too. When I finished my religious spiel, Karyn listened patiently and respectfully. Then she flat out told me how it was with her. She explained she wouldn't be with me if I didn't at least consider conversion to Christianity. And at some point in the not-too-distant future, I would have to unconditionally accept Jesus Christ as my savior and practice Christianity as an integral part of my life. Otherwise, she wanted no part of me.

Karyn's ultimatum scared me, because Sheryl had told me the same thing. Either I had to join the church, or I couldn't marry her. From Karyn's perspective, I had to become a Christian wholeheartedly, or she wouldn't be a part of my life either. Of course, I didn't walk. I ran—fast. I left Karyn sitting on a chair by her patio table eating the Chinese food we had just been sharing. Her reaction to my leaving was only a sad and lonely silence. And when I closed the door behind me, I never thought I would see Karyn again. Apparently, she also thought there was no future for us either, because she didn't try to stop me.

Luckily for us, Karyn called me at my apartment after school the next day. She came over that evening. She discussed the extraordinary connection we had already established and that we couldn't simply discard our feelings and potential future so arbitrarily. However, we both were plagued by our own consciences. And to be judged with moral turpitude by our family, friends, and peers, was a frightening prospect. We knew it was morally wrong to be together before I was legally divorced entirely, and we debated whether it was worth the guilt we would certainly be haunted by or not. The end result was that we didn't want to lose each other. Although the timing for us to meet couldn't have been more inappropriate, we both knew we had a special bond that had to be pursued to its fullest. So we searched for, planned, and found precious moments to be together while I was waiting for my divorce from Sheryl to be final.

When I finally called Karyn from jail, dialing her number tore the last cell of emotional strength I had from my mind. I had already concluded that she would dump me immediately without hesitation, because I had lied to her. I told her I was going somewhere else, not with Sheryl for the long weekend. I felt sorry for myself due to my stupidity and lies, because I not only caused Sheryl's death, but that my lies and deception were about to cause me to lose Karyn too.

When I called Karyn on that Monday morning, she couldn't believe what she heard. When I told her I had been with Sheryl over the weekend, and that she died so brutally in the wreck I was responsible for, she was totally confused and distraught. I tried to explain to her Sheryl's request to go away with her one last time; Sheryl wanted to prove to me that she could compromise her ways, especially in the religion department, and she was prepared to do what it took to save our marriage. For Sheryl, the trip was a new beginning. For me, it was closure. Of course, Karyn couldn't understand anything I said. All of what came out of my mouth was suspicious, and to her, it looked for sure like I had lied and deceived her all along. To Karyn, we had just been a fling while Sheryl and I tried to get back together. When we hung up our phones a few minutes later, I never thought I would ever see Karyn again.

About 10 A.M. the morning after Sheryl's death and my arrest, my phone calls were finally finished. My brain felt pretty much fried, and I was completely alone. Sheryl was dead. And, only God could save me from the monsters eating me alive. In my mindless stupor, I turned toward the main booking area about twenty feet away from where the jail phones were. I tried to hail a guard to take me back to the tank, but when I finally caught one's attention, he moved me to an isolation cell instead of the drunk tank.

My new residence was a five-foot by seven-foot concrete box. It had a narrow wooden bench at one of the long ends of the cell, a toilet immediately inside the heavy metal door, and another disgustingly filthy sink abutting the stainless steel toilet. The door had a tiny window in it about eight inches square and five feet up from the cement floor, and a food tray slot about groin high. That was it. There was just barely enough room for the squished, three-inch foam mattress the guard threw into my cell behind me when I stepped in. When I spread the mattress out and lay on it to relieve some of my piercing back pain, my feet and ankles hung over one end onto the cold cement floor. The single blanket the guard had tossed me besides the mattress was too short to cover my body and my bare feet at the same time. Of course, the cops had also removed my shoes at the booking desk earlier afraid I might use the laces to hang myself. On top of everything else, the jail was freezing cold. And like a fat, ready-to-be-butchered beef after slaughter, I felt like I had been placed in refrigerated storage.

I tried to sleep or just rest my eyes, but my efforts were fruitless. At the same time, I also realized I needed medical attention for my back. I couldn't straighten my body and back without agonizing shots of stabbing pain attacking every bone, muscle, and joint. Mostly, I lay hunched in the fetal position on the mattress on the concrete to stay warm and to try to alleviate my discomfort. About the only time I arose from that position was to urinate or to get a drink of water. The pain was too unbearable to do anything else. Even when chow times came along for supper or breakfast later, I couldn't muster up the physical strength to lift myself off the concrete to fetch the slop from the slit in my cell door. I don't think I would have been able to conjure up the mental motivation or the physical strength to eat anything even if I had been able to get up.

My mind was buried in a constant, relentless fog of guilt and remorse. I couldn't dream. I couldn't fantasize. I couldn't conjure up a happy place anywhere in my mind. It seemed I was sucking fumes, and I was being slowly and methodically squashed like Sheryl had been. I didn't know whether I would live or die from the physical or emotional pain at that time, or if I would end up insane in a psychiatric unit somewhere blubbering like an idiot forever. How could I face my children, my friends, or Sheryl's family ever again, I thought? I began to believe that forever, as long as I lived, I would never be able to look into anyone's eyes again.

Without moving from my fetal position, I prayed to God again and attempted to repent of my sins. I told him I wasn't worthy of his mercy. I told him I had done many bad things. I had lied. I had cheated. I had hurt many people throughout my life because of my pride and selfishness. When I finished spilling my guts to God, I pleaded with him that, if he could somehow see into my mind and heart right then, he would see that I was finally ready for him to come into my life. He was my last resort. I bared my soul to him, and as I did, I cried like a hungry baby looking to suckle his momma's breast. Although I knew it was probably disrespectful to God not to kneel with folded hands, I knew that if God was really out there, he would understand my human frailty.

By mid-morning Tuesday, I still hadn't slept at all. My back pain was beyond the horrendous stage. When I mentioned my back pain to the guard supervising the morning chow delivery, he said there was someone outside working on my bail. I should just try to be patient and wait to see my own doctor when I was released in a little while. I didn't know who was trying to spring me, but I was elated just the same. For the first time since the accident more than thirty hours before, I had a positive emotion of some sort. I couldn't distinguish at the time whether it was a selfish emotion to finally feel a little good about something, or I was just happy to finally be able to see my kids and be able to take care of the funeral business. Either way, I didn't care. I only wanted to breathe some free air.

For the next nine hours, I chomped at the bit waiting for a correctional officer to retrieve me for the bailing procedure. I waited and waited some more. With no sleep, unrelenting emotional trauma, and severe back pain ganging up on me for so long, I was way beyond the edge of insanity. It seemed that every time I heard a noise during those long hours, I was like a man with a noose tied tightly around his neck awaiting the inevitable kick over the side of the bridge he was being hung from. Every sound in the jail penetrated my innermost core as I anticipated all of them were finally coming to liberate me. I was a nervous wreck, but still no one came. Totally distraught, I finally fell asleep about 4 P.M. I hadn't slept in about forty-four hours.

About five o'clock, I was rudely awakened by the clank of jail keys against my steel door. I jerked awake out of my dead sleep expecting to hear that someone finally posted my bail. But I was wrong. What I did hear was that my attorney had come to the jail to talk to me, and I needed to follow the guard to an interview room. When I asked the correctional officer why my bail hadn't been posted yet, the guard told me I had better discuss the matter with my attorney. I knew that was bad news right away. But I didn't know until a little later though exactly how bad it really was.

With great difficulty, I managed to hoist myself up to my knees with the help of the bench as a leaning post. The cop noticed my obvious pain, and he kindly offered his help. I hung on to his arm for leverage to stand up, but spiking back spasms drove me back to my knees. It took quite awhile to conquer the pain enough to get up, but somehow I did. I felt like an old grizzled grandpa with a cane. It felt like my spine was tied in knots and twisted like an order of curly fries from a greasy burger joint. But at least, I made it to the interview room without being carried on a stretcher. I was worried about my kids, and I prayed to God again silently to allow my attorney to vanquish me from my private hellhole.

My attorney was waiting patiently for me as I finally hobbled into the interview room. Without wasting any time, he asked me if I needed medical attention, because it looked to him like I should be in a hospital somewhere. I had massive black bags under my eyes from the stress and lack of sleep. I hadn't washed. My fingers and nails were like raw hamburger, and dried blood hung on them as if I had dipped them in red paint hours earlier. I told him the CHP cops had asked me at the accident scene if I wanted medical attention. But I refused their offer. I also informed him that I didn't have the energy or interest to get cleaned up in the miserable excuse for a sink in the drunk tank, or the isolation cell either for that matter. I was in too much pain, and worrying about my kids had been weighing on my mind too heavily to care about how I looked.

About five seconds into my attorney's questioning regarding my medical problems, I cut him off abruptly and asked him who it was that tried to bail me out earlier and why it hadn't happened yet. I couldn't understand in the dementia of my frayed mind what the hold up was. First of all, my attorney explained in detail that, when I hung up the phone with Mark on Monday morning, he and Tammy had gone directly to my house to be with my kids. Although they were horrified and shocked initially, they were also worrying about what was happening to me in the jail and if I had to go to prison for twenty years.

In a flash, the news about my kids triggered a flood of tears. They gushed out of me like a broken water main. I regained control after awhile, and compassionately, my attorney began to encourage me, in that, I was quite fortunate to have such loving children, and that I should start thinking about them instead of dwelling on Sheryl's death. He went on to explain that Mark had contacted Sheryl's brother, and he had called the rest of Sheryl's family. Again, I began to cry. Some of Sheryl's family and I had some differences in the past, but to me, we were still family. And I loved them all as such. I envisioned their initial horror-struck emotional reaction, and the unimaginable pain I had caused them all. I knew then that the emotional and psychological pain I was experiencing was minuscule compared to theirs. It would be multiplied a hundred fold in all of the mourning and grief I had caused the entire family. I felt I didn't deserve to live.

A few minutes later, I recuperated a little again. Although I knew my emotions were hovering on the edge of my sleeve still volatile and un-manageable, I knew I had to get a grip on myself. So I forced myself to converse reasonably with my attorney in order for us to figure out the best plan of attack to get me out of jail.

My attorney went on to explain that the bondsman required $10,000; ten percent of the actual $100,000 bail for the gross vehicular man-slaughter charges I was facing. But when Mark arrived at the jail to post the bond, the guards told him and the bondsman my bail had been raised from $100,000 to $200,000. Naturally, when my attorney told me this nauseating news, I was stunned. When I mumbled my disbelief and questioned my attorney why the bail changed so drastically, he informed me that there were some members of the community who were cam-paigning to raise my bail so high that I couldn't afford to bail out. Upon hearing the news of Sheryl's death, several of them had even taken up arms. Their weapons were the pen and ink and the mighty phone mes-senger. A great and formidable loathing emerged in their psyches, and their fingers began to dial their faithful recruits. Their propaganda was dispersed, specifically aimed to support Sheryl and to destroy the one who killed her.

By the time their phones finally cooled, my attorney told me candidly that I was in the deep end, and he hoped I could swim. Within hours of the public notification of Sheryl's death, approximately thirty professionally written and typed letters were hand delivered to the district attorney's office. All of them had the same orchestrated theme for the district attorney's consideration: no matter what happens, you must make a judge believe and understand that under any and all circumstances, Randy Wiens shouldn't be permitted to bail out of jail. The instant he is allowed to bail out, he will grab Logan, his youngest son, and flee to Canada, his country of citizenship. He won't take responsibility for his actions. He will run from them.

In addition to the castigating letters, members of the campaigning monster made personal visits to the district attorney's office to verbally convince them of my miscreant character. By Tuesday morning the day after the accident, headlines appeared in the paper about the accident. Opinion articles denounced me as a disgusting human. And word of mouth spread like wildfire to all who lent an open ear. Thus through the media, a vile and repulsive picture was painted regarding my character: Randy Wiens shouldn't be permitted to bail out of jail. His bail should be revoked unconditionally. Or it should be raised so high that it would become unreachable. Randy Wiens, the maniac, couldn't be allowed to roam free. He should have to spend the rest of his life in prison. That is the only justice that should be allowed by law.

Although my attorney's words were a lot softer than my own imaginings, his words still screeched around and against the inside of my skull. Then, as if that wasn't enough, he unleashed another atomic bomb.

"If you are convicted on the gross vehicular manslaughter charges, you will be sentenced to prison for a four—, eight—, or twelve-year term. Most likely, you will get the middle or upper term due to the outside community influence," he told me in his business tone.

As he imparted the words, I could only stare at him in shock for several minutes. I had been sitting upright in my chair interested in my counsel as best as I could due to my back spasms. But when I heard the news, I collapsed against the back of my chair in total disbelief. My heart sunk. My soul ached. I was totally convinced I was a horrid abomination to all of mankind, and I was only worthy enough to be cast out of normal society into prison.

"What happens now?" I asked my attorney sadly through pursed lips.

I was barely able to eke out the sounds as I slouched back in my chair, totally distraught. I didn't know if I was going to be able to survive the relentless emotional onslaught or not. The consequences of my actions were emerging from their vast and hideous caves. They swarmed my mind like killer army ants pursuing some delicious live flesh.

"The first thing to do is stop hanging yourself," my attorney said flatly, without beating around the bush. "For your own sanity, and your kids' sake, you need to smarten up right now and realize there's nothing you can do about what happened. You made a mistake, and there was a tragic accident. It's done. And yes. It's terrible. But now there's business to do for you and your kids' future."

"What do you mean?" I asked bluntly, sitting up in the chair as best as I could in my extreme physical discomfort.

"First off, if I'm going to be able to help you, I need to know all the details about the accident from start to finish. You can't leave anything out," he explained plainly.

"What good will that do?" I asked him impatiently. "I already told the cops I was drinking and driving, and the breath test proves that I was over the limit."

"Yes. That's true. But, we don't know if the blood test will verify the Breathalyzer test number one. If it doesn't, they had no probable cause to arrest you in the first place. And two, in order for you to be convicted of gross vehicular manslaughter, the police have to prove that you committed some other traffic violation in addition to the DUI/vehicular manslaughter, like speeding or weaving, for example," my attorney continued aggressively. He was trying his best to make me understand that my burial hole wasn't finished quite yet.

"I can tell you straight up I didn't commit any other traffic violation for sure. Sheryl and I were driving along at the regular speed limit just talking when the car came across the line on the corner. There was nothin' I could do but swerve to get away from killin' everybody in a head-on crash," I explained a little excitedly, hoping that there might be some kind of light in the darkness I seemed to be mired in.

"If that's the case, we're in good shape. The onus is on the D.A. to prove the "gross" part of the charges in addition to the DUI itself. And if I were you, I wouldn't convict myself on the DUI just yet either. Anything can happen at the lab. Or maybe there is a loophole in the cops' arrest procedure somewhere," my attorney told me clearly.

"What happens if I'm convicted of the vehicular manslaughter charge without the gross part?" I questioned my attorney, calmly this time, with a new hope that maybe I wouldn't have to go to prison.

"That is complicated. There is no definitive answer. Mostly, it depends on how vociferous the community is out there in the media. In a small community like this, public opinion and outcry plays a huge part in the political process. The D.A. and all the judges are elected officials, and if they want to keep their jobs, they have to seriously consider community opinion," he continued.

As soon as my attorney explained the community's view would negatively affect my case, especially my sentencing, I felt totally dejected again. The encouragement my attorney fed me helped briefly, but I knew the nature of the beast. When an angry community mob got its hooks into something, I knew the bad guy wasn't likely to escape its ripping talons.

"What about my bail?" I asked my attorney. I was scared. I wanted my mommy. I wanted to go home.

"Mark's workin' on that as we speak. He's tryin' to get some help from some of your other friends. Your bail has been raised to $200,000 now. It's because the letters delivered to the D.A said you would skip bail and flee to Canada with Logan," my attorney explained to me frankly. His eyes avoided mine when he noticed my ire had been provoked when I heard him speak those nasty words. My attorney and I had known each other for a long time, and he knew very well that I had the reputation of never backing down from a fight or confrontation with anyone, or for any reason. He also knew the running-away to-Canada-with-Logan story was only a ploy to hold me down under the water for as long as possible.

"That's ludicrous," I spat back at my attorney in total disgust. "They are tryin' to make it look to all the world that I killed Sheryl maliciously, and now that I had, I'm gonna take Logan and run to Canada and away from the consequences and my responsibilities too?"

I totally understood all of the monster's resentment, because I knew all too well the abhorrence I had for myself. But when people were out there flipping lies all over the planet, it made me mad. It seemed the monster was baring all its teeth and diving for my throat for the quick kill. There was no stealth about it. Immediately, I knew I was going to have to start gnawing back on them if I was to survive this thing at all. It was bad enough that I killed Sheryl. But the lies and slander forced me to engage in the battle for pure survival.

"I completely understand your frustration, Randy. But I can tell you their behavior is human nature. You and I would do the exact same thing, and knowing our competitive nature, we would probably be a lot worse than them. For now, all you can do is keep a cool head and run the gauntlet. We will do the very best we can to get you out of here in time for the funeral and to minimize your prison time. All I can say is try to be patient. And you need to know there are many people trying to help you out there. Try to get some rest and don't be so hard on yourself. What's done is done. No matter what happens to you, you have to stay strong for your kids. Their future depends on you now," my attorney said sincerely. He made a lot of sense too.

"I'll try. Just please ask Mark to take care of my kids till I get out of here. Also, can you tell Mark I have the twenty grand for the ten percent of the bail, but it's gonna take a few weeks to get it. I can pay him back soon if he can somehow raise whatever it takes to get me out now. I have to make arrangements for Sheryl's funeral. I can't miss it no matter what happens. I would never be able to live with myself if I couldn't go," I implored him.

We shook hands strongly in friendship, and my attorney walked out of the jail interview room leaving me alone with my thoughts. My mind was raging its contempt for those who were after me so viciously. However, like my attorney said, I would have felt the same way if the shoe were on the other foot. I would have defended my young and stayed loyal to my friend too. So, all I could do was wait—wait for bail—wait to see my kids—and wait for Sheryl's funeral. I begged God for his forgiveness again.

The guard delivered me back to my isolation cell. Thoroughly dehydrated, I immediately began to drink furiously from the water outlet in the sink by the toilet. I sucked it up like I was a camel at the end of a weeklong trek across a barren dessert. About a gallon later, I collapsed onto my cot on the cement. I was so tired that I couldn't even pee. For the first time in many, many hours, sleep finally came.

CHAPTER 4

Pride's Consequences

Two days after the accident, I was moved to Sandy Mosh, the county's satellite jail a few miles down the road. I figured the move's purpose was to keep me in isolation in protective custody so they could watch me more closely. I assumed the jail cops considered me to be a suicide risk. That was normal procedure in a death case like mine. Although I never seriously considered suicide as an option, I was plagued with constant doubt and guilt regarding my children's and my future. Besides that, I didn't want my kids to ever have to explain to anyone why their dad's head-meat and marrow were scattered all over a floor or a back wall somewhere.

My new quarters were similar to the isolation cell at the main jail. God must have put one of his guardian angels to work too, because there were several more deputies I knew who went out of their way to help me out. During a brief conversation with one of them, we discussed the main reason why I was isolated. I found out it wasn't because the cops thought I might commit suicide. They knew me better than that. It was because I was an ex-cop. I had forgotten, but inmates in the jail system were notorious for killing cops or ex-cops as soon as they were detected. To all members of the criminal element, cops were equal to child molesters as the worst scum on earth. Being dead was all we were good for. So I had to be housed separately for my personal protection.

I expressed my boundless gratitude for the guard's concern for my welfare. I was also grateful I didn't have to physically combat any of the other inmates who may have recognized me from years earlier. I had Sheryl and our kids on my mind, and I didn't need the distraction for sure. By chow time on the evening of the third day after the accident, I felt my mind and body were beyond repair. I hadn't budged from by bunk since my move to the Mush, and I still couldn't sleep. The conversation with my attorney plagued every cognitive cell, and the looming horror of my inability to attend Sheryl's funeral with my kids continued to plague my skull.

I didn't hear him enter my cell during my desperate search for la-la land. But somewhere on my way to total unconsciousness, a correctional officer rudely awakened me with a smack on my foot. He told me I had visitors when I emerged from my stupor. I had no idea it was visiting time, and I had forgotten I was allowed to receive visitors during my initial incarceration. I also knew I wasn't bailing out yet. The guard would have told me if I was.

I hobbled to the visiting room upon the guard's command, sat down on a round wooden stool facing a large piece of see-through plexi-glass, and stared at the closed door where I assumed the visitors would enter. The cop informed me that I had several people waiting to see me, but I only had a half an hour total for all of them. So I knew I needed to budget my time. I remembered those jail rules from years earlier, and I successfully held back my contempt for them so my privilege wouldn't be stripped. Compassion for criminals was a rare commodity. I desperately needed to see a friendly face besides my attorney's.

When I saw my brother's big ugly mug duck under the doorway, and my sister and my mom on his coattail, I promptly broke down into another unstoppable crying jag. All of our eyes met as they entered the room. All three of them felt my agony, and they cried with me. As they sat on the round stools on their side of the glass, all of our hands seemed to reach up to the glass simultaneously and press against each other. I grabbed my phone and talked to them all. We ached to be able to touch and hug each other. But that was against the rules. Mom explained that as soon as she got the call from Mark she tried her best to fly out on Monday. But there were no flights from Kamloops, British Columbia, Canada until Tuesday. Before she booked the 1500-mile flight, she got Darryl and Connie on the horn and asked them if they wanted to accompany her. Mom was going no matter what. She was extremely riled and adamant. Not even a blockheaded team of mules could have reined her in. We all laughed while we cried as Darryl joked about the mule story, how mad Mom became at every little delay at the airport, and how she cussed at the pokey drivers in traffic keeping her away from her son who needed her.

The cop came in again fifteen minutes later. He told my brother, sister, and mother they had to leave and that I had more visitors. My mom had told me that Mark was going to spring me soon, and that I just needed to try to be patient. We all laughed again when she said the word patient, because they all knew that was a word that didn't exist in my vocabulary. They left with all of us waving wildly at each other while we all dropped more crocodile tears. But before the door could close behind them, Mom ran back the few steps to the phone and told me she would be there for me when I got out no matter how long it took. Our hands met on the glass one more time. We smiled at each other with tear-filled eyes. Then she was gone.

Mark walked through the door less than a minute later, and I started bawling again like a hungry newborn calf. He immediately expressed his unconditional love and support for me. Then he proceeded to talk fast as there was so little time left in our visit. He explained about the bail situation and how he was struggling to get a judge to set the final bail due to the public's outcry.

"I have the $20,000 for your bail. Coach and Steve pitched in some to help out, but the judge on your case is thinkin' about raising it to $300,000 now, or not allowing you bail at all," Mark explained anxiously.

"You mean to tell me my bail is not even set yet?" I almost yelled back at Mark in my total frustration. I couldn't believe the monster's ruthlessness out there. But I knew I was helpless. All I could do was to trust Mark and my friends to get me out somehow.

"You have a bail hearing tomorrow. If they set the bail, whatever it is, we'll get you out. I've already made the arrangements with a bailsman," Mark continued.

"Don't worry about the money. I just need a few weeks to get it," I explained to Mark humbly. I tried to express my gratitude, but Mark wouldn't have any of it.

"Forget it. You'd do the same for me. The important thing is to get you out so you can be with your kids. And if you have to go to prison, we'll take care of your kids till you get out. So don't worry about stuff. Everybody knows it was an accident. You have many friends and family out there who love you and are rootin' for you," he said encouragingly. I still had absolutely no control over my emotions, and I began to cry again.

I didn't know it until Mark's visit, but by the time I was moved to the satellite jail, Mark and Tammy had already proven their true magnificence as friends. When Tammy said on the phone earlier that they would take care of everything, she wasn't kidding. They had seen to my kids' needs. They did all the dirty work to make all the necessary phone calls. They had taken time off work to take care of my business. Besides all that, they had personally thrown in $15,000 out of the $20,000 total for my bail. They hawked the equity in their house, and both of their retirements as collateral for the bondsman just so I could get out of jail and be with my kids at Sheryl's funeral.

My visiting time was over before we knew it. There was still so much to discuss, but we were powerless to buck the system. I just had to suck it up and take my lumps like a man, like my dad used to tell me every day when I was a kid. Mark and my family were gone, but at least I knew my kids were doing okay under the circumstances. I was greatly relieved to know I had so many friends and family for support. Between the public outcry outside the jail bars and all of the negative consequences due to my actions, my friends and family were a godsend. I tried my best to wait patiently to bail out, but I couldn't help distressing if I was going to get out in time for the funeral or not.

The next day or so was gruesome—physically and emotionally. I ate very little. I felt so weak I didn't move much from my cell-bunk except to pee and to try to stay hydrated. While I reflected on the recent events in my life, it was quite interesting to me what I was able to endure for the four days in jail after the accident. The comforts of home had ceased to exist. In fact, nothing in my life was the same. I had exhibited such a disgusting behavior that society's rules saw fit to strip me of all of my comforts and privileges. Water was suddenly a vital commodity for basic health and survival, and the thirst-quenching beer, hot morning coffee, ice-cold milk for dinner, and delicious homemade foods became only fantasies conjured up in my mind. I couldn't dial a phone at will just to shoot the bull. My clothes were filthy and bloody. And I smelled so badly I could hardly endure my own stench. Besides all that, I was starting to think I would be a cripple with my back out of whack as badly wracked as it felt. The sad thing was that I knew all of it was going to be my existence for many years to come in prison.

A little later, God granted me one of his countless miracles. Finally, four days after the accident and the night before Sheryl's funeral, Mark bailed me out. For whatever reason, the judge decided to set bail at $200,000. By the time the cop came to get me from my cell, I had all but given up hope. In a daze, I hobbled out of my cell. I trudged along behind the guard as well as I could muster, and slowly, we continued down several long hallways and through many steel doors that opened and shut with great crashes. All of them echoed eerily like doors in a dark dungeon in some lost castle. Slowly, my mind began to register the reality of my release. I was finally going to be able to put that part of my hell in my rearview mirror, at least until I headed to prison.

I halted abruptly at the last door while the jail cop searched for the right key. Through the small plexi-glass window, I could see about twenty-five of my family and friends waiting patiently for me to come out. I couldn't believe my eyes. I had just been the cause of Sheryl's death, and Kodi, Logan, my mom, Darryl, Connie, and several friends had come to support me. The spectacle was very strange to me, to say the least. When I walked out of the door, I forgot my physical pain altogether, and I didn't cry. I could only smile sheepishly. I walked slowly to Kodi and we hugged. Hard. I looked into her eyes and our eyes welled up. She said it was okay. She knew it was an accident. Logan was next. He said it was okay too. Then systematically, I slowly made my way around the room hugging and smiling. But the strangest thing was happening. No one was really speaking. Their warm smiles of forgiveness overwhelmed me. Everyone continued to watch my emancipation as I tried my best to hug my immeasurable gratefulness for their love and support for me. It was truly God's graciousness that allowed me that extraordinary pleasure.

I rode with Mark and my kids back to my apartment when we finally walked out of the jailhouse. We ate and talked about the accident and my jail experience for hours. Then I slept. My bed felt like heaven. And I slept. I didn't awake until about seven the next morning, and when I did, I knew the day was going to be another monster. It was the day before Sheryl's funeral, and it was also the day of Sheryl's formal viewing. On top of that, it was the day I had to face Sheryl's family and friends.

However, before I could physically endure the viewing, let alone emotionally, my first order of business was to seek help for my back. The only thing I could think of to do at that early time in the morning was to start calling chiropractors out of the yellow pages and pray one of them could take me before the noontime viewing. God must have been hearing my prayers, because I found a chiropractor who was game to treat me right away. I think he felt sorry for me after I gave him the brief version of the accident, its outcome, and the rest of my story, because he was willing to treat me at his office an hour later.

After I saw the chiropractor, I really started to believe that God existed and he truly did grant miracles. From the doctor's x-rays, I could plainly see that my back was twisted into several odd-shaped pretzels. But, after he snapped me around for about fifteen minutes, every vertebra in my back felt like it was back where it was supposed to be. I didn't feel 100 percent normal physically, but my back was mobile once again. And I had flexibility enough to move and bend without unbearable pain shooting throughout my body. I was still quite stiff; I had to go back for several follow-ups later on, but the fact my pain was all but gone gave me a new faith in miracles to be sure.

I had driven to the doctor's office by myself, and when I walked out of his office, a new hurricane of guilt swept through me. For a short time, I had felt pretty good because my back was okay again. However, I caught myself thinking of me—yet again. Sheryl was dead, and I was still walking around healthy. I wasn't mangled, crushed like a bug, or crippled for life. I was healthy. I might have been messed up mentally, but I was healthy otherwise. All I could think about was how I didn't deserve to be walking or talking or breathing any more. Sheryl needed to be the live and healthy one—not me. Consequently, as I drove the ten miles back to my apartment, the thunderclouds of shame opened once again and drowned my cheeks with their acid rain.

Sheryl's funeral was an incredible celebration. Over the years, Sheryl had earned the reputation as being the epitome of daughters, friends, and athletes everywhere. She was loved and respected by all who knew her. And on a scale of one to ten, Sheryl broke the high end of the scale to pieces with her courage, determination, high moral standards, and character. Hundreds of people thronged to pay their respects to Sheryl; to all who attended, and to all who knew Sheryl, her loss was extraordinarily tragic.

For me the funeral was an awesome tribute to my wife. And as I sat in the front row beside my kids, my emotions were completely out of control. My brain was still working, thinking, and reasoning properly at all. But it seemed like every few seconds, thoughts of Sheryl and what I had done to her triggered uncontrollable tears and sobbing jags. The speakers lauded Sheryl for her infinite enthusiasm for life, and for her constant efforts to help everyone in need. I cried. I cried my support for all of the accolades Sheryl had earned in her life. I mourned her death at the same time.

From time to time, I glanced over to my kids sitting beside me. Their eyes were also red and awash with tears, but they seemed to be in control of their emotions somewhat. I wasn't. Every time I seemed to start to get a hold of myself, the horrible image of Sheryl being methodically and cruelly crushed under the truck would cast me immediately back into deep despair. The sobbing would always continue as if on cue.

Sitting at the funeral in my emotional psychosis, I prayed to God for his forgiveness over and over and over. As I prayed, I also began to try to reason and understand why God allowed me to live and Sheryl to die. After all, I was the drunk driver—the animal—the detestable creep who was responsible for Sheryl's death and the hurt I caused everyone. Why was I not killed, or maimed, I thought? Why did Sheryl have to die so awfully? Why couldn't I be the one dead and Sheryl still alive?

Sometime during the dilemma inside my head at the funeral, I began to rationalize that, by allowing me to survive the accident unscathed physically, God was forcing me to atone for my sins by making me suffer. If God had taken my life instead of Sheryl's, I would never have realized the hurt I had caused my family due to my selfishness and stubborn pride over the years. Sheryl had told me countless times not to drink and drive. She even said that she hoped I wouldn't kill someone someday. She also said she hoped it wasn't one of my kids when it happened. But, noooo! I wouldn't listen. No way. Not Randy Wiens. I was above the law and nothing bad was going to happen. I could handle my liquor.

The funeral ended. A few days later, I began the inevitable process of mounting my defense. I was facing four, eight, or twelve years in prison for gross vehicular manslaughter. Although I had admitted full responsibility for drinking and driving to the cops at the accident scene, and to God, and I confessed my sins to everyone I came in contact with, including my attorney, the district attorney, the judge, and Sheryl's family, the powers that be were working diligently to make it the maximum term allowable by law. The idea of spending one minute in prison puckered my sphincter, let alone twelve years. So I embarked on the battle of my life literally.

The initial visit with my attorney after Mark posted my bond turned out to be just a continuation of the devastating consequences I was already facing. The blows seemed to destroy most of the remaining self-esteem and emotional strength I had left. Besides the consequences I had been dealing with thus far, my attorney kept on beating me up viciously like I was the heavy bag in a professional wrestler's daily workout regimen. He informed me that it may cost as much as $50,000 to retain his services from initial counsel to sentencing and beyond. And he needed $10,000 up front just to start. Additionally, he said that because of the dynamics of my case, including the powerful influence of all the outside forces, I should prepare myself for the worst. In other words, there were people out in the community who were working tirelessly to send me away for twelve years for gross vehicular manslaughter.

To be totally honest, this possibility scared me to death. I knew that public opinion, especially small community power, had incredible clout in the judicial system. I knew I had messed up very, very badly, and there were many people who loved and respected Sheryl. Consequently, in my paranoia, I believed the great enemy out there was picking sides for Sheryl's cause and against me. I knew some only fought for the drinking and driving cause itself, and they saw my case as an awesome opportunity to use me as an example for all of society's benefit. In their minds, a higher prison term would naturally serve as a strong deterrent against drunk driving everywhere the second the sentence was administered.

In my grand paranoia, I understood. And I was afraid. Twelve years in prison? What would happen to my kids, I thought? Would they be able to enjoy success without their mother or me around to help them prepare for life? Would they be ok? I detested myself because of the pain and anguish I caused them and everyone else.

However, the mortician wasn't finished his banging on my coffin just yet. He continued his hammering. In other words, my attorney informed me that, if I were convicted of the felony, I would be deported back to Canada upon my release from prison because I was a Canadian citizen. I would never be allowed to return to the United States again because of my convicted felon status. In society's eyes, I would be labeled as a scoundrel and a villainous character. If I did cross the Canadian border at any time, I would be facing twenty years in a federal prison somewhere for violating federal immigration laws.

From those ugly thoughts, my mind tail-spinned down the slippery slope. It slid out of control into the cruel and grotesque money monster. Simply put, if I decided to fight the deportation proceedings upon conviction of the felony charges, an immigration attorney would cost an additional $20,000 to $40,000. At the same time, I knew my children would need me more than they had ever needed anyone in their lives before. So I knew I would have to pay whatever the fee was, even if there was only one chance in a million that the immigration attorney could prevent my deportation. Why? Because after prison, I knew I had to be around my children and their families for my own sanity, as well as, I had to make up for all the heartache I caused them all, even if it took forever. And I was willing to spend every last cent I had in the world to prevent my alienation from them. Only in that way would I be able to feel like I hadn't abandoned them and that I tried my best to fix what I had broken—their faith and trust in me as their father. I had already dishonored their mother and our family. I felt I had to make it all up to my kids somehow, someway. I knew I would crack up for sure if I didn't.

The train wreck inside my head became relentless in its destructive force. The steel and cast iron mental strength I had garnered over the years was gradually twisted and obliterated. Nothing did any good until I finally decided to escape from my personal pity party. I forced my mind to think about, and begin to understand that, my friends, my family, and my blind faith in God's miracles were all I needed. I didn't know it at the time, but from the second the accident happened, I had God, family, friends, peers, and students to support me faithfully and unconditionally.

As part of all that support, a multitude of support letters arrived at the jail, the DA's office, and the judge's chambers. When my attorney informed me of the overwhelming communications, my brain was triggered to reflect upon some of the events and my behavior and thoughts while I was waiting to bail out of jail. I was especially inspired when I remembered that even my students had offered me their unconditional love and support. They went so far as to investigate and find out the name of the jail pastor in charge of ministering to the inmate population. When they found out who he was, they contacted him personally at his home, and they convinced him to deliver a book to me in the jail called *Hugs For the Hurting*. The book contained a myriad of stories, scriptures, and sayings to encourage and inspire the emotionally afflicted like me.

The book and its contents were incredibly appropriate and wonderful. Some of my students had even carried the book around the school campus to obtain signatures and encouraging comments to me from other teachers, students, and administrators. And, for the next several hours, I couldn't sleep anyway, so I read far into the night. Even when the lights were extinguished for the night in the entire jail, I remember hunkering against my steel cell door to capture the narrow beam of light slipping through the tiny window about five feet up on the metal cell door. There was barely enough light to distinguish the small print, but it seemed that every word I read completely mesmerized me. My emotions flowed freely, and I wasn't embarrassed about letting it all go, because there was no one around to see or hear me sob. Every message, every story, every saying, every scripture cut me to the quick like a hunter guttin' a bull moose. I had been desperate for some form of peace or solace or some tenderness from somewhere. But then I realized I found it. No, I had it all along in all the people out there who cared about me.

The following is a compilation of some of my eighth grade students' endearments. As a special bonus, my school administrators and teacher peers also wrote some kind words in *Hugs For The Hurting*. I will cherish them forever.

Mr. Wiens,
You were the best teacher I've ever known, and you are a wonderful person. I will keep you in my prayers and I will never forget you. You are such a great person and nothing will change that. Love always . . .

Mr. Wiens,
We all know what a wonderful person you are. I'm so sorry to hear about this. My thoughts and prayers are with you. Thank you for being my best teacher and idol to me. You always will be. Love always . . .

Mr. Wiens,
It's hard to imagine what you must be going through in there, but all of us in Core 2 are praying for you. We also heard the teachers called a special assembly for tomorrow afternoon to tell all the students what happened to you and your wife. We are all sad about everything, but we all know you are tough and you will be okay. Just believe and trust in the Lord, and someday, all of your troubles will seem like a bad dream. We love you Mr. Wiens. Take care, and God bless . . .
P.S. By the way, be careful in the shower.

Mr. Wiens,
You are by far my favorite teacher. You need to know that all your students support you no matter what. You need to hang in there and don't take any nonsense from anyone like you always teach us. You always teach us to get back on the buckin' bronco no matter how many times that mean ol' nag throws you. Well, we are all telling you to do the same. Get back on that horse and send him to the glue factory. You can do it. We all know in our hearts you can. We love you . . .

Randy,
We met with the students today and they, along with all of us, wish
you the best. You are sorely missed at school, and all your students are
nagging us constantly about how you are and to give you their love
when we come to visit you. Hang in there. We know you can do it. We
will try to visit soon. Keep your chin up. May God bless you and show
you His infinite mercy and forgiveness . . .

Mr. Wiens,
I am sure all of your present and past students would have loved to
sign this book and send their love and prayers . . .

As I made my way through the *Hugs For the Hurting* book, I slowly
began to realize that I had so many family members, friends, and supporters on the outside that I knew immediately I needed to stop feeling
so sorry for myself. I needed to realize and understand that, even though
there were some people out there trying their best to destroy me completely, I had a much stronger weapon of love and loyalty fighting cou-
rageously for my cause. And as I started to understand the true magnitude
of that power, I cried again and again in gratitude to Him. I was so very
thankful for all of my blessings in life, and I knew somehow, someday, I
would be able to hold my head up in the streets and face my friends
once again. I knew it would be a long time coming. But I knew for sure
it would come at some point down the muddy trail.

Above all others, Mark and Tammy were literally heroic in their
unconditional support for my children and me. They not only offered to
take care of my kids while I was in prison, but they risked their house,
their retirement, and everything they had in the world financially so I
could be with my kids and go to their mother's funeral. Ranger, Kodi,
and Logan's lives had just been dynamited to smithereens. Their life as
they knew it was gone forever. But my friends were there to pick up the
pieces. They taxied me around because I lost my license. They became
Logan's legal guardians. They cared for Kodi's needs as well as my granddaughter Carlie's. And it was all mind-boggling to me. I never expected
any of it. Until I finally meet my maker, I will never be able to fully
understand the magnitude of their complete selflessness. For all of what

Mark and Tammy did, my debt to them can never, and will never, be paid in full.

There were so many people who ran to my rescue when I needed them most. It was inconceivable to me. After the funeral, Coach Hughes, my friend of twenty-seven years, called me and told me he was coming over. He said, "Be home. I have someone I want you to meet." Of course, whenever Coach or I used that tone of voice with each other, we both had learned to heed the call and come running, whatever the reason happened to be. It has been like an unwritten law or rule throughout our friendship.

Anyway, when he showed up at my apartment an hour later, he had another man with him. He was also a Christian like Coach. Well, Coach's wisdom and insight regarding me was right on the money, because when he introduced me to Philip, we formed an instant bond I can't explain. Of course, Coach's motive was to finally capture me into his Christian fold. He used the accident as a perfect opportunity to convince me that without accepting Jesus Christ into my life as my personal Lord and Savior, there was no way on the planet that Randy Wiens could ever live at peace in his mind. Coach had been trying for years, just like Sheryl had done, to make me realize that I, like every other human individual, can't survive spiritually, emotionally, or psychologically without God commanding my life's helm. Coach knew that God was the only one who could forgive me. And until I allowed him to do just that, my own emotional healing couldn't begin.

When Coach cut Philip loose on me, I was ripe for the picking. Even through all of the tragedy and trauma I had experienced and endured somewhat successfully throughout my life, I still wasn't tough enough to endure the unsympathetic assault of gloom and doom in my life and mind after the accident. I was dreadfully desperate for forgiveness by someone or anyone. I was broken—shattered like a stomped light bulb into a million pieces of wretchedness. One minute my light was on and shining. The next minute, my mind and might were hurled into never-never land where only God's miracles could resuscitate me.

Well, God sent Coach. Coach brought Philip. Coach told me I was going with Philip to a Bible study group the next day, and I didn't have any choice in the matter. In my complete brokenness, I didn't have the energy or the fight to resist his command. So I went with him like a puppy on a leash. Philip also became my personal taxi service for all the business I had to take care of. He called me daily to offer his help to my kids and to me. But mostly, Philip became my friend. God had blessed me with Philip, and I learned an incredible amount about Christ under his direct tutelage. He graciously took me by the hand and began to show me the Lord's love and humility. Although he wasn't alone in his quest for me to find peace, he was a main contributor.

Karyn also played a major role in initiating my marathon walk with God. I had lied to her. But she forgave me. Karyn forgave me because she believed I was finally ready to know God like she did. She knew my spiritual pump was finally primed. And like the devoted and loving warrior woman she is, she went straight for my jugular. She wouldn't see me, but she did encourage me to go to church. She suggested I introduce myself to the Lord and to begin my walk with him for the sake of my children and my own inner peace. She also introduced me to many other Christians, and all of their love and graciousness flowed in boundless fashion as well. Her church peers embraced me, and without judgment, they opened their homes and their hearts in earnest to ease my pain. God had blessed me with Karyn months earlier, but I hadn't realized it, just like I had never realized how Sheryl had blessed my life for twenty-two years.

Even though I had accepted Christ as my personal savior after the accident, and I sincerely tried my best to think and to live in a Christian-like manner, I learned to hate insurance companies with a passion. Sheryl had recently died, but the trauma it caused in my mind and life was irrelevant in their eyes. All my life they had chomped at the bit hounding me for prompt payment of their insidious premiums. But when it came time to pay the policy benefits upon Sheryl's death, the red tape they subjected me to was inhumane. First of all, in my mind, my kids came first for a change. I didn't want to disrupt their lifestyle or their emotional state any more than I had already done. Consequently, I became desperate for the insurance payout so I could ensure that they wouldn't be in need of anything. Too many people had already doled out a lot of cash to take care of my kids. I was desperate to fulfill my duties as a father.

Also, my attorney needed his fees up front. I needed to reimburse Mark and Tammy the $20,000 they coughed up to bail me out of jail and so they could get their house and retirement out of hawk. I needed to pay house payments, car payments, food, and other monthly bills like everyone else on the planet. But the insurance companies simply didn't care. All I could do was wait and pray my kids would have what they needed, and to continue to make excuses to my friends and my attorney why I hadn't paid them their money. The funny thing about the whole mess was that I was the only one obsessed or worried about the money. My attorney had known me for years, and he knew I was good for it. He told me not to worry about it. When the insurance companies paid, he said I could pay him then. Same deal with Mark. He told me to stop sweating such a little thing. It was just money. But I felt a sense of urgency I hadn't felt before. I needed to get my affairs in order as fast as I could, and the sooner the better. The judicial system had given me a very short leash. I was headed to a home behind steel bars, and faxes and computers were non-existent in the big house. Phones were also going to be a rare commodity, because there were no friends where I was going this time.

During the time I was mounting my case, at no time did I try to snivel out of the felony DUI charges and my responsibility to Sheryl, her family, or society. I knew I deserved to go to prison for my filthy behavior. But I didn't believe I deserved a longer sentence than I was justly due. Although my attorney said we could try to find a loophole in my case somewhere to try to exonerate me altogether, I told him I was guilty and I wanted to plead guilty. However, I told him I definitely wanted to combat the "gross" part in the gross vehicular manslaughter charges I was faced with. Why? Because I didn't commit a separate vehicle code violation besides the DUI. And I didn't want to serve twelve years in prison if I only had to do four.

Six weeks after Sheryl's funeral, as I sat perusing my deportation papers, the phone rang rather rudely. I was horribly depressed because the cops still hadn't disproved the "gross" in the charges. When the phone rang, I immediately prayed that the call was from a representative of an insurance company. Instead though, it turned out to be my attorney calling me with the most magnificent news I had heard in a long, long time.

"Randy. Are you sitting down?" my attorney said, more excitedly than I could ever remember him communicating before.

Yes. What's goin' on?" I answered quickly. I had been totally disheartened from the harsh deportation information, and I was trying to think positive thoughts hoping for something encouraging.

"You are no longer being charged with gross vehicular manslaughter. The most time you can get now is four years in prison!" he blurted, almost yelling his enthusiasm.

"What happened?" I almost yelled back at him, in total shock and relief at the same time.

"I just received the final CHP accident report, and it clearly states here in black and white that they could find no evidence of a vehicle code violation besides the DUI. That means the whole shootin' match changes for you. Now, the minimum jail term you can receive is one year in county jail with five years probation when you get out. Or you can receive sixteen months, two years, or four years in state prison depending upon what the judge finally decides. Whatever the term is though, you will have to serve eighty-five percent of it. Because vehicular manslaughter is considered to be a violent felony in the California Penal Code, you will also be branded with one strike under the three strikes law. Simply put, the strike makes it mandatory for you to serve eighty-five percent of whatever the final sentence is. There is no appeal. That part of the sentence is set in stone." My attorney explained all the details as fast as he could.

"What? You're kiddin' me? I don't believe it!" I said, trying to keep from falling off my chair in my excitement.

The numbers eight and twelve seemed to rush through my brain like Star Trek's Voyager at warp speed. The news meant I wouldn't have to do eight or twelve years in prison after all, like my brain had been programmed to believe. I would only have to do four years maximum at eight-five percent. That translated to 40.8 months with good time and work time taken in to consideration. I still was convinced I would be sentenced to the maximum term allowed by law on the charges I was facing due to the intense pressure from the powers that be. But I thought at least the four years was much easier to stomach than the eight or twelve years I had been plagued with.

I didn't stay on my cloud number nine for very long though. The idea of going to prison at all, or even back to jail for one more minute churned my guts. Besides that, I began to question my newly found faith in God. I wondered if He really had forgiven me and if I would really ever be able to forgive myself for causing Sheryl's death.

A few days after the great news about my charges, I visited my attorney to discuss the deportation proceedings I would have to deal with when I was released from prison. My attorney confirmed that if I was convicted of the felony vehicular manslaughter and I was sentenced to more than one year, then my deportation would be automatic upon my release from prison. There was no possibility of appeal. If I was convicted of the felony and sentenced to less than a year, then I wouldn't be deported according to the federal immigration laws. Of course in my dementia, and my lack of faith in God, I expected the worst. Consequently, I resigned myself to the fact I would be in prison for almost four years. I also began to prepare my mind to accept that I would be deported and never be able to legally return to the United States for any reason. I knew that if I did return, even to visit my children, and I was subsequently caught, I would face up to twenty years in federal prison for the violation.

My mind crashed again. I had built a quality life with Sheryl in California, and the only home my kids had ever known was in California. Canada was almost completely foreign to them all. They all had visited Canada with me on several vacations, but they often expressed their heated dissent when I suggested we move to Canada as a family for a better quality of life. Instead of growing up in a concrete jungle type of environment, I had always been intrigued with moving my family to Canada so they could also experience the awesome nature and outdoor lifestyle Canada offered. But the idea of snow and ice and thirty below zero weather had always been a frightening prospect to them.

All of these thoughts raced through my mind uncontrollably. The only time I would be able to see my children would be if they came to visit me in Canada. But I knew that would cause problems too. It would be several years before any of my children could afford to travel the 1500 miles to Canada. And I sure wouldn't have the money to give them for traveling. My bail, my criminal attorney, and my immigration attorneys would have eaten up all the money I had and would have received from insurance. Plus, the fact that I would struggle to find an employer who would want to hire an ex-con and pay a half-decent wage made it all seem worse. The bottom line was that I had caused everyone a filthy and unfathomable heartache. All of the horrible consequences seemed endless. I started to think that I was better off dead too.

My sentencing date finally arrived. My mother, brother, and sister had flown back down from Canada, and my side of the courtroom was filled to capacity with my family, friends, and supporters. All of them were worried about me having to spend any time at all in prison, while the other half of the stuffed courtroom lobbied strongly for the maximum prison term allowable by law. It seemed that there were two formidable battalions of gladiators lined up to do battle. And when I turned around to face them, I was immediately confronted by another emotional scourge. I was so embarrassed and sad that I had caused everyone to be there. I thought back to a time not long before that when all of them had been in my house for dinner or a visit, including all the members of the other team at one time or another. It was sad that they had become the enemy that wanted me hung.

But after the last dog was hung and not me, the judge ruled. When she did, I was absolutely shocked when she cast her decision to the courtroom.

Paraphrased, she said: Mr. Wiens, the court has studied your case in great detail. You have pleaded guilty to vehicular manslaughter, and thereby, you have accepted responsibility for your poor choice to drink and drive. Further, the court believes that you acted without malice and your wife's death was a tragic accident. Although there has been strong argument to the contrary, the court believes the facts of the case speak for themselves. At this time, the court hereby sentences you to prison for a period of sixteen months. You are immediately remanded to the custody of the bailiff.

As the judge informed the packed courtroom of my sentence, I looked over at my attorney in disbelief. I glanced back at my family and friends blankly. I wasn't going to prison for twelve years, or eight years, or even four years. I only had to serve eighty-five percent of sixteen months, which in turn, calculated out to be about thirteen-and-a-half months. I could do that standing on my head, I thought.

As I was being handcuffed and shackled by the bailiff, I made eye contact with my family and friends one more time. It seemed everyone on my side of the courtroom had tear-filled eyes. They were all very sad for me. They knew I was in for the ultimate test of a lifetime. We all had heard the same war stories about prison. Gangs, rapes, drugs, and killings were all the horrible truths. They knew, and I knew, prison was going to be no picnic.

CHAPTER 5

The House of the Gladiators

The last shackle clicked into place around my right anklebone, and the bailiff escorted me out of the rear of the courtroom down the hallway past the judge's chambers. I didn't see my family or friends anymore after that. As I hobbled in the direction of the jail about a block away, a loathsome loneliness engulfed me. I was sad. I was sad for all the people I had disappointed so grotesquely. I was sad because I had caused so many so much pain. And I was sad for myself.

It didn't take long to cover the few hundred yards to the main jail booking area. But during the short trek, my shackles self tightened. The bailiff had neglected to double-lock the metal connectors properly, and every movement caused the shackles to tighten by themselves. When I told the bailiff about the pain, he blew me off. He said I would be at the jail in a minute. He would take them off then. Just then, I realized I had better not antagonize him. I had already caused myself enough agony. So I simply kept my lips zipped and fought through the torture.

It seemed like a long walk off a short pier. But I finally hobbled up to the outer doors to the same jail booking area where I first heard Sheryl was dead after the accident. The bailiff, who had me in tow by my left elbow, had been guiding me through the parking lot of the jail like I was a neck-reined cattle pony. When we reached the door, he had some worthwhile advice for me before he delivered me to the same holding cell where a dozen or so other convicted felons awaited the prison bus.

"If I were you, I'd keep my mouth shut in the holding cell. You never know who is on the hunt or scoping you out for future use," he told me frankly, while he unlocked the heavy steel door casually.

At first, I didn't know what he meant by his remark. However, like a bad dream, a past experience suddenly triggered in my brain when I was a cop. It had something to do with a skinny kid fresh out of high school who was convicted of auto theft and several burglaries. He also was awaiting his bus to prison. Unfortunately, for the young whippersnapper though, the wait was just long enough for him to yap some immature remark to a weathered old con on his way through the county jail system for another eight-year stretch for armed robbery and mayhem. To the con, the skinny kid was simply a punk and a toy that needed to be trained properly regarding basic respect. The kid needed to learn when to talk, what to say, and what not to say when he did spout his naivety. Unfortunately, in this story though, by the kid opening his mouth at all, it didn't matter what came out of it. He was out of line and automatically disrespected the veteran con.

The dream was short, and as the brief vision ended regarding the semi-naked kid bent over the wooden holding cell bench and the hardened con going at him like a crazed animal in heat, I thanked the bailiff for the advice. My main intention from that second on was to keep my mouth shut tight.

Somehow, I managed to chop-step the last forty feet or so to the booking counter without falling over. My feet and ankles were numb from the vise-like steel clamping them so tightly and preventing my blood from flowing freely enough to allow proper limb function. When the bailiff eventually unhooked my manacles, my ankles were black and blue. He didn't care much though. He just relinquished control of me to the jail booking guard like he had done it a few thousand times before. The jail guard fingerprinted me again and told me to go stand by the holding cell about fifteen feet behind me. I did as he ordered like a good little convict. While he walked around the counter to unlock the holding tank door, I noticed a dozen or so other sentenced convicts already prepped for prison and awaiting our bus.

However, before the guard could find the right key, a familiar voice seemed to jump out of nowhere from behind me somewhere.

"Hey, Wiens! Hold on a minute," the friendly voice said. He was an old friend in the sheriff's department. He still worked in the jail after all that time.

The jail cop and I turned toward my friend's order simultaneously, while the other sentenced inmates in the tank watched intently through the heavy plated plexi-glass. I didn't realize it then, but every inmate's contact with the cops was highly scrutinized by all other convicts. If there was any reason to believe a fellow convict was receiving special treatment from the cops at all, that convict would be seriously hurt or killed before someone could blink an eyelash. In prison, cons were scorned and taken care of in brutal fashion if they became friendly with the cops. The cops, all cops, were the enemy. To the cons, they had nothing coming, just like convicts had nothing coming from the cops, simple as that.

As my friend approached us, he nodded to me subtly before he came into the inmates' view. He knew the game and the score very well in his long tenure. He was just trying to look out for me the best he could. Instinctively, I showed zero body language acknowledging my friend. And when he got close enough, he faced me with his back to the cons so they couldn't read his lips or hear him speak to me.

"Don't talk. Don't react to what I say to you in any way. Just listen. Guard, wait for me by the printing area," my friend said to me sternly and without looking at the guard.

"I need to educate you quickly. Your life and or your virginity may depend on it. I know you remember a lot about jail and prison, but I still want to make sure you haven't forgotten a few vital tidbits for your safety. I want my friend to come back in one piece and not be someone else's piece," he told me frankly, genuinely concerned about my safety.

"First and foremost, don't trust anyone. Only talk to people when you absolutely have no other choice in the matter. Second, keep your mouth shut where you're goin'. That includes talkin' to any cops. The less you talk, the less exposure you have to the main population, and the less information they will know about you to use against you. You may or may not understand what I'm sayin'. But listen to me. Talk to yourself, talk to the bedpost, or talk to a toilet. Maybe that way, they will think you're psycho and not bother you. Also, cops have snitches all over the place in prison, and you definitely don't want to be caught in the middle of any drug, sex, or gang activity. Keep to yourself, and always have your ass to a wall somewhere. Even though you have old meat, there are plenty of sickos who would like a taste of it. Last but not least, always be prepared with some of that hockey roughness and meanness you have. I guarantee you will be confronted. Everyone in prison is tested repeatedly to see if they can take care of themselves physically or if they can be used as a sex toy or punk," he explained to me clearly, slightly curling his upper lip in a subtle smile still facing away from the other cons. I knew that even though he smiled, he was dead serious.

Without another word, he turned on his heel and quickly walked off. I waited only a minute or two for the guard to come back, but during that short time, I had a chance to glance through the plexi-glass and around the inside of the tank. I tried to observe and get a quick picture of what the other inmates looked like and if they had been watching me during the commander's speech to me. Of course, I was being eyeballed like a monster python sizing up an unwary warthog in a jungle somewhere.

When the guard opened the door, I was scared to death. I forgot about Sheryl. I forgot about my kids. I forgot about everything except to prepare myself for the worst, including fighting to the death if that is what it took. When I stepped in, their smell alone was different than normal people. The air hung thick with old sweat like the thousands of athletes I had been around all my life. Every face was haggard and unshaven, while their orange and yellow jumpsuits hung on them loosely. Many of them had rolled up their long sleeves and had taken off their tops because of the unbearable summer heat and humidity. Almost every inch of their exposed skin was covered by tattoos of some sort or another. I didn't look or stare at any of them to distinguish what gang affiliation they represented. I was also careful not to make more than a brief eye contact with any of the cons. In jail or prison, eye contact with unfamiliar people was considered to be disrespectful and was avoided at all costs to avert trouble. I remembered that little gem from my law enforcement days.

As I made my way down the center of the holding tank, I felt like I was running the gauntlet. Every eye in the tank scanned and scoped me out. My intention was to simply shut up and sit on the far end of the room by the toilet where I had spotted an empty seat through the plexiglass, but about half way across the tank, a hunter was already sniffing out his prey.

"Hey. Homey. Where ya goin?" a stocky, fully tattooed white guy asked me sardonically.

Instantly, I knew I was already being tested. My intention was to be a mute, but I had just been backed into a corner. Without thinking I responded. "I'm gonna take a leak, then I'm gonna sit right there and mind my own business like you need to do," I responded just as sarcastically. I stared at him square in the face and pointed to the empty seat without looking at it at the same time.

I knew if I showed any weakness at all, I would be easy pickings. So I simply continued on to the toilet and began urinating. Fortunately, the urinal's position was such that I could plainly observe any movement the con made with my peripheral vision.

"How much time you catch?" the same con said a little less aggressively this time.

I could tell he was trying to backtrack. It was obvious he didn't expect my aggressive response. I knew I had done the right thing immediately by returning his arrogance. Otherwise we would have been duking it out already. He really didn't want any trouble. It was all simply a game. It was the same game every inmate in every jail or prison had to endure. How each of them played determined how easily or harshly the convict's time was spent behind bars. However, the sad thing about it was that I realized I was one of them. I had the same jumpsuit, the same convict status, and the same stigma as the lowest scum on earth.

I calmly finished my business at the toilet and zipped up my jumpsuit. As I turned away from the toilet, I looked right in his face again.

"I'd rather not talk about it," I said to him in an even tone. I was trying hard not to instigate any further confrontation with him or any of the other sentenced cons watching the scene intently. Then I proceeded to sit down slowly without making any more eye contact with anyone. It was his move, and I prepared myself for anything. But nothing else happened. Apparently, by my standing up for myself, I had garnered a little respect.

Conversation in the holding cell was almost nil. And about fifteen minutes later, three prison bus guards called us all out of the tank one by one. They shackled and cuffed us. They led us to the bus in the sally-port outside the booking area doorway. As I hobbled along at approximately arm's length behind a black con, I stared directly at the ground. I wanted to be as inconspicuous as possible. Besides that, I began to contemplate future altercations I knew were inevitable. I began to worry about myself and my own behavior and reaction to further trouble. I worried about how I was going to be able to avoid doing battle with some of the idiots I would be around for a long time. I wondered how I was going to be able to avoid fighting and getting involved in activities I didn't want any part of like gangs, their endless games of intimidation, and their lust for power and control over everyone not in their gang. I knew myself too well when it came to my short fuse. That bothered me a lot.

We all loaded up like fattened cattle prodded through a chute headed to slaughter. One of the prison guards stood up at the front of the bus when we were all seated and strapped in securely. He proceeded to inform us in his condescending tone that we were on our way to DVI (Deuel Vocational Institute). It was a prison in Tracy, California. It was nicknamed the Gladiator School. I knew he was playing his little intimidation game too when I noticed several of the old cons smirk when the guard spit the words at all of us. He used the Gladiator School term as a shock tactic. His intention was to scare us virgin cons and to humor the weathered and experienced ones. Before he finished, he made sure every one in his payload knew the rules of the bus too. Absolutely no talking was aloud. If we were caught talking, we would be forcibly removed from our seat, dragged to the steel cage in the back of the bus, transported to DVI with the rest of the load, and then placed or dragged to the hole for six months before our file was reviewed.

While I rode the bus quietly vexing, an old white con struck up a conversation with me in spite of the rules. We were towards the back of the bus, and he told me if we whispered, the sound of the bus would block our voices. I didn't want to talk at all, but I realized right away it might be in my best interest to listen. The con was obviously weathered. I thought maybe I could learn something from him. I was right too. I learned that the reception centers had several purposes. The main one was to segregate violent and non-violent convicts from one another. Also, the cops wanted to disintegrate gang affiliations as soon as possible so one particular gang didn't have the manpower to physically dominate other gangs. This was done to maintain an equal balance in numbers regarding race. They didn't allow one race to be too dominant over another; otherwise race wars and violence could not be avoided. But basically, all the reception center's motives were to minimize violence and maximize safety for everyone, especially the guards. The con also explained that all convicts were expendable. Cops weren't.

During the long one-and-a-half hour bus ride, the con went on to tell me I would spend anywhere from thirty to ninety days at DVI. The time in Tracy's prison would be the most difficult for me because of my rookie status in the prison system. He told me the experience would be a valuable education for my survival wherever I was sent eventually.

About a half hour before we pulled up at DVI, the old con finished with a strong warning.

"This place is where the young and dumb and old alike must learn to play the game or become someone's personal property sexually. Either you can handle it, or you can't. If you can, you will simply chalk this up to a harsh experience and go about your life a better person for it when you get out. If you can't, your guts will be the painting on the prison walls."

Consequently, much of the rest of the bus ride to the Gladiator School was spent in hard deliberation. I worried about what was in store for me in prison. I wondered if God really was out there somewhere looking after me, and most of all, I wondered if I would ever be able to forgive myself for Sheryl's death. Again and again, the vision of Sheryl's body being slowly snuffed out because of my ignorance and stupidity was a haunting burden I simply couldn't shake. I wanted to cry so badly. I wanted to sob my misery to the world, and I really didn't care if I was in a prison bus headed for hell or not.

But then, just as suddenly in my delusional state, my mind snapped back to reality. I realized if I cried where I was sitting right then, I would ultimately be signing my own death warrant. I would be displaying a gross weakness. The predators hovering all around me were like kids in a candy store stalking fresh jars of candy. If I showed weakness in any form, it would be like chickens on a grasshopper for sure. The other cons would see me cry and store it in their memory banks. They would come hunting at their earliest opportunity. So I didn't cry. I just sat. I just sat and gazed wearily out of the darkly tinted, steel barred, prison bus windows; chained and shackled.

The slog to the Gladiator School was extremely laborious emotionally. I tried to think about happy thoughts, like my kids and friends. But I fantasized about Karyn especially. I knew my kids would be fine under Mark and Tammy's care and tutelage, so my ardent worrying about them had subsided somewhat by then. However, I was in desperate need of something soft. Too many things had been harsh and brutal. Karyn's vision seemed to be the only light at the end of the torpid tunnel I was mired in. The memory of her femininity and the thoughts of her compassion, grace, and mercy seemed to linger on my lips like sweet nectar. I found out quickly that if I concentrated hard enough, Karyn's incredible tenderness was the only thought that could break the impregnable barriers to the pleasure center in my brain.

After a short time, thinking about Karyn softened my mind up pretty well. It wasn't nearly as hard and negative and cynical like it had been for so long since the accident. I even started to think about my professional baseball days again and the incredible accomplishment it was to play at the Triple AAA level. Baseball memories melded into hockey memories and the flashes of brilliance I once had with the puck on my stick. They in turn gave way to fantasizing about horses and dogs, my favorite mammals in the whole world. I remembered the Black Stallion books I read as a young teenager and the young boy who rode the black so wild and carefree. He never had a care in the world as long as the wild horse was running between his knees at full gallop. I remembered the countless days Rascal, my shepherd mix, and I would wander the high country of Canada when I went up there during my summer vacations from teaching school. He was the best friend I'd ever had, and loyalty was his middle name. All of those magical thoughts took my mind off the gruesome reality of going to my new prison home—for a little while anyway.

The bus finally pulled up to a fearful prison gate. The fanciful thoughts I was enjoying so vividly vanished immediately when the air brakes hissed us to a dead stop in front of it. To me, the gate was the doorway. It led through to the inside of the great monument symbolizing my gross moral turpitude. It was topped with concertina wire. The gate itself was hewn with thick wire and steel. The concrete walls seemed to surround the entire world. Everywhere I looked outside the bus, I saw monstrous walls of cement reaching to the sky. They all were bonneted nastily with the razor sharp cutting wire that wouldn't be vanquished by any human's flesh.

The only way in or out of the place was through the heavily guarded gate, or through the three-foot thick concrete walls, or by a flying machine of some sort. Escape was impossible it seemed, not that I had really thought about it much. But, it did seem a little like overkill. Who in their right mind would even attempt an escape from these modern prisons, I thought. At the same time though, I thought about all the movies I had watched in my life about prison and escape stories. But then, I realized they were only fantasy. I was living in the real world, passing through real gates to live in a real prison because of my disrespect for society's laws.

The guards at the gate seemed to flock out of the guardhouse in droves to inspect the bus outside, and inside, before all of us convicts de-bussed. They strutted around like old mother orangutans inspecting their young for ticks and other cooties. Only in this case, they were searching for any weapons, drug paraphernalia, or contraband the bus guards might have missed somewhere back on the dusty trail.

The guards looked mean and antagonistic. So I didn't try to make eye contact with any of them. I had enough trouble keeping my own mental processes intact let alone combating an indomitable force. I learned from my police experience long ago that few people ever crossed the law and won. Most succumbed willingly, and those who didn't brought the wrath of cops a hundred fold. Except for a woman scorned, attacking or hurting a cop reaped the wrath of all their Greek gods. In other words, a cop's gods were all the other cops within radio distance.

The gate officers funneled back into their cubbyhole alongside the prison gate when they were completely satisfied all us convicts were clean. Then the bus lurched forward once again. The driver didn't even have time to shift out of second gear before he pulled up again by an expansive sally port in a billowing cloud of dust encompassing the entire bus. The bus door flew open immediately. A different troop of prison guards stormed onto the bus. They seemed to bark orders at us all at once as they aggressively made their way single file down the aisle with their puffed out chests and combative tone in their voices.

The cops were so organized; it was like they were intent on accomplishing a dangerous mission with minimal casualties. No one was going to keep them from accomplishing their task either. They knew precisely, in what chair exactly, members of the Black Guerrilla Family, Mexican Mafia, Nortenos, Surenos, New Order, Nazi Low Riders or any other gang members were seated. One by one, the guards extricated the gangsters from their seats and off the bus and towards the reception area. They were taking no prisoners and leaving no doubt who was in charge either. All I could do was wait my turn. While I did wait, a new fear rushed through my body. I shivered from its weight on my soul. This was it, I thought. I wasn't coming out of that hellhole for over a year—if I came out at all—alive—or in one piece and unmolested.

Before it was my turn to debark the bus, the last Nazi Low Rider passed me from behind somewhere. As he hobbled past my seat about half way down the aisle, I glanced up at his face briefly, and then towards the back of the bus. I didn't have much mobility due to all the tools tying me down like a hog-tied heifer. But I could turn my head enough to see the rear of the bus was emptying rapidly. I could see plainly my turn was coming up soon, and I mentally prepared to enter my new home. I knew I had to be ready for anything, including any potential confrontation with one or more of these mean-looking gang members somewhere down the road. And that thought sent another shot of fear through my neck and head. Again I shuddered.

As I turned my head to the front again, the back of a Nazi Low Rider's huge square head caught my attention rather rudely. But luckily, it also snapped me out of my terror. My eyes seemed to glue onto a large tattoo on the side of the con's neck under his ear. A multitude of other tattoos completely covered the rest of his neck. I could see many of them finished far below his jumpsuit collar, but the tattoo in dark black and blue letters depicting "IRONMAN" stood out like a sore thumb. Just then I froze in my seat. For a split second, I couldn't move. A guard growled my name from the front of the bus somewhere. I was going in.

The name "Ironman" intrigued me somewhat though, and I continued my observation of him until he disappeared down the steps of the bus. I imagined he was a well-weathered con who knew all the ropes. He was definitely no first timer like me. I guarantee you that. It was too obvious, especially when the guards swarmed around him as he hobbled off the last step of the bus. They weren't taking any chances at all with this guy. At the same time, watching the gathering around Ironman and the obvious respect everyone was giving him helped me take my mind off my fear. And I was grateful for it. I knew I was going to need all my faculties and smarts to get through this mess.

Ironman was at least six-feet, three inches tall and 240 pounds of muscle rippling through his jumpsuit. He was like a white panther with cruel eyes just waiting for the perfect moment to strike. He exuded meanness and power at the same time as he carried himself like a seasoned veteran among children. And strangely, my eyes seemed to be drawn to his stature even more. He was mesmerizing, and for no apparent reason, I became very, very scared of him. I became scared of him and everyone like him in that whole nightmarish place.

Somehow, it made perfect sense to me to get my mind off Ironman and the other gang bangers as fast as I could. I guess God was with me, because almost instantly, I began to reflect upon the time and effort the prison system put in to their segregation policies. It looked to me like the system's diligence minimized the violence exponentially, and it saved many lives and serious injuries when the gangs in smaller numbers snapped and went off on each other.

But like every war, I knew there were always some who escaped and lived to fight another day in vengeance of their dead comrades. Consequently, even though segregation solved some bloodshed, I learned a little later in my new prison education that gang-affiliated cons were infinitely tenacious in their mission to attain control and power over all others. So, I did the most reasonable thing I could think of. I stopped obsessing. And when I got the order to move out, I exited the bus with the last group of white guys not affiliated with a gang of some sort.

The traffic cop commanding the double doors leading into the prison from the sally port was about the size of a Budweiser Clydesdale. It looked to me like he could eat a horse in one sitting and still crave an entire sweet cherry pie before his first belch. As I approached the door chop-stepping about four convicts back, I noticed that every con followed the giant's arm signals and brief commands without making eye contact with him even for a split second. I thought that was kind of humorous, and without thinking about it, I looked right into his eyes when it was my turn to go through the unshackling process.

"You must be from Texas," I told the gargantuan man casually with a slight smile escaping my lips.

As the last word came out with my little smile tacked onto it, I thought to myself what a complete fool I was. I shouldn't be looking at this guy or talking to anyone. I should simply be minding my own business. There would be plenty of time to defend against confrontational men and situations for the next thirteen-and-a-half months. I thought how stupid I was for exposing myself like that. However, just as I began beating myself up yet again, the guard's retort was a surprise.

"Only steers and queers come from Texas. I'm from Canada," he responded calmly, returning a slight smile and simultaneously motioning me towards a Caucasian-only granite holding tank.

Well, I have to say that I was pleasantly taken aback. Not only did he see the movie, *Officer and a Gentleman*, because that is where he stole the steers and queers line from, I had a fellow Canadian around. Also, I had come across a guy who wasn't as mean and as nasty as I had perceived every prison guard to be since they picked me up at my hometown jail. Although I wanted to tell the guard I was from Canada too, I realized I might have said too much already. I had forgotten to be part of the puppets and not talk to or make contact with anyone, especially the cops. I knew I had failed to heed my friend's advice again. I was lucky before, but I began to wonder how long my luck would last if I didn't play the game the way it was culturally in the prison system. Contact with others would surely bring trouble soon enough without me initiating more.

When I was passed off to the unshackler, I looked around sheepishly to see if any of the other convicts had heard or picked up on my short exchange with my fellow Canuck. But I couldn't tell. There were so many holding cells in the area full to the brim with new arrivals that I didn't have time to look around enough. I just hoped my stupidity wasn't noticed.

When I was directed through the single revolving door, I noticed immediately that it only turned one way, so once a convict was inside, he couldn't get back out unless a different door ten feet down the wall was opened with a key by a guard. It alleviated the need for one full-time guard standing at the door opening and closing it every few seconds for a fresh con off the bus. And it was like Grand Central Station at Christmas.

In the middle of that array of thoughts, I found an empty seat, again by the toilet. I started to think the toilet was where I would be forever after what I had caused for so many people. Anyway, as I sat without talking to anyone, I continued my private analysis regarding the revolving door. I realized after a few minutes that it wasn't constructed because of the prison system's motivation to save money at all. It was for the guards' safety first and the convicts' safety second. There were at least thirty convicts in each of the ten holding cells in the immediate area, and I imagined the terrible chaos if a gang, a group, or even a single con got the idea to storm the door as the guard opened or closed it one of the hundreds of times during the course of a day. The guard at the door or in the receiving area would be massacred or taken hostage for sure. It might even cause a riot situation. But, they had it all figured out though. And, the revolving door was only one tiny trick in their trade.

My daydreaming about the revolving door was abruptly interrupted a few minutes later when I happened to look around the holding cell nonchalantly. I was trying my best to keep my wits about me and not expose myself to any more verbal or non-verbal contact with anyone. In my first cursory observation, I noticed right away that Ironman was directly across the room from me about fifteen feet, and to my right about four bodies. He seemed to be heavily engrossed in a conversation with two other white guys who were obviously gang members like Ironman. I couldn't hear what they were saying, but it was obvious Ironman was running the show. He was doing all of the talking, and his underlings were doing all the nodding. They were also being respectful to him. They constantly averted their eyes from direct contact with Ironman's, but he stared directly at each of them as he spoke. I perceived he was a boss or leader of some sort, and I tried to remember from my police experience what the bosses of gangs were called. I knew gangs adopted somewhat of a military structure, and I remembered something about soldiers and Captains and Lieutenants, but I couldn't remember the common term for their supreme commander.

I continued my scan of the holding cell and counted twenty-nine other white cons. A few of the others looked like gang members too, but they didn't seem to have friendlies from their gang in the cell. Otherwise, I thought they would be conversing like Ironman's crew was. Most of the room was made up of scraggly, unshaven, and severely depressed looking customers whom I imagined could all cut another's throat if trouble started. But, for me, I just glanced around again briefly. I didn't dwell on anyone in particular to avoid instigating any undue contact.

I did scrutinize the action outside the holding tank in the main reception area though, and I wondered how long we all would be holed up in our hot and humid stink-room. It smelled like an old pile of jock straps the trainer hadn't washed since the beginning of a long baseball season. Anyway, I counted nine correctional guards through the thick plexi-glass. Four of them were evenly dispersed at the corners of the squarely constructed main receiving area, and they all were heavily armored as if they were anticipating trouble. They all had batons firmly gripped with both hands, and several canisters of mace and pepper spray hung from their midsections. Also, they had riot shields over their faces and thick helmets covering their domes completely. Their entire dress was made up of a single black jumpsuit extending up from black, steel-toed boots similar to the goon squad's garb I was familiar with in my law enforcement days. They were prepared for anything, and their show of force was meant to be a deterrent to any potential inmate uprising.

Every thirty minutes, a different four-man set of guards would replace them, and thirty minutes later, the initial set would return. Obviously, a thirty-minute stretch under the high pressure conditions, plus the fact they were just standing and observing inmate movement, was long enough before a break was needed. I don't know where they went in the off times, but it didn't seem to matter to anyone much. The fact was that security was a big deal, and inmate control was vital.

The other five guards had specific duties as well as the goons. They closely monitored every inmate that exited the buses and entered the general receiving area. As the inmates entered, one cop would instruct each inmate to hobble up to a bench, kneel up on it, and wait to get unshackled. Another guard halted all the other inmates outside the door until the bench was clear. After the shackles were released, the guard would unhook the con's cuffs and instruct him to follow another guard to the holding cells. The inmate's race and his known gang affiliation, if any, determined what cell he was placed in initially. Each con was delivered to the fourth guard waiting by a revolving door where he would be searched again briefly for any obvious weapons or contraband. After the search, like a fish head-bashed with a club after the hook was taken out, the fourth guard would direct the con into the bucket.

The fifth guard, and last of the nine, was the strip searcher. He would retrieve one con at a time from the holding cell through the key-locked door. However, before he opened the door, the closest goon would walk over to the door as a formidable back up. He would press a speaker-system button on the outside of the door and gruffly bark an order to all the cons inside the room to move quickly away from the door and glass. When he was satisfied they all complied appropriately, the goon would call a con's name over the speaker and order him to stand by the door.

Everyone else was ordered to stop talking and not to move until the beckoned con was removed and the door was locked again.

The same process continued for hours, and it all ran like clockwork. During the several hours I awaited my strip-search, it seemed a new bus arrived every hour or so. Fresh cons would enter our holding cell through the revolving door, and different cons were ordered out to be stripped and issued their prison garb.

During the long wait, I had plenty of time to think. So, I continued my prison education by analyzing some other important aspects of the system. I figured the more I learned, the better chance I had of surviving the whole awful predicament I had caused for myself. I combined my police experience with new reasoning that, when new arrivals first entered the reception area, knowledge of individual inmates was limited to other law enforcement agencies' reports and communication. Although most inmates already had a prison rap sheet, and the cops knew everything down to the color of their body-moles, it was all about gangs and violence. Gang members weren't always obviously detected, and their close affiliations with fellow comrades weren't always known or up to date.

In other words, recent crime on the street may have involved new or old counterparts, but there weren't enough cops in the world to keep up with the dynamics of the gang activity. So, the receiving area's main purpose was to sift out gang members from others of different gangs to avoid gang wars and to maximize safety for everyone. Also, The cops wanted to separate members of the same gang from each other so they couldn't band together. If they were able to group up, it was likely they would join forces to manipulate the system. They would gang up on and hurt or kill rival groups, and ultimately, they would wreak havoc on everyone in the system.

Every once in awhile, I had to get up off my bench seat to drink from the wall fountain by the toilet to stay hydrated, and sometimes to urinate. I was fortunate I didn't have to have to have a bowel movement during my stint in the holding cell, because there was only a three-foot high, four-feet long cement retaining wall separating the toilet from the other cons' views. While others seemed to show no embarrassment when they defecated, probably because they were seasoned veterans in the system and learned it was all a part of the game, the whole scene seemed so vile and base to me that humans had to be subject to the experience at all. But I also knew that was the nature of the beast I had created for myself.

Chapter 6

Ironman

I didn't notice Ironman and his two buddies horn my seat and the two next to me when I was getting a drink one time. As I turned around from the wall fountain, I immediately had an antagonizing shiver crawl up my spine. I had unwittingly put myself into a vulnerable position when I got a drink. My butt wasn't to the wall like my friend advised me earlier, and when I turned, I wasn't prepared mentally to deal with the incursion.

Many things ran through my mind all at once when I saw Ironman staring at me, daring me to say something about him taking my seat. He had already run the other two cons off to make room for his friends, and all three of them waited for my reaction. I knew if I didn't do something about them stealing my seat, I would be considered weak like the others. Ultimately, Ironman and his crew would basically have control of the cell, and I would be a punk for backing down and letting their intrusion stand without retaliation of some kind. On the other hand, I was also aware that, if I took them on head to head, I might be hurt, killed, or receive additional time for fighting if I was able to inflict some damage on Ironman, and or, his boys.

However, my state of mind at the time wasn't normal according to the acceptable standards in every day average society. In other words, I just didn't care. I figured, whatever happened, happened. Without thinking about it much, my reaction became a casual glance about the room initially, and then a calm, but stern, stare directly into Ironman's eyes. I knew it wasn't the prudent thing to do under the circumstances, but I also knew that I didn't want to be anyone's punk either. If I allowed Ironman or any of his boys to railroad me, by doing so, I would be considered churlish in the eyes of all the others. Consequently, even they would take a shot at me later. It would be open season on Randolph.

I was the only one standing, and all the other cons watched the action in earnest when my eyes met Ironman's. They all knew it was my move, or puppy-dog my way across the room to the only empty seat left by the glass and the revolving door, one or the other. And, I had stalled long enough.

"How's it goin?" I said calmly to Ironman. "Do you mind if I have my seat back?"

I didn't avert my eyes and I didn't blink.

"You gotta be kiddin'," Ironman snarled back at me without taking his eyes off mine. "Waddle your old gray-haired ass over there where you belong before you get smashed," he continued as he motioned to the empty seat at the same time.

"Look. I don't want any trouble, but if you continue being rude, one of us is going to be embarrassed in front of all these guys," I said calmly, trying to maintain a monotone and not show him or anyone else that I was scared to death.

I knew the fight was on for sure now. There was no turning back. But, it didn't come from Ironman. I should have known there was no honor in gang warfare. They had to dispatch their underlings to do their dirty work.

As soon as the last word escaped my lips, Ironman turned his eyes from me and looked directly at one of his soldiers. When he nodded to him subtly, the soldier stood up, slowly and warily walked the three or four paces over to me, and positioned himself directly in front of me nose to nose. Well, it wasn't exactly nose-to-nose. It was more like my nose even with the top of his head, so I had to look down just a little. I had found that to be common in my life as I was six-feet, four inches and a forty-four-year old wiry guy to boot.

"You have about two seconds to sit your ass down before I smash you," he yapped in a combative tone.

While he yapped, I prepared myself for a sucker-punch mentally, but I didn't budge even slightly when he tried to stare me down and intimidate me into crawling away. Of course, that wasn't in my blood. I was too stubborn and mule-headed to back down from any little skirmish. So, I just did what I do when backed into a corner with no respectable escape.

"Look, sonny. Why do you want to beat up an old guy? I'm not bothering you," I mocked him playfully, but I readied myself for his first movement at the same time.

The soldier was a young whippersnapper, drunk with power and eager to earn respect from his boss, his other comrade, and the rest of the cons watching the suspense building to an inevitable boil. My hands were still open, but they still hung at my sides. I didn't know what to expect from the young man for sure, so I just stayed prepared for anything. I knew at my age, I was at least twenty years his senior, but that didn't seem to matter to Ironman or his stooges. Intimidating and attacking geriatric cases like me seemed to be in their bag of tricks to gain respect and heighten their power. So, I just waited patiently. It was his move.

"I said Sit your old ass down," he yelled at me this time, losing his cool.

As he spoke, he brought both of his hands up to my chest and tried to shove me backwards forcefully. However, I had my feet planted firmly, and I leaned into the shove enough to prevent myself from being budged. In the same motion, as his hands met my chest, I hit him in the face so hard with by best right that he became airborne a little. He flew backwards and landed at Ironman's feet. Then, I just waited. No one said anything. No one did anything, except watch the soldier bleed like a stuck pig all over the holding cell's floor. Blood seemed to spew like a geyser from his nose. He rustled around a little on his right side trying to regain his dexterity in his dazed condition, but I figured it would take awhile. For sure, I didn't think he would be giving me any more trouble.

Ironman didn't look at me, and neither did his other stooge. The youngster who confronted me didn't know where he was for a few seconds, and when he did realize what had just happened to him, he kind of crawled to his seat and hoisted himself up onto it. His buddies didn't help him a lick.

"If you want some more of me, I'll be right over here," I said flatly, glancing at Ironman and casually walking to the empty seat by the glass and the revolving door.

"By the way, you can have my seat. The view is probably better over here anyway," I told Ironman politely. He didn't move a muscle, he averted his eyes when I looked at him, and he didn't sic his other dog on me.

However, in seconds, every con in the tank started talking to his nearest neighbor. Also, in the next hour or so, about ten cons conjured up friendly conversation with me. Although I didn't spill the beans too much about myself personally, we did discuss the vehicular manslaughter charge I was doing time for, and the other cons were willing to share their charges as well. What was so frightening though was the fact that I knew I had better be very, very careful from that point on. I assumed Ironman would want his vengeance because I pulverized his soldier so handily, and I didn't know if I had just signed my own death warrant or not.

All the action had taken place in a span of only a few minutes, and luckily, it was all over so fast, the guards or goons didn't see the altercation. At least, I didn't think so at the time, because none of them came in to tie me up and banish me to the hole. In fact, like the earlier clockwork, the guards and goons kept their program running as smooth as a baby's butt. On schedule, one of them would open the door every half hour or so to fetch another con for a strip search and to drop another fish into the bucket. So, all I could do was wait patiently for my turn. I wanted out of that place, and I reckoned if I could get to a cell of my own, I wouldn't have to put up with any more nonsense. The only thing I wanted was to mind my own business, do my time, and go home to my kids in one piece.

Before one of the goons called my name over the speaker about an hour later, I experienced some interesting action in the holding cell. I can honestly say that it was one of the most disgusting situations I had ever witnessed in my life. I had to walk by Ironman, his healthy soldier, and the busted up one to relieve myself, and I consumed some water another time, but none of them even looked at me. I didn't know if they were planning something later or not, but I kept myself turned enough to keep an eye on them anyway.

As soon as I walked back to my seat and sat down, my attention was drawn to Ironman and his stooges yakking about something intently. I could almost guarantee they were formulating a plan of some sort to inflict serious physical damage on me, but after a few seconds, I understood the real motive of their conversation. Ironman had been keenly watching the guards' movements outside the glass. When he perceived the coast was clear, he nodded to his healthy dog as a signal of some sort. Simultaneously, the wounded soldier moved slyly to my left and stood close to the glass as a lookout. Instinctively, I prepared to stand up if they rushed me, or if one of them approached me to closely.

The next thing I knew though, the first soldier took a few steps over to the toilet and not towards me, sat down on it, and proceeded to expel a number two. In the meantime, Ironman and his injured soldier watched the guards and their movements carefully like they didn't want the guards to know their buddy was on the toilet. One time, I even heard Ironman tell the guy to hurry up. It was time for the goons to retrieve another con for a strip search.

I watched all of them like a hawk. I didn't trust anything about them. I knew that sooner or later they would attack. I had disrespected them all, and I was positive I would have to face one or all of them again at some point. But, a few seconds later, I saw the soldier give himself a reach around with the toilet paper he ripped out of the dispenser between the sink and the toilet. Suddenly, totally surprising me, the soldier stood up and reached into the toilet bowl with both hands. I couldn't actually see his hands enter the pile of excrement I imagined he was fumbling in, but his arms disappeared down behind the retaining wall enough that I perceived the search was happening for sure. The soldier quickly rose up, glanced at the cops to see if they were watching, then spun around to the sink. When he first stood up, I noticed his filthy brown hands cradling something in his hands before he turned to the sink. He engaged the water and washed whatever he had found in the gunk. It wasn't long before he glanced around to the cops one more time to make sure he wasn't detected, then he sat down on the far side of Ironman away from the window. Immediately, the lookout walked back over to his associates and sat down closest to the window, leaving Ironman and the dung grabber concealed from full view of the window in case the cops looked in.

Ironman and his soldier seemed to be fervently tending to a task of some sort. Just then, I decided to walk over for a drink. I was curious, and while they were distracted, I thought it was a perfect opportunity to check out the situation regarding the manure hunt. When I reached the water fountain, I glanced over to the three stooges and noticed a large pile of tobacco on a piece of plastic on the wooden bench between Ironman and the healthy soldier.

Well, it finally clicked. I remembered back when I worked in the jail. Some of my corrections training dealt with the various ways inmates smuggled drugs, paraphernalia, and contraband into the system. And, now it all made sense. Somewhere back at the jail where the soldier was sentenced, he had rolled up a package of tobacco very, very, tightly, wrapped it in a piece of cellophane, and stuck it up where the sun doesn't shine. I reasoned immediately that, no wonder they didn't come after me when I decked one of their dogs. They had more important business at the time. They needed my seat, and the other two, so they could use the toilet when the coast was clear. The tobacco was just their top priority at the time, because they all knew they would be strip searched shortly. They didn't want to be caught with, or lose, their stash. Tobacco was like gold in prison. It commanded a tidy sum in trade or for future favors. No wonder I wasn't attacked, I thought. In a blink of an eye, a daunting fear engulfed me. I instantly became more scared than ever.

I wasn't surprised when each of the gang members took a quick turn on the toilet to pack their smaller packages up their chutes. I didn't know the real risk they were taking of getting caught by the cops when they were strip-searched. But, I didn't care. I just wanted out of there—fast. Now that the tobacco gold was taken care of, I didn't know if I was next on their hit list for humiliating them earlier.

God must have been watching the action closely too, because just then, a goon bellowed my name over the speaker right in my ear. I got up casually, but inside, I wanted to bolt for the door. Everyone stepped back from the door as they had been ordered a dozen times since I first arrived, and I followed the stripper cop willingly. I tried not to make eye contact with anyone. I just followed on the guard's heels to another room on the far end of the reception area.

There have been only a few times in my life where I was completely and utterly humiliated. However, the first prison strip search I had to endure at the Gladiator School was at the top of my list for sure. First, I was ordered to shut up, follow every instruction to the letter without thinking for myself, and only speak if I was spoken to. It sort of re-minded me of my dad and mom when I was a kid when they always yelled at Connie and me. We had no respect, and we were only sup-posed to be seen and not heard.

Anyway, I complied like I was a young child ruled by a vile dictator. I removed all of my county jail attire like I was commanded to do and placed it all into a large rolling hamper about the size of a cord of fire-wood. Completely naked, I was exposed to two female correctional of-ficers I hadn't seen before handing out prison garb to several other cons a few feet away. Although I had never felt so violated right then, it got much worse in a hurry. The stripper cop ordered me to open my mouth wide so he could closely inspect the inside of my mouth; I had to turn my head and fold one of my ears forward, then the other; I was told to bend over at the waist toward the cop and rustle my scalp. (I didn't have much hair. Logan had buzzed me the day of my sentencing.) I was or-dered to lift my testicles as high as I could while the cop bent down even with my groin for a close inspection; I was instructed to turn around, face the wall, put both my hands on the wall for support, and lift one foot at a time backwards so the bottoms of my feet could be examined; Last, but definitely not the least, I was ordered to step away from the wall backwards, bend over at the waist as far as I could manage, spread my cheeks wide, and cough twice aggressively. Now, I have to say, that was uncouth and uncivilized. To be violated in that way was egregious, to say the least. However, it also seemed appropriate in some strange way. Why? Because I knew I deserved whatever medicine I got for what I did to Sheryl, my kids, and all the rest of them.

The strip search finally ended, but then I had to parade by the female cops totally naked to receive my prison issue of clothes. I tried to cover my groin with my hands the best I could, but when I reached their counter full of clothes, one of them smirked and made a comment to the other female about me being a fresh fish. I thought that was rather rude, especially because they didn't care at all that I heard their derisive remark. But, I kept my mouth shut. I received my clothes and stepped to the side and put them on as fast as I could. When I was fully dressed with my spare garments in hand, I was ordered to stand outside the room until I was told to move.

Three other fresh white fish and two other white gang members were already standing against the wall where I was positioned. From my vantage point, I saw that the receiving area was still running like clockwork. All the goons and guards looked mean and dead serious. And, all the inmates mulling around in the holding cells seemed to be worried like I was. I had no clue what would happen next, or if and when Ironman and his dogs would get another whack at me or not. As sure as I was standing there in prison, at the Gladiator School in Tracy, California, they were coming. I felt it in my bones.

Again, God had his divine plan all worked out for me like all the rest of us churls on planet earth. Ironman, who apparently had been stripped in a different room, seemed to pop out from nowhere. As my fortune would have it, he was ordered to stand by me. Of course he was, I thought. God was testing me. He wanted to know what I was made of. He was punishing me for my grotesque behavior when I chose to drink and drive and cause Sheryl to die so brutally. Now, it was my turn. God was exposing me to Ironman as many times as it took for God to discharge his punishment on me. It was all part of the plan.

When our eyes met, I averted mine from his right away. I figured I better not disrespect or antagonize him any more than I already had done. A few seconds later, another white fish completed our gaggle, and a goon and one guard gruffly ordered us to follow them. We weren't allowed to talk to anyone, and had to look straight ahead until we got to where we were going. Of course, part of God's plan was to place Ironman and me at the rear of the pack, with Ironman bringing up the rear. I wasn't allowed to turn around so I could keep my eye on him, and I was starting to freak out. I just knew the monster would get me from behind. I was absolutely and completely vulnerable, and he knew it.

I was dumfounded that it never came. We all ended up walking about a block down several cement hallways. On the way, we passed a dozen or so prison wings that housed all the other convicts at DVI. We passed lines of other cons being escorted to various other places in the prison, while our line followed like baby chicks after their momma. I didn't know where we would all end up. I only knew we were headed for a concrete cell of our own down one of the cell blocks sooner or later.

It came sooner rather than later. The goon led us through a thick, steel gate into H-wing, one of the housing sections in the Gladiator School used for newly inducted convicts. As we all passed through the gates, I was downright stunned by the awesome demonstration of brilliant architecture sprawled out before me. As we lined up against the wall like good little convicts, I had a chance to survey the cellblock I was going to be living in; it was colossal. It was at least one football field long and about eighty feet wide. It had four tiers, each about fifteen feet high stacked on top of each other like a mountain of shale. Everything was grayish in color and constructed of concrete and steel of incalculable proportions. It was breathtaking to me that a structure like that could even be built. It was equal in magnitude to many of the grand and enormous ballparks I had the pleasure and privilege to play in. It was a shame though. There was no honor or satisfaction in being there in prison. It was the exact opposite. It was disgraceful, humiliating, and dishonorable. I was a convict, the lowest scum on earth.

Just as I was really getting into feeling sorry for myself again, the goon and escort guard disappeared. But, three other H-wing guards moved in synchronized fashion to our fronts to give us our initiation speech.

"Make no mistake about it. We are the masters of your universe while you are here. For those of you who have had the pleasure of visiting our fine establishment before, welcome back. You know the program. The hole is real close, as you know, for those of you who insist on screwing up. For you rookies, learn from your cellmate if he is a veteran. If he isn't, do what you are told when you are told. Learn our program here as fast as you can. It will go better for you if you do. If you fight or give us any trouble, you get to visit the hole for a few months till you figure out prison is our home. It is also our program and our game, not yours. You are only visiting until you are moved to your destination prison. Respect goes a long way in here." The cop rattled off the speech like he had done it a few thousand times before.

The speaker continued with some specific instructions, and I began to panic.

"Everyone will be paired up. When I call your names, find your cell down the block as fast as you can, get inside it, and get on your assigned bunk until you are told otherwise," the cop rattled off his spiel sternly.

I even started to shake a little. First off, Ironman was standing right next to me, and I knew for sure he had murder on his mind. I didn't know when it would come, but like death and taxes, the piper had to be paid. By the end of the day, my skirmish with his soldier would have been spread like wildfire all over the prison. To save face and to regain respect, he would have to do some physical damage on me sooner rather than later. If he didn't, or he didn't order one of his dog soldiers to do it for him, he would no longer have any clout in the system at all. And, in prison, especially the Gladiator School, gangs killed, rioted, and manipulated for power to gain the upper hand.

The inside of the Gladiator School was like a magnificent colorful battlefield with valiant warriors laying their lives down for the cause. By the end of the first day in the joint, I learned that the only difference was that a multitude of enemies were in the same theatre of war jockeying for the same terrain, instead of just two foes battling one another. Individually, gangs mirrored enormous grizzly bears marking their territory, and anyone who infringed upon it was mauled immediately and unmercifully.

At DVI, like all other prisons in the California Department of Corrections, the infrastructure of the individual gangs themselves reflect that of the United States military somewhat. The bosses of the gangs are labeled as generals, who are followed by captains, lieutenants, and then the grunts or soldiers. The generals make all the major decisions. He orders his officers to make sure a job is done to the letter as they are commanded to do. The officers, in turn, supervise the job he is given, but the grunts usually do the majority of the actual work itself. From time to time though, the general and his officers do the dirty work if the threat of the enemy was imminent, or if they trapped in a firefight they can't avoid.

In prison, there are literally dozens of different gangs vying for a piece of the power and control pie. Included, there are a myriad of white gangs, black gangs, Asian gangs, Mexican gangs, and many others included in the mix. Strangely, the portion of the state, country, or community a particular gang calls its home determines what other gangs are enemies or allies. Race is not a factor. In other words, even though the prison system is dominated by racist convicts, whites don't always affiliate and team up with whites, for example. Sometimes, whites are mortal enemies with other whites. Similarly, blacks don't always join with other blacks, and Mexicans don't always band with other Mexicans. And, so on.

It was easy to notice that Ironman was well known by all the veteran convicts whether they were gang affiliated or not. It was obvious he had some power around there too. Other cons avoided him like the plague, and all of his underlings cowed to him automatically when he was around. So, basically, I knew I was in deep trouble.

While I stood there in line distressing, the H-wing guard continued his distribution of us convict pairs and our cell designations. And, of course, God was having a field day.

"Wiens, Randy! Tier two. Cell two-one-five lower. Branch, Clavin! Tier two. Cell two-one-five upper. Move out!" the cop bellowed.

Naturally, Ironman was going to be my roomy in prison. God saw to that. God knew it would take someone or something of Ironman's caliber to punish me properly. At least, that is what I obsessed about on my long walk through H-wing to get to my new house.

Ironman got the jump on me to our cell too. I didn't know why he wanted to precede me to the cell, but I knew his motive was evil whatever it was. I could sense it. So, once again, I prepared for the inevitable battle. The Gladiator School nickname began to make more sense to me every step I took it seemed too. And, I knew I would have to be at my very best if I wanted to survive the brawl coming just minutes away.

I climbed the catwalk stairs up to the second tier about half way down the cellblock scared to death. I anticipated a hard-fought battle similar to the myriad of scraps I engaged in often in my hockey days, but this one reeked of even tougher consequences. In hockey, all the players were layered up with body armor that would vanquish a hundred-mile-an-hour slap shot. Sturdy helmets encased our heads, and most of us wore thick plastic mouth guards. The only way we ever really got hurt in a fight was if a punch landed around the nose area, which wasn't very often. However, on the flip side, I have been in fierce battles off the ice as well. When I was a police officer, and when I occasioned some drinking establishments from time to time, I participated in many fisticuffs with no gear or equipment at all like Ironman and I were about to do. It was one on one with us. There were no guards in the cell, and his soldiers were segregated, so they couldn't do his dirty work for him.

For sure, I assumed one or both of us would be seriously hurt shortly. Gang members like Ironman had the reputation of being ruthless. Plus, they all fought dirty. Fairness never existed in their vocabulary. For me, I have had blood in my eyes many times too, but I couldn't remember a time ever when I fought to hurt someone maliciously or when I had to fight to preserve my life. But, again, I knew that was the nature of the beast I had created by drinking and driving. My home, only God knew how long, was in Gladiator School. DVI was no place for weakness. The faint of heart perished quickly in prison, and only tenacious physical and mental toughness allowed a convict a chance to survive. Even then, the chances were poor, and I knew it as surely as I was about to be standing in front of the Ironman.

So, I prepared. I prepared to do whatever it took to stay healthy. It was Ironman or me. When I trekked the last forty or fifty feet up the steel stairs to the second tier, my eyes followed Ironman as he disappeared into number 215 about thirty feet ahead of me. I was fixated on his movements like a starving mountain lion on her final approach on dinner. I approached the cell extremely wary of the other hunter starving for my intestines and liver for lunch. None of us had eaten since early that morning, and it was getting close to dinnertime for both of us. I edged up to the door and stole a quick look around the opening slowly. Immediately, I noticed Ironman with his back to me. I was surprised to see he was fumbling with his bedding preparing the bottom bunk, which had been assigned to me. Of course, I had to say something about that.

"Hey. Clavin. What's up with the bunk?" I said calmly, as I stepped inside the minuscule concrete cell, eight-feet long and six-feet wide. Suddenly, the hydraulic door shut abruptly almost jamming my right foot in the base of it. When I rounded the corner into the cell, I had moved into a defensive stance ready for anything Ironman had planned, but my preparation went out the window when the door closed so fast and ruined my defensive posture. In the cell, about three feet from the Ironman, I felt pretty darn vulnerable and helpless. Fear grabbed my guts right then like a lion on a jugular.

Ironman wheeled around to face me almost nose to nose like his soldier and I had done earlier. This time though, it actually was nose to nose. I didn't have to look down at all. And, eyeball-to-eyeball, Ironman was a man built like a pachyderm. He had taken his shirt off for intimidation purposes I am sure, and his massive arms and shoulders spewed from his torso like a forklift, all of which I assumed were constructed from thousands of prison push-ups.

"You don't really want to push me about the bunk, do you?" he said sarcastically with his purplish and pulsating veins popping out from the side of his oversized baldhead.

At that moment in time, I didn't know for sure if he was just testing me or he was simply going to finish me off in one bombing run I would have no chance of defending against. I was positive he probably hadn't been directly confronted by anyone very often in his life. He was too formidable physically, and when he added a callous and cruel tone to his physical presence, I imagined very few people on the planet would challenge him. He seemed too dominating and impregnable.

However, I was no slouch either, although I was so scared I almost peed myself when he stood face to face with me as the cell door closed so abruptly. It seemed like an instantaneous combustion at that precise second. One minuscule second I was physically and mentally prepared to do battle with Ironman and do whatever I had to do to him to save myself, and in the next flash of time it looked like I was dead for sure. Obviously, I was correct in my assumption and fear that he wanted my throat badly when he spoke. When I noticed his veins bulging out on his head and neck like a million tributaries on an aerial photograph, I was convinced he wasn't acting. His bloodshot eyes bore into mine, and he was sweating profusely. I assumed he had been thinking about evening the score with me since I kicked his dog, and as he stood waiting for my response, I could sense he was readying for an attack.

"That depends on you," I said boldly, but still calmly. I didn't want him to smell my fear, and I figured if I could get him talking a little, maybe he would calm down and not kill me with his bare hands.

"What do ya mean?" he said aggressively, not backing off an inch.

"I mean, if you're asking me if you can have my bunk, I'll give it to you no problem. But, if you are telling me you're just takin' it, then we are gonna have a problem like me and your buddy had earlier," I explained flatly, matching his hostile stare.

CHAPTER 7

Horseshoes and Hand Grenades

I knew for sure if I showed any hint of weakness right there, he would be all over me like a tidal wave. But, unexpectedly, Ironman's eyes changed from wanting to kill me deader than a doornail to more of a relaxed gaze. He dropped his eyes briefly, apparently to diffuse the bomb a hair away from detonating. However, I knew the last thing I could do was relax and let my guard down. I believed in my heart I couldn't trust this guy at all about anything. For my own personal survival, I had to assume he had ulterior motives for softening so suddenly due to the whooping I gave his soldier and the embarrassment I caused him in front of so many other cons.

"Look, Clavin. The last thing in the world I want is trouble with you. We have to share this hole for no tellin' how long, and we need to be able to get along. There isn't enough room in here for ants to move, let alone two mules like us. So, what do ya say we shake hands and not come out fighting? This is a tough deal as it is. We don't need to cause any more trouble," I told Ironman easily, still not knowing if he averted his eyes just to bait me so I would drop my guard.

"I agree," he said, more affably this time. I was a little shocked at his retreat, but I was so grateful, a tiny shot of relief penetrated the pleasure center in my brain.

"I've got enough problems on my mind too. But, I'm still takin' the bunk. You are a peckerwood, and peckerwoods have to learn who's really in charge of things in the system of things around here. You will live a lot longer that way," he continued, a little less arrogantly.

"You can have the bottom bunk," I responded quickly before he had second thoughts about kickin' my face in.

"It isn't worth scrappin' over. However, I'm not going to be disrespected by anyone. I'm no one's punk. To start with, you need to educate me on what a peckerwood is. That already sounds like an insult," I informed him frankly. I was still apprehensive and suspicious regarding Ironman's motives. I still didn't know for sure if the fire was out, and I wanted to put it all to bed and get on with making my own bunk.

"A peckerwood is prison lingo for a white guy who has never been to prison before and who doesn't know squat when it comes to staying alive and healthy," Ironman chuckled a little when he said peckerwood. It was obvious I was in brain surgery territory, but I only knew tiddlywinks.

As he continued, he backed off completely and sat back on his bunk while I still stood by the door for my first formal prison lesson. I took a step forward unflinchingly and chucked my spare clothes and bedding over Ironman's head onto my bunk. Ironman didn't even blink when I approached him. He sat fearlessly. He was completely aware of my every movement. When he didn't react to my infringement on his bunk so closely, his coolness signaled to me immediately that he wasn't one accustomed to back down from anyone, no matter who it was. No wonder he was a general in a gang, I thought. Generals were proven soldiers and ultimate leaders. They were fearless in the face of the enemy, and when it was life or death, a good general would sacrifice his own life for the common good of his troops.

I stepped backwards a few paces and leaned against the hydraulic steel door. I knew I had to give Ironman the respect he deserved and had undoubtedly earned. I paid close attention to everything he said and did. When he twitched, I was ready. When he moved his eyes, I tried to read him. Although what Ironman seemed to be willing to teach me was immeasurable, I was convinced it was only the calm before the storm. Why? Because there was still the little matter of me kicking his soldier's fanny and the embarrassment that resulted. And, generals simply don't forgive and forget an attack on their dignity so readily without planning and strategizing a counter attack of some sort at some point in time. I reasoned that maybe he was just toying with me and waiting until I slept before mounting his attack. I knew generals often used surprise as a valuable tactic, and I also knew that gang members fought dirty. They manipulated the circumstances so the conflict would be fought on their terms. Advantage was everything. Damage to the homeboys would be kept to a minimum that way.

"Another thing, if you're as smart as you think you are, you prob'ly oughta listen to me 'bout a lotta things. First, I'm a general in the Nazi Low Riders. We believe that whites are the supreme race on our mother earth. It's our duty to educate all whites to that fact. Other races are inferior, and they must bow to our rule. At the same time, there are some white gangs that need educatin' too, because they don't believe as strongly as the NLR does that whites must rule unconditionally. However, our power rivals any gang in here, and it's our job to make sure all new fish and everyone else learn the ropes fast. Furthermore, it's all about show in here, and the more manpower we can command and get organized, the better. That means we all stay alive longer. Power intimidates most guys, and it is a deterrent to a lot of bloodshed," Ironman explained casually, this time without any nasty tone in his voice.

I wasn't shocked at Ironman's vehement attitude regarding his philosophy. Sadly, I had a lot of experience with racism when I was a cop and when I played baseball, and I realized Ironman would never be swayed from his erroneous beliefs. It was his mindset, and no peckerwood, or anyone else, was going to change his views. I imagined he would have died first.

"I appreciate everything you teach me. I know I am dumber than a bag of hammers when it comes to surviving in here. And, I have to admit; I desperately need your help to make it in here. Thank you for your help," I said to Ironman, placating him.

This time, I felt like a load of logs was just hoisted off my back. At least Ironman was talking, and he didn't seem to have murder on his mind at the moment. However, I knew I had better appease his hostility even further, so I went along with the racial nonsense for a while until I could get my bearings around my new home and the prison system in general. I had just barely entered my new diggings, and I still hadn't had any time to think about anything but preserving my guts for future use. I wanted them to continue aiding in my eating and digestion for several decades to come.

"For right now, the only thing I'm gonna tell you about has to do with usin' the can. If you have to go, before anything hits the water in the pot, flush. And, keep flushing until nothing hits the water anymore. That way, I don't have to hear it, and it keeps the smell down. Now, I need to use the can. I need a smoke." Ironman lectured me like I was his student in a social studies class. This time though, he was the teacher. I was the student.

Ironman stood up quickly right then and took his first step towards me. My foot had been on the toilet during the last portion of our discussion, and I moved it willingly. I stepped toward him at the same time, and as we passed each other in the breadbox-sized cement cell, we didn't make eye contact. We both turned sideways simultaneously and respectfully of each other in our tight quarters. I realized then and there that life in that cell would be another hell on earth. I wondered what Ironman had up his sleeve for me. And, I wondered if I would catch another term for hurting him badly if that is what it came to. I had never been more alone, and deathly afraid, in my life.

I was tired of the gross exhibition earlier regarding the tobacco, so I turned my back to Ironman while he sat on his throne. I knew he knew he was the king in the Gladiator School, so I ignored his detestable arrogance and his nasty odor as best as I could under the circumstances. Although I still didn't know if he was waiting for me to show my back so he could seek his revenge, I concentrated on making up my bunk and stashing my extra clothes neatly in one corner at the foot of my bunk anyway. I figured if he was going to get me, it was going to happen whether I obsessed about it and stayed paranoid or not.

So, I used the one-foot square desk, and the stool that folded under it, to climb up on my mattress and lay down. It had been a long day already, I thought, although I chuckled to myself when I realized I would be able to spell "long days" very, very, very well by the time I got out in thirteen-and-a-half months.

I completely ignored Ironman until the dinner chow arrived an hour later. During that time, I stayed horizontal. I only stared at the ceiling and reflected on all the events that had taken place already that day. It was the first of June, it was hotter than an egg frying on a sidewalk, and I was sweating like a pig in my cement tomb. My roommate was a psycho from hell, and it was the first day I had ever been imprisoned. I was six-feet, four inches tall, and my bunk was only six feet long. I couldn't extend fully, so I felt tied up like a bad sailor's knot constantly. My back was killing me. I had forgotten about the excruciating pain caused by the accident for most of the day because of all the other action, but the minute I laid down, I was stiffer than a fresh piece of plywood sliding off a green chain. And, time was my enemy as well as Ironman. Time haunted me. It played games with all my cognitive senses, and it tricked me into fantastic mind games I couldn't win. Of course, God was watching, and I thought he must have been having a field day. He always did when his constituents were stubborn and bullheaded and didn't recognize him unconditionally as the only one with real power over anything and everything. And I knew his power too. I had known it since the night Sheryl was slowly crushed to death.

Jail was like a slap on the hand compared to prison. In jail, one had the impression he only had a short stint to endure before he was sprung and able to enjoy the supreme pleasures of the flesh once again. However, in prison, I had to learn fast that thirteen-and-a-half months were a lifetime. And if I wanted to ever experience the magnificence of life's little pleasures again, I figured I'd better attend Gladiator School intently and be a fiend in my learning of the system.

As a result, I began by watching Ironman work. I didn't want to talk to him any more than I absolutely had to, but I did enjoy his ingeniousness in his manipulation of other cons and the prison system in general.

He was truly the king, and I suppose, among all of us other derelicts cast from society, he deserved the credit he was due.

First, I learned a new method of fishing shortly after Ironman retrieved his tobacco and washed himself in the sink. He seemed to be having a nicotine fit, and I assumed he needed a cigarette before chowtime. I became intrigued in his expertise when he tore part of his sheet into several long, narrow strips. He tied the ends together into a fishing line about twelve feet long. At receiving, we both had received a small plastic bag containing a disposable razor, a tube of toothpaste about the size of a small thumb, a small bar of soap, and a toothbrush just long enough to reach the back teeth in a normal-sized head. Not being educated in prison practices of survival, I was surprised when Ironman tied his disposable razor at one end of his fishing line to use as a hook. Next, he dropped to all fours and put his face down to the cement floor like he was listening for a train coming down the track miles away. Before I knew it, he started yelling at the top of his lungs.

"This is Ironman in 215. I need a light. Who's next door?" Ironman bellowed.

At the time, I was wondering why he was yelling so loudly. I thought the guards would surely hear the racket and come running to confiscate the tobacco and the light, if Ironman was able to even find one. There was no smoking allowed in the prison, and tobacco was illegal contraband worthy of being sent to the hole for if a con was caught with it. But, I realized the guards probably couldn't hear Ironman's yapping through the din of the 200 other cons screaming to each other throughout all of H-wing.

The cops didn't come, and Ironman had a light within minutes. Another NLR soldier two cells down heard from another con in the cell between us that it was Ironman doing the hollering. Of course, for his general, he disconnected the light fixture on the ceiling of his cell in minutes, touched the hot wire with the ground, and with the sparks that flashed like miniature lighting bolts from the fixture, he ignited a rolled up piece of toilet paper. To my further surprise, the toilet paper acted like a wick. The soldier quickly tied the wick on to the end of his fishing line and whipped it out of his cell through the two-inch crack at the base of his cell door. Apparently, from Ironman's prone position, he could see the soldier's extended line with the wick on the end of it about six-feet down the catwalk outside our cell. Immediately, Ironman shot his line out under our door. Masterfully, on the first cast, Ironman snagged the lighted wick with his razor-hook, and within seconds, he was puffing like a steam engine struggling up a monster hill fully-loaded with lumber.

It wasn't long after that when chow arrived, and I was ravenous. Also, I was severely depressed from the predicament I was in, and I felt eating might take my mind off my misery for a while. But, I couldn't have been more mistaken. The slop the guards slid through the slot in the door was disgusting. First of all, it stunk like rotten cabbage. I couldn't even identify what it was, except it was mostly dark and runny with a few pieces of some sort of soy product protruding out of it. Yum! I thought right away. I can't wait to dig into this feast. It is as good as my momma's turkey dinner at Thanksgiving. However, I quickly got off the humorous deliberation when I suddenly recognized the only thing I was thankful for was that I was still alive. Ironman hadn't killed me or had a chance to sic his dogs on me yet.

The rest of the evening was uneventful, except that I continued my education by watching Ironman's antics. When chow was over and the guards retrieved the food trays, he started yelling again. This time though, he stood upright and screamed through the crack in the steel door in the direction of his soldier two doors down. Ironman ordered the soldier to send another light over and to read the kite he was going to send back. I garnered some extremely valuable knowledge in the next few minutes. I learned that no information is sacred in prison. I learned that, by writing and sending notes, or kites, to the right people, anyone, at anytime can find out the scoop on another con in the blink of an eye. As a matter of fact, in about thirty minutes, Ironman found out there were about fifty whites on our wing, including a dozen peckerwoods, forty blacks, forty Mexicans, thirty Asians, and the rest were classified as others out of 200 inmates. Now, to the layman like me, these numbers didn't mean much at first glance. However, it didn't take me long to realize the numbers were crucial in Ironman's and other gangs' world of intimidation and violence.

Obtaining an accurate scouting report is often the difference between life and death to gang and individual gang members in prison. Similar to any military theatre or athletic competition, in order to win, gangs desperately collect intelligence on other gangs' physical numbers, who their leaders are, their style and known strategies. This way, gangs know who and how many they are up against, and especially, how aggressively they can inflict their influence and power in the system.

For example, during my 24/7 education, I received a master's degree in prison manipulation and guerilla warfare by closely observing Ironman's movements, his endless communication by kites with his soldiers, and by keeping my ears open. I learned in a day or two that Ironman's Nazi Low Riders had superior numbers compared to some other gangs housed in H-wing and inferior numbers to others. Consequently, he knew his gang faced serious competition for control of H-wing and the entire Gladiator School in general.

And, that was the ultimate prize. Control. Control over other gangs, control over the flow of drugs and contraband in and out of the Gladiator School, and control over other convicts' destinies in general. Although Ironman held the keys, or in other words, he commanded his ship of Nazi Low Riders, other gangs had chieftains of their own who were formidable in their own right. They offered themselves as conquerors too. They also commanded ferocious soldiers who fought to the death for their own piece of the pie. And, none of them cared a lick who or what they had to do to claim that treasure and booty.

Ironman and I didn't converse at all until the next day. In the meantime, I counted my lucky stars and thanked God for his blessing that Ironman was tired and fell asleep early the first night. Of course, he snored louder than a tired bulldog, and sleep for me was impossible. All I could do was to pray and to think. I begged God for his forgiveness over and over, and I prayed for him to grant me the strength to overcome my fears. I asked him to give me sleep and to keep me strong and healthy. I asked him to take care of Karyn and my kids if I was hurt or killed. And, I prayed for Ironman to look deep inside himself and realize that I wasn't his enemy. I just wanted to do my time without bothering anyone. Just then, I fell asleep planning to apologize to Ironman the next day. I thought that maybe, just maybe, I could appeal to his sense of decency.

For the next two days, Ironman and I talked very little. I tried to strike up a conversation with him on several occasions, but it was clear I was like a scorned woman. He was no longer interested in toying with me, testing me, or pretending he didn't want to pull my heart out of my chest. I reasoned that, because I manhandled his comrade so easily, he was spurning me. He was kicking me to the curb as trash, and it was obvious his mind was festering like a boil in need of being lanced. He seemed to storm about the cell increasingly belligerent and disrespectful. It was as if he was a riled steam engine building up a head of steam for a meddlesome mountain pass in British Columbia. And, as his courage built, he began to peck at me like a chicken on corn in the farmyard. He would brag and tell me how fearsome he was and how he had beaten and killed so many rival gang members and civilians for no more than a handful of change or a smoke when he wanted one. He would tell me how charming he was and how many women he had molested and talked out of their panties. He would rant like he was the king of the world.

In the meantime, I was actually scared to get off my bunk. I had never witnessed the kind of rage this man exhibited before in my life, and I thought for sure my life was over. Although I was burdened with a high degree of anger myself, mine seemed like it was like a pop can getting ready to blow in the fridge compared to Ironman's volcano. I just didn't see myself confronting this monster, or anything positive arising out of any of it if I did. So, again, I just talked. I didn't know any better, so I just stayed on my bunk and talked. Besides, I had the only defensive position in the cell. If he attacked me from below, I thought he would have to reach up, and his blows would be less devastating for sure.

"Ironman! What's up with the constant pacin'?" I said to Ironman out of the blue during his continuous two steps up and two steps back.

He was like a caged animal looking for a crack to spring. He never looked at me, and he never spoke to me directly, but it was quite obvious he was on the hunt for blood.

"You haven't earned the right to talk to me, stupid!" he said caustically, like acid on an eyeball.

When he spoke this time, he glanced up at me from by the door about four feet away. By his expression, it was clear he noticed that I had hoisted myself up into a sitting position on the side of my top bunk facing him when he made his last turn for the door. But, when he saw me staring at him blankly and unintimidated, he halted immediately. I figured I had the advantage, and he knew it too.

"I thought I told you I wasn't going to be disrespected," I responded to Ironman's derisive remark curtly, and I stared hard into his eyes.

I knew it was on now, and there was no turning back. I felt I had lived in fear for the last two days, and I hadn't slept a wink fretting about this idiot. He was as disrespectful and uncouth as they come, and it was obvious he wasn't going to back off. So, I knew it was time to find out who was the biggest grizzly in the bush.

"Do you know who I am!?" he growled back at me.

His veins were popping out on the side of his head and neck again, and he was flexing his arm and shoulder muscles for additional effect. He puffed his chest out and clenched his fists; it was quite apparent he was utterly stunned someone was standing up to him. He was definitely new to the experience.

"Yeah, I know you very, very well," I said, flatly.

"Whaddaya mean, you know me?" he argued back.

"It's very simple. You're like all the other blowhards who just yap constantly, but nothing really important comes out," I said to Ironman calmly, but he knew I was taunting him too. "I've decided if you were gonna do somethin', you would have done it by now. Actually, I feel quite safe right now," I said more aggressively this time. I had grown tired of the bickering, and I just wanted it over with one way or another.

Before Ironman could pounce, or respond to my latest snide remark, our cell door slid open. Ironman jerked around to the door slightly confused at what was going on. He was surprised when he realized he had forgotten it was time for our wing to hit the yard for an hour of exercise. He got a hold of himself just as quickly though. When he stepped out of the cell, before he went out of view down the catwalk, he said we would continue our little fracas in the yard.

Well, I have to say, I almost peed my prison pants right then and there. First, I hadn't been able to relieve myself for so many hours, and I thought I would explode like a water-filled balloon I used to nail my kids with in the summer. I had been so scared I didn't want to get off my bunk. Plus, I knew Ironman held the keys for all of the Nazi Low Rider gang members in the entire prison. He was their boss-hog. Although only H-wing wing was being released for exercise, I knew Ironman would send all of the H-wing soldiers he commanded after me in the yard for sure. He called the shots. He ordered the hits. And, what he said was law. In other words, I was marked for a hit.

I thought I would just stay in my cell at first. That way, I wouldn't have to battle an army by myself, and it would still be one on one. At least I would have a fighting chance that way. However, God wanted me in the yard. I felt it was another test. He was testing my will and my courage. He was wondering if I was ready to surrender completely, or if I was going to carry the flag until the last dog was hung. I had opened the can of worms, and God wanted to know if I was willing to eat what I opened.

About a minute later, a prison guard appeared in my doorway while I stewed about the sour pickle I was in. He was perturbed that I hadn't left my cell and gone to the yard yet. He told me in his vilifying tone that this wasn't a Holiday Inn, and I had to do what I was told when I was told. When I tried to explain that I didn't know the rules yet, he informed me it was mandatory for everyone to go to the yard when their time to go came up. The guards could shake down all the cells for weapons and contraband and not be disturbed that way.

I complied immediately. I wanted to spill my guts to the cop about Ironman's intent to smash my brains on the concrete, but I knew if I did and Ironman or any other con found out I snitched, everyone in the prison would want to kill me. And, I figured Ironman and the Nazi Low Rider gang were enough enemies for the time being. I didn't need any more.

I slipped my prison jumpsuit top on quickly, and I hustled out of my cell down the catwalk. From my vantage point on the second tier, I was amazed by the size of H-wing once again. But, I didn't dwell on my new home very long. I knew I had better prepare for the carpet-bombing from Ironman's soldiers in just a matter of minutes, and I knew there was no hole or bomb shelter anywhere around where I could escape it. Again, I felt God was laughing at me during the whole parade. He was telling me that I had no control over anything. Only he did.

There were three stragglers like me at the rear of the herd when I caught up to them exiting H-wing and heading for the exercise yard. Second from the end, I strolled along. The pack had set a slow pace, like they really had any control over anything any more than I did. It was their way of rebelling I suppose.

Anyway, after passing several more wings of convicts, and after trekking through many concrete halls, we all poured into a gigantic open area surrounded by forty-foot granite walls with tornado-like rolls of concertina wire spread generously along the tops of them. Almost immediately, I noticed that the assemblage of convicts split into a myriad of segregated groups according to race and gang affiliation. It looked to me like they were all being herded into their various corrals without the herders.

I spotted Ironman immediately standing in the middle of about six or seven of his cronies. I assumed they were his soldiers, because all the other races and gangs had split off and huddled up too. The only ones who hadn't grouped up were other peckerwoods like me looking for a friendly roost. We had no protection and we were vulnerable to the wicked predaciousness surrounding all of us. We had nowhere to go. Sure, there were four gun towers, with guards patrolling outside them ready to blow a brain out if trouble ensued, but that didn't help me right then. By the time they joined the action, I would already be a carcass waiting for the shovel.

Cautiously, I walked slowly around the outside of the yard. Luckily, an old man about sixth-five years old caught my attention and motioned me over to him. He looked harmless enough, so I took a few steps over to him. He was standing with a few other whites, who were neither gang affiliated nor peckerwoods. They were old cons who didn't want to play the gang game and who had somehow survived several prison stints each.

"How's it goin' youngster?" the old con said to me affably.

"I'm doin' okay at the moment, but it in a few minutes, I might not be healthy anymore," I replied. I managed a small smile.

"Whaddaya mean?" the old guy said inquisitively, while his older buddies listened to our conversation intently.

"Unfortunately, I've rubbed Ironman the wrong way by smashing one of his soldiers in receiving the other day. To make it worse, the guards paired him with me, and now he wants me badly," I explained, and glanced across the yard at Ironman still staring me down at the same time.

"I know Ironman and all his goons," another old con piped in right then. "He's a mean mutha, and his Nazi Low Riders don't take no prisoners neither. I'd be real careful if I was you."

"I'm open to any suggestions you might have. I'm outta ideas myself," I said casually, wondering if God would miraculously zap one of the geriatric boys into Superman, or Batman, or Spiderman, or any other super hero who could vanquish the nasty boys for me if I asked him nicely.

"I only have one," the original old con told me enthusiastically. "If you're confronted by Ironman's stooges, 'cause I guarantee he won't wanna do the dirty work himself, call Ironman out directly. If you call 'im out, he will have no choice but to go one on one with you. It is an unwritten rule in here that gang leaders can't deny a personal challenge in the presence of their soldiers, and when they are challenged, no soldier can help him in any way," the old con explained plainly.

"You mean if I walk over there and call Ironman out, I won't get jumped by the rest of them?" I said to the old con, a little surprised at the experience and insight these old guys were willing to share with me.

Apparently, I was like a sore thumb like all the other peckerwoods. We stood out in the crowd, and every other convict could pick us out of the line up from a mile away. I suppose we all just had the deer in the headlights look or something. It was all so strange.

"Yeah. But, are you willin' to enter the lion's den?" the second old con asked me frankly, while all of them stared at me. They were all probably wondering if I was stupid enough to challenge Ironman in front of everyone, or I was just blowing smoke and pretending I was entertaining the idea to begin with.

"I don't have any choice. If I don't, his goons will do me for sure. If I do, then at least I will have a fair chance," I said to the old group, as I glanced over towards Ironman and his crew once again.

"You might be right. But, remember, there're guards up there with big guns prayin' they can plant a lowlife. They'll cut ya down like a cow-corn silage chopper," one of the old cons reminded me sternly.

"Thanks. I never expected anyone to help me out. I appreciate it," I stated calmly, as I looked right into the eyes of the old con.

I knew I had a decision to make then, and it was possible it might be the most important one of my life, literally. It was simply a question of taking action or not. When I glanced over the heads of all the old cons, I noticed Ironman and his clan was all sizing me up like I was the only little darling at the dance. To them, I was a prime peach, perfect for picking. I wanted to run, but there was nowhere to run to. I looked around the yard and noticed it was pretty calm, and no one besides the old cons and Ironman's cronies were eyeballing me. The gun tower guards were pacing back and forth searching for a target, and the yard guards stood in small groups in their goon-gear prepared for some gang to go off on another one. To me, it appeared everyone had his own soup cooking. However, in Ironman's eyes, I was his main dish.

Ironman stood encircled by his gnarly looking associates, and they all seemed to be milling around like a bunch of cocky roosters. They all had their shirts off as they strutted around cockily, and every inch of their midsections, torsos, arms, shoulders and necks were one continuous tattoo like Ironman's body was. They stood out like a grand spectacle, and without being told, I knew it was part of the intimidation game. They wanted everyone in the yard and in the prison to know who was claiming title to the real estate. For me, I just didn't want to die.

I figured if it had to happen, it might as well be on my terms. So, I thanked the old cons for their help once again, and I told them I would return the favor some time if I lived through my walk into the python pit. Slowly, I started walking towards Ironman standing head on to me across the yard about one hundred feet away. I stared directly at him as

I walked. It seemed like I was Little Joe Cartwright facing down Jesse James and his horde of ruffians. I saw his lips move subtly, and his soldiers casually dispersed in different directions so the guards couldn't pick up on their strategic maneuver. I saw right away what they were up to, and I froze. They wanted to circle and come at me from all directions. I was sure of it. Suddenly, I heard a friendly voice from behind me somewhere.

"Hold on there, peckerwood," the voice said cordially.

I swiveled around on my heel slowly. I was careful not to be too abrupt in my movements so I wouldn't attract undue attention from the guards or show my fear to Ironman and his soldiers. I was shocked to see another white bald guy in his early thirties. He was at least six-feet tall and carrying about 210 pounds of lean muscle, and he was approaching me unhurriedly. He also was an obvious gang member, and about two-dozen swastika-covered soldiers of his own shadowed him. They followed the leader of the pack about ten feet back, and when I made eye contact with him about fifteen feet from me, they stopped in their tracks.

"What's goin' on?" I said to the guy suspiciously. I didn't know if he was part of Ironman's gang I didn't know about, or if he and his gang were friends of Ironman's, or if he just wanted to jam me about being a peckerwood. Whatever it was, I thought it was time to surrender. There were way too many adversaries in this jungle for me to keep track of, let alone battle all of them. Anyway, just as I was about to tell him, "OK, you can be my daddy," he stopped about four feet away and smiled at me.

"My name is Psycho. Jed just told me Ironman's been jammin' ya pretty hard cause you thoroughly educated one of his soldiers the other day in receivin'. Is at right, or not?" he asked abruptly, as he pointed back in the direction of the old cons.

As he studied my mug intently, I couldn't tell if he was sizing me up like his momma shopping for a ripe tomato, or he was wondering if I really did knock Ironman's gorilla down out of his tree.

"That's about the size of it," I replied, still wary and wondering how many cat lives I had left in my bag.

"Well, nice to meet you. What's your name?" he said friendly-like, as he stepped closer holding out his hand for me to shake.

I have to say that gesture surprised me. It seemed I was getting shocked every other time I took a breath. I also didn't know if it was a ruse, or it was a genuine appeal for friendship.

"Randy," I replied apprehensively, and shaking his hand strongly at the same time.

"This is your lucky day. Ironman and his clones just happen to be our main competition in town, and we would like to help you out. We have a helluva lot more clout than they do around here, and we don't ever let' em muscle our guys. So, you in?" Psycho asked me enthusiastically, but at the same time, I knew he really wasn't asking.

In a short minute, I had to make a choice, one that I would have to live with whatever the consequences, just like drinking and driving and causing Sheryl's death. I could either continue on my crash course with Ironman and become mincemeat in a few seconds, or I swap for Psycho's game plan.

However, I knew that Psycho's help wouldn't come without a hefty price tag for sure. Gangs and their leaders always have ulterior motives in every situation, and it was always about personal gain. It wasn't charity, and it wasn't out of the goodness of his clandestine heart. I knew his motivation was to advance his position in his gang's eyes, and more importantly, in all the other gangs' eyes in general. And, if I chose not to accept his poisonous offer, I would have him and his gang on my trail as well as Ironman's.

"That depends. What'll you expect in return?" I asked Psycho point blank, as I waited anxiously for the hammer.

"First off, anyone who's got the hair to stand up to Ironman, I want him on my side. Straight up, I want you in my gang. If that ain't you, it's okay. We don't force anyone to join us unless they want to. As far as the debt you'd owe me, I expect you to back me up if I ever need it. Other than that, I expect you to learn some basics from me about bein' a white guy in prison so you don't get killed by a few thousand other cons in here," Psycho explained frankly in his recruiting speech.

I took a few minutes to contemplate Psycho's proposal, but my feelings were clamped in a vice. I knew for sure there was more to it than what Psycho was portraying to me in our brief communication. He would undoubtedly call in his marker if he wanted a hit or back-up on one of his search and destroy or rape and plundering missions just like all gangs did when they had a puppy on their leash. The fact was I knew it would be like that with me sooner or later.

I didn't stall or hesitate very long before I figured that getting tangled up with Psycho couldn't be any worse than tackling Ironman in front of everyone. The chances were pretty good I would either get shot by the guards, or I'd get stabbed or mauled by some gangsters if I did. There was a chance I could challenge Ironman and take him, but I was flat out too scared to take that chance. I knew I was probably selling my soul to the devil, but with Psycho and his mercenaries, I would at least live a little longer.

"I don't want to be in any gang for sure. And, as far as backin' you up, that's automatic where I come from. When someone does me a favor, I always pay him back somehow. It may take awhile, but I always pay my debts. Just don't expect me to be your punk, your gopher, or your brainless stooge that you can stomp on anytime you get a hankerin' to. I won't do that," I explained to Psycho aggressively. I wanted to make sure he knew I wouldn't be his puppet.

"Fair 'nough," Psycho said shortly, while at the same time, he motioned two of his soldiers over to us.

While Psycho summoned his boys over to us, I glanced at Ironman and his gang briefly, and I could see clearly they had stopped crowing. They all had redressed and huddled up, and they weren't gawking my way anymore. To be quite honest, I was amazed and impressed. Ironman seemed quite formidable. But apparently, Psycho was carrying a bigger stick.

Psycho introduced me to Bam-Bam and Magician, and for the next few minutes or so, we all yakked about me regarding what I was in prison for and what I did for a living on the outside. I also received some life-and-death schooling. Bam-Bam and Magician alternated in my personal training and instruction, in that, they informed me that whites were absolutely not allowed to eat or drink after a black guy or a member of any other race or color other than white. In other words, I could sit by them in the chow hall, because the guards didn't segregate us during mealtimes, but I couldn't touch another non-white's food or drink.

I could talk to a non-white, if I was asked a question, but I couldn't initiate the conversation. I couldn't associate with anyone other than whites for any reason, even if he was a long-lost adopted family member. I couldn't use the same soap as another non-white con, or any other hygiene item. I couldn't share my clothes or bedding, I could never sit on a non-white's bunk, or allow a non-white to sit on mine.

Although the training was only an immediate crash course, Bam-Bam explained to me quite succinctly that if I didn't abide by all of the basic rules willingly and to the letter, every white convict would want my head on a platter. It was all about race in prison, and if a white guy crossed the white-line paved clearly for him, he would crash head-on with every other white con in reaching distance. All I could really do was to agree and to nod my approval of the racist program Bam-Bam laid out for me. Although some of my best friends were non-white guys out in the real world, I thought about my personal physical survival. I thought I had better learn the prison culture as fast as I could so I could eventually go home in one piece.

In the meantime, Psycho already had a plan formulated in his head. It concerned Ironman and my future as a peckerwood or live human. He had already given or heard the race lecture a million times before me, and while Bam-Bam and Magician talked at me, he headed straight for a group of armed cops standing by the basketball hoop where the blacks were playing four on four. As he approached them, I noticed all three of the cops stop talking to each other. It was obviously out of whack to every cop and con on the yard that Psycho, or any other con, would be bold enough to talk to the cops for any reason, but Psycho did it all so subtly it was evident to everyone in the yard he wasn't earning any favor from the cops. In fact, he became so animated in his short speech with the cops, it looked like he was arguing with them fiercely about something no one could hear. Of course, it was all part of his game, so other gangs or whites didn't demolish him later for sucking up to the cops.

Anyway, about a minute later, the yard horn shattered the air like an old destroyer's blast would have done in the fog at Normandy. Immediately, every con hit the ground. Magician told me to get down fast, or the guards would pop a cap in my rear. While we waited for a few seconds for further orders, he further informed me that, when yard time concluded, every con had to sit on the concrete yard whether it rained or not so the guards could manage the disembarking with minimal casualties. When the cops were satisfied everyone was concordant, a guard would command us by tier and cell number over the loud speaker to rise and follow the yellow lines painted on the cement out of the yard. The strategy minimized riots and violence during the transition back to our cells. If we swayed from the line at all, the tower guards had free rein to open fire. According to Magician, all the cons knew the procedure. And it was up to the friendlies like him to teach me the idiosyncrasies of prison life so I wouldn't die prematurely. Magician stated to me very clearly that there were enough brambles in the bush that bashed skulls, stole souls, and snuffed out lives in a heartbeat. There was no point in getting the axe over stupidity or for lack of education.

The guards roared out our cell and tier numbers, and like cattle through a chute, we hustled through the yard, out a set of massive steel doors, down the many halls again, and back towards our cells. Meanwhile, some yard guards were positioned strategically around the yard, and others were stationed like infantry in battalion-like force around the gate ready for a charge. I was heeding Magician's counsel to the letter. I knew if I didn't, the tower guards might nail me whether I knew the rules or not, or the other cons would perceive me as weak and bend me over for sure.

However, after the first step I took following a black guy at the end of my particular line, I realized I was headed right back into the Devil's lair. I had been distracted by the preparation-for-exit melee in the yard as well as the guards' bellowing, and I had forgotten where I lived and with whom. Suddenly, I knew Ironman would be waiting for me in our cell. He was at the front of my line. Instantly, I was so scared again, I almost peed my pants. My mind raced and I couldn't think straight. Every step I took, I knew I was one step closer to the ultimate duel. I began to think about Psycho and how meaningless and worthless all that hubbub was in the yard when he said he would help me out. Well, where was he now, I thought. I was going back to my cell, Ironman would already be waiting to bushwhack me for sure, and I would have no choice but to kill or be killed. It was all too clear.

Just as I entered H-wing, my eyes automatically followed the path up the stairs I had to trek to my cell. When my eyes located my cell in their scope, they became fixated on the rectangular opening as if it was the pathway to my execution chamber. It seemed like every step I took, I could feel the lethal injection taking control over my whole body. My skin crawled like it was infested with fire ants, and electrical shivers chased each other up and down my spine. Somehow, I just knew God had only been testing me up to that point. Now, it was time for me to pay the piper. No more games. No more reprieves from Psycho, or tobacco hunts, or lucky horseshoes like during the accident.

As I reached the stairs leading up to tier two, I grabbed hold of the rail so I wouldn't fall backwards. It seemed my inner perturbation was making my physical dexterity lame. But, I guess I still had one horse-shoe available somewhere, because just then, I heard a woman's voice yell my name from behind me somewhere by the opening to H-wing. I wheeled around towards the cop's voice and noticed her motioning me back to her station. I started walking back to her, but as I did, I glanced back up to my cell above and behind me. Of course, Ironman was leaning against the side of our open cell door casually watching the action. He must have heard the guard call my name too, I thought. He lurked like a rattler under a rock waiting for the rat to crawl close enough for a deadly strike.

During the time it took to cover the sixty feet or so to the guard, I thought about squealing to the cop about the inevitable fight I was headed for when she was done with me. I didn't care anymore if I would be labeled a snitch or not. My confidence was shot, and I thought there was no way I could survive the battle with Ironman. Even if I did, it would be open season on Randolph by every one of his goons from that second on.

Out of the blue, another horseshoe surfaced instead before I could spill my guts. When the cop told me to sit in her office, she told me curtly I was being moved to a different cell in H-wing. She refused to elaborate when I asked her for an explanation, but she did say, "Ask

Psycho. He's your new cellmate." Immediately, I had a new and incredible respect for Psycho. He had made the move possible. He had saved my bacon after all. I don't know what Psycho told the guards in the yard, but it was obvious that whatever he said, the guards took him seriously. I guessed that Psycho told the cops to move me unless they wanted the Nazi Low Riders and the New Order gangs to go off on each other at the first opportunity.

Ironman was escorted to a holding cell right away, and I packed up lock, stock, and barrel. When a cop led me to my new home down on the main tier, Psycho was waiting for me with a devious smile plastered all over his face.

"What's up, Homey?" he stated simply, like I was his long-lost friend from home or something.

"I don't know what you said to the cops, but I was just about to throw in the towel. Thanks for whatever it was," I replied cautiously, wondering if I was a rat caught in the same trap I had been with Ironman. He was being a little too friendly for my liking.

"Don't worry about it. You looked like you were worth rescuin'. And, we're always scoutin' out worthy new comrades. Besides that, what you did to Ironman's soldier, and what you were willin' to do to Ironman in the yard, I want you with me, not against me. What do ya think about that?" he informed me pleasantly, while he studied my face and eyes intently. It was obvious he was going to school on me to see what made me tick.

"Let's put it like this. It's obvious I'm a heckuva lot better off now than I was a few minutes ago. And, I greatly appreciate your help," I said with a chuckle, although it was feigned a little. I didn't want Psycho to know I was still scared and I didn't trust him as far as I could throw him.

Psycho and I didn't talk much for the next several hours. I stowed my gear and we both sprawled on our bunks. The only thing he really said for quite awhile was that I needed to flush before I dropped one, just like Ironman had ordered me to do. That way, my natural bodily functions wouldn't be so disgusting. I obliged of course, because I definitely didn't want to get off on the wrong foot with my new cellie. Besides that, I wanted to use Psycho for my own personal gain. I figured the more information I could sift out of him during my stint at the Gladiator School, the easier life would be in my prison over all. I also thought if I could live long enough to hunt up a few more horseshoes, I might be able to experience the outside world again someday.

CHAPTER 8

The Nazi's Nazi Nemesis

Time is God's greatest disciplinarian. When a human has nothing but time to think, and to contemplate, and to reflect, his internal monsters become infinitely more hideous and intensified than if they were just passing through the brain somewhere in a single thought. The curse of time isn't merciful. It simply doesn't care who you are, what you are, or how much material wealth you have killed yourself and others for during your lifetime. It is incessant in its vilification, and there is no reprieve.

In prison, time became a fascinating phenomenon to me. For twenty-three hours a day, for the next three days straight in Psycho's cell, I laid prone staring vacuously at the concrete ceiling. It was utterly impossible to sleep, or physically or mentally shut my brain off at all. When I did doze a little, it seemed my mind would flash Sheryl's distorted face in front of my eyes time, after time, after time. It would come out of the blackness of that horrible night a few months earlier, and my eyes would jump open again uncontrollably. I must have conjured up Sheryl's configuration a million times during that stint. No other thought had the power to vanquish it.

In those three days, I calculated I spent only one hour a day distracted from Sheryl's apparition. However, during the short stays of execution, Sheryl's image never left my mind completely. It hovered inside my brain like a vulture even when the chow trays came every morning at 5 A.M., and every night at 5 P.M. It circled when lunch was delivered in a brown bag with breakfast, and no matter what mind game I tried to invoke to make it disappear, I was powerless to stop it.

I had no other contact with anyone outside the cell. I was alone. Psycho slept in the bunk below me and hovered around the cell like a caged madman, but I was alone. Sometimes, Psycho would stand at the cell door for countless hours and stare through the tiny, thick plexi-glass window about chin-high on him. He seemed to be anticipating the prison kites, or written messages passed from cell to cell by inmates, landing at his airport. But, even when the guards didn't allow the infor-mative deliveries, he stood there anyway just in case something hap-pened in our cellblock somewhere. I understood why he watched so carefully though. He was in command of a huge army of soldiers, and it was up to him to be diligent and sift any and all information he could from any possible source available. He would even strike up conversa-tions with the cops as they made their rounds every couple of hours, and he would talk to them through the window like they were long-lost friends. Many times, they had the most accurate intel, and I was positive that is why Psycho played the game with the cops. They knew the game too, but to minimize animosity with the heavy hitter, the cops placated Psycho like I did.

While I sat in my prison cell completely demoralized, a sad loneli-ness engulfed me. There was no softness. There was no hug. There was no sensual kiss. There was only the monster called time, and in its steely blackness, it was a vile and sordid enemy. Slowly, in its crafty deliberate-ness, it stole my heart from my chest like a vindictive fox.

On the morning of the fourth day in my new home, Psycho started picking at me for conversation right after he ate breakfast. It seemed he was on a mission to save me, or something. At least, that is what I thought at the time.

"Time to rise and shine, peckerwood. You need to start eatin' and stop feelin' sorry for yourself. I've been eyeballin' you and your blank stare at the ceilin' for days now, and it's time for you to learn something. Besides, we'll be called out for showers in awhile, and you stink like some ol' goat cheese I dug out of a dumpster a few years ago," he yammered enthusiastically, like he was a teacher and I was a student he was trying to motivate.

"Whaddaya mean it's shower time?" I asked half-heartedly.

The word shower seemed to jump-start my brain instantly. I hadn't had a shower since I was sentenced several days before, and I was already way past the point of being rank. I stunk so badly, I couldn't even stand myself. I was even surprised Psycho hadn't stabbed me by the end of the first day together because of it. I had tried to wash my pits, butt, and body with the minuscule bar of soap the guards so graciously gave me in receiving, but it didn't seem to have any effect on the gruesome odor that emanated from my every pore. I couldn't remember smelling that nasty even in my worst times as an athlete when I wouldn't wash my jock-strap for weeks because of my laziness. At least then, a washer and a shower were always available when I needed or wanted one, or I just couldn't stand the stench any longer. Things were different in prison though. Being or feeling clean was a valuable and rare commodity. Being or feeling clean in prison was like having a pot of gold big enough to buy the world, but rarely was it within reach.

Convicts weren't usually permanent fixtures at the Gladiator School. It was only a brief respite for them. Until their paperwork was completed, they were classified at a certain security risk level, and a destination prison was chosen by the corrections staff, they stayed put. In the meantime, personal hygiene items were almost non-existent. The system didn't care if the temporary residents stunk or not. To me, it looked like the cops were taking their own hit out on us by not allowing regular showers and providing us with enough hygiene items. They had storerooms full of the products, but they were stingy with them. It was like pulling teeth with a pair of rusty old pliers and without anesthesia.

The standard prison issue included a tiny bar of soap, a three-inch toothbrush, a single disposable razor, and a two-inch tube of toothpaste with a circumference about the size of a penny. The soap was issued to perform many duties. It was meant to be used as a deodorant, shampoo, shaving cream, and as a washing tool in general. The bottom line was that, when a con ran out of the skimpy prison issue, tough luck. The con stunk up the joint with his body odor until he was moved to his destination prison, or his cellie couldn't stand the stench any longer and loan him some of his supply of hygiene items, if he had any left to loan.

Basically, when it came to frustration regarding my cleanliness, or lack thereof, during the initial two months in the prison system, mine could fill the hold of a giant ocean liner. I realized very quickly that I had taken my usual personal cleanliness for granted my whole life. I was completely spoiled, and I didn't even realize it. I lived in a decadent society where I could shower two, three, four times a day if I needed to or just wanted to. But, in prison, I waited all week for a short splash of that deliciously beautiful and sensual commodity—water—to run over my body for a few precious moments. It became one thing among many I began to appreciate and no longer take for granted like I had done as a spoiled and arrogant free human.

"We get a five-minute shower twice a week, and today's one of 'em. We have to be ready when the door opens, "cause five minutes later, it closes. The guards yell when we gotta minute left. Wet or not, if we aren't inside when the door closes, we go to the hole for a week," Psycho told me frankly.

"How many get out at one time?" I asked Psycho curiously. I was trying not to let on that I was still scared of Ironman and his soldiers, and I didn't want to get caught with my pants down.

"That's an excellent question. Now you're startin' to think a little. Usually there are eight at a time, and they usually open four cells in a row until one tier is done. Then, they start on another one. While we're talkin', you need to know the scoop on Ironman and his soldiers too. While you were poutin' the last few days, I've been gettin' a lot of kites about Ironman. He's still up on tier two, but he has several of his soldiers here on tier one, only a few cells down the road. That means we need to be careful. Although there are a lot more New Order comrades than Nazi Low Riders in H-wing, the way the guards open the doors determines how many of us and how many of them will be let out to shower at the same time. So, when the doors open, watch yourself. If they try somethin', lotta times it's right out of the gate. Look in every direction, and don't let your guard down for a second. The only real safe place is being locked in here." Psycho lectured me sternly, and while he talked, I perceived from the intense look on his face that he was gearing up for potential battle.

Strangely, Psycho's candor all made perfect sense to me. It also cast me out of my depression in about two heartbeats. It dawned on me that it was imperative to mentally prepare myself for battle immediately; I couldn't waste any more time whining about my problems. Like a light switch turning on and illuminating a dark cavern, I started thinking rationally and strategically. I was positive Ironman wouldn't have forgotten the altercation between his soldier and me. Secondly, Psycho embarrassed him even more in the yard in front of the entire wing by calling me back from challenging him. And, that little tactic showed Ironman up deliberately. It was obvious that Ironman had to retaliate, and soon, if he was going to be able to save face with his fellow gangsters or maintain any power at all in the entire system. He was humiliated along with his entire gang. He had no choice but to strike back as strongly as he had ever done before. Keeping his position at the helm and preventing his ship from capsizing depended on it.

In addition to all of that mess, it was clearly apparent that information was readily available through message-kites passed around the prison by trustees and even guards sometimes. And, by the prison system's own hand, it allowed the crude communication structure to operate unmolested. Apparently, that was the cops' way of learning the heartbeat and plans of all the gangs and ultimately maximized the cops' safety. If they didn't allow kites to be passed, they wouldn't be able to detect much of the ceaseless brewing of malice rampant in the entire system. So, they allowed handpicked trustees to roam the prison wings for an hour in the morning and an hour at night. Every convict and cop in the entire Gladiator School knew what was going on. That is why I was still alive. Information passed through the yard so fast that Psycho was able to intervene before I reached Ironman.

There wasn't much the cons didn't know or have the capability of learning. They knew the gang in charge as well as its leader. They knew who his lieutenants and soldiers were. They knew who was targeted for death, stabbing, beating, raping, and plundering, even though we were all locked up behind bars. They even knew what was happening in other prisons all over the California.

Every time a new inmate would check in to school, he was promptly grilled for tidbits of information on other gangs, new laws recently passed, or any other piece of information that might be available to advance the interrogator's, or his gang's, position and influence in the system. I wouldn't doubt it if they could find out what color of underwear I wore on the street if they really wanted to.

It was all uncanny, it was strangely interesting, and most of all, it was very, very scary. If they ever found out I had been a cop, there weren't enough cops in the entire country to stop all the gangs, cons, and especially Psycho and Ironman, from whacking me immediately. Oh yeah, I am sure they would rape and torture me first, get their fill of my old meat, then kill me. Everyone was watching like a hawk. They were watching because blood was on their mind, and control and influence was the omnipotent prize.

"So, what's the plan? Do we stay together, am I on my own, or what?" I asked Psycho probingly, although I was desperately hoping it was the former.

I had already learned that being the Lone Ranger in prison was the least desirable position to be in. I knew I was alone romantically and intellectually, but I knew without a doubt that I needed some homies with some clout for my physical self-preservation. The enemies were too many and too powerful to brave it alone. It would be suicide if I tried. The fiasco in the yard was a joke. The only one I was kidding was myself. God knew it. He knew he had to send Psycho in after me before I reached the point of no return. If I was really going to be honest with myself, I knew that, without physical back up, I would be hunting bear with a fly swatter. And, that was God working too, and I didn't even know it.

"Cellies are like the wife and kids. You have to be willin' to die for 'em. If you aren't, then the word gets around real fast, and you get dead real fast. It doesn't matter how many are out there, we stay together. That's why I picked you as my cellie. You looked like you could take care of yourself. Got it?" Psycho stated, bluntly, and it was clear he wasn't playing around.

"I understand completely," I replied just as sincerely.

Psycho and I didn't exchange any more words until the doors opened for shower time. In the meantime, I sat on the edge of my top bunk like I was Mike Tyson's challenger awaiting his decimation. All I seemed to be able to think about was how long the madness was going to continue. The waiting was killing me more than the thought of being gang raped by Ironman's Nazi Low Riders.

Just as Psycho flushed, the steel door slid open.

"Follow me closely and keep your eyes peeled. I'll give you a thumb up if it's clear. A thumb down means we go to war," Psycho told me firmly as we stepped out of our cell.

I quickly scanned the entire wing. I noticed immediately that Psycho had scoped out the situation as well, and we caught each other's eye when we saw the coast was clear. He gave me the subtle thumbs sign up from his side, and we followed four black guys and two Mexicans to the showers. All of them looked around apprehensively and suspiciously too. They had enemies like everyone else in the system. We all marched quickly towards the shower stalls about fifty feet towards the guard's office. We only had five minutes to shower and return to our cells.

I was the last one in line to reach a showerhead. There were eight open stalls, so the guards could scrutinize every con in the shower closely. In this case, there were three cops monitoring our group from their roost up and on the end of the third tier closest to the H-wing exit. From my law enforcement experience, I knew the prison showers spawned many of the hits that took place when the guards were distracted by other duties or action on the tiers. That is why only eight cons were released at a time. The cops knew that if one or more of them attacked another con, they could manage the problem. Correctional officer and convict casualties could be minimized until reinforcements could be called in, although ultimately, the strategy prevented riots and mayhem in general.

The water was already blasting out when I stepped into my stall. Slyly, Psycho had grabbed an end one. Although it didn't appear to me there was any immediate danger, I suppose Psycho was acting on wisdom he had garnered over his eighteen years in the system. A con could never be too careful, and Psycho knew it. The end stall prevented the enemy from surrounding him for a rear attack and offered minimum exposure to the other cons if they unexpectedly charged him.

I tossed my towel and prison boxers over the rail like everyone did, and quickly ducked under the strong flow of lukewarm water. I calculated I had only about two minutes for an actual shower, so I did what I could in the time I had. The water felt sooooo good on my head and body. It had been about five days since my last shower, and I felt like a nomad finally finding a rich oasis after a year in a waterless desert. I thrust my face up close to the nozzle to feel the maximum force of the spray. I think I may have been a little insane at that point, because strangely, I thought the stronger the force of the water, the more I could wash away my guilt and my sins. If I could wash away my sins, then I would finally be able to start forgiving myself for what I did to Sheryl and our kids.

I didn't want to dwell on my misery right then, because I wanted to cherish the privilege of reducing the stench emanating from my body. I soaped up and rinsed as fast as I could, but before I knew it, the guard's one minute warning rudely jolted me out of my watery bliss. I caught Psycho's eye for a second, and he summoned me with a subtle head-jerk to get back to the cell. Frustrated at the Gladiator School's medieval nature of maintaining personal hygiene, I begrudgingly grabbed my towel, put my boxers on quickly, and slipped and slided towards my cell on the flimsy shower shoes I was allocated in reception.

About fifteen feet from my new ground floor cell, all hell broke loose. Out of nowhere, a horn blasted so loudly, my eardrums felt like they were caved in momentarily. At the same time, I located the other cons in my shower group. They seemed to be hitting the deck as if they were ducking a bomb barrage. I immediately followed suit without thinking. Actually, I must have been thinking, because the image of a tower guard blowing me away flashed through my mind when I saw Psycho go down.

Less than a second later, I heard a guard yelling over the sound system for us to get down and stay off our feet, or we would be shot. We could sit and watch the show, but that was it. Like a grand hog led to the slaughter, I followed everyone else's gaze as they stared straight up to the top of tier three on the opposite side of my H-wing. In the same bat of an eyelash, I witnessed a frightening sight. As I clued in on the action above me, I saw a white convict flying through the air. When my brain picked him up and acknowledged what was happening, the con's body was descending past the second tier. In mid-flight, I noticed the body was flailing madly at the air like he had just learned how to skydive, but his parachute didn't open. I could clearly see his mouth gaping, and a horrible scream was shattering from it through the entire wing.

When his head splattered on the cement on tier one directly in front of me, I could only gape in horror. It seemed surreal, like a gory movie on the big screen with surround sound I had watched somewhere before when I was free. I imagined he must have been able to gain a pretty good head of steam for the size of the mess on the concrete floor. He had come in for his landing on the side of his bald head with nothing to break his fall, and the nauseating thud that ruptured the air sounded like a target watermelon exploding from a high-powered gunshot. It was a sickening sound. But, the blood and portions of brain oozing out of the con's shattered skull all over the cement were even worse. Splatters of blood were strewn in front of us about twenty feet away, and the little droplets of dark red liquid looked like a grotesque gravy the prison guards had spilled when they fed us for chow the night before. The bald guy was obviously dead. He didn't move. He didn't spasm. He didn't squirm.

In about thirty seconds, a dozen goons stormed through H-wing. Four of them pulled up in their haste in front of us with their military rifles pointed at us in case we decided to take part in the melee. The other eight took the stairs two at a time up to the third tier. All of them were in full riot gear and they looked like they were in no mood to take any prisoners. They were a formidable bunch that I assumed had a lot of experience in these situations. In fact, I knew they were specifically trained for that type of duty. They were professionals, and they took their jobs seriously.

Before that minute, I didn't think to look back up to see what had caused the con to plummet in the first place. But, when I did, I was convinced he was chucked over the side of the railing above me. Otherwise, why was he flailing or screaming to begin with, I thought. I also noticed five other white cons and two blacks sitting up on tier three, and it looked to me that all but two of the white guys were gang members. They appeared to be headed to the shower on tier three when the incident occurred. Thus, I concluded that a gang hit had just occurred.

Anyway, when the goons reached the other seven cons sitting on their tier like my group was, I realized I had perceived the situation accurately. While six of the goons violently manhandled the three cons closest to the stairwell, four more of them held their rifles on the other four. One on each arm, the six goons escorted the three cons down the stairs, out of H-wing and to the hole until an investigation could be conducted. In the meantime, the four goons up on tier three locked the remaining cons back up in their cells, and the four goons guarding my group locked us up. Visibility from our cell window was next to nil, so Psycho or I couldn't watch any of the cleanup on aisle one.

Back in the cell, Psycho was eyeballing me closely to see if I was squeamish or not about what had just happened.

"Guess who that was?" Psycho asked me after I had dressed back into my prison issue and climbed up on my bunk.

"I'm guessing it was a hit of some sort," I responded calmly.

"You guessed right. It was one of Ironman's lieutenants. I had some of the skinheads do me a little favor so Ironman and his crew get the message Homey don't play," he said just as casually. Apparently, the skinheads were another Nazi group friendly with Psycho's gang.

Right then, there was no doubt in my mind that Psycho was a force I hoped I would never have to reckon with. I thought if he had that kind of clout, he was carrying an awfully big stick. I also imagined Psycho could reach out just about anywhere in the entire prison system and tap some adversary on the head with that stick if he was wronged, or if he just wanted to send a message like he had just notified Ironman and his comrades. No. Tapping would be too slight and feminine to describe Psycho's capabilities. Ordering a hit a thousand miles away on the other side of the state, and having the enemy's skull crushed at will, would be more like it, I thought.

"What happens now?" I asked Psycho, trying to get an idea of the trouble I might be in when we were released for chow or showers next time.

At the same time, I figured I better continue placating Psycho. My cellie was the supreme commander and general of the entire New Order White Supremist gang, a guy who had the ultimate wallop to squash me like a defenseless bug under his boot whenever he felt like it. I definitely didn't want to get on this guy's bad side, and I thought it would be a good idea to engage in conversation with him so he would get the idea I was sincerely absorbed in his interests. The bottom line was that, I pacified Psycho to make sure he was comfortable and confident I was on his side. I was scared to death of the man. His racist views, judgments, and overall abhorrent values and ideas were the filthiest attitudes I had ever experienced in a single human in my life. And, I was expendable. I was useless to him if he ever detected I wasn't with him all the way. It was without a doubt his way or be paved under the highway.

"You prob'ly don't have to worry 'bout it. After a killin' or stabbin' or fight, there's usually an extra long lockdown on the whole prison. The cops are gonna need time to find out what happened, and to save a gang riot, they lock us all up and throw away the key," Psycho explained matter-of-factly, as if the chaos was an everyday occurrence to him.

"What does lockdown mean exactly?" I asked him curiously.

"It means we don't get outta here for any reason 'cept maybe to shower and change laundry once in awhile. And, there's no guarantee that'll even happen. Keeping us caged is the only way to stop the problems. No. That's not really right. It never stops the problems, cause they never stop. They can be delayed, but they don't stop. Lockdown also gives the guards a break and excuse to keep us locked up until the warden decides to cut us some slack. In the meantime, they don't really have to deal with us for whatever time the lockdown ends up bein'. We get fed in here, and trustees can deliver laundry. The only thing they really have ta let us out for is a shower. It's supposed to be twice a week, but in a problem this big, that can be yanked too," Psycho explained, while he reclined on his bunk, and I did the same on mine.

"How long do you figure we'll be here?" I asked Psycho inquisitively. I wanted to get an idea how long the madness would continue so I could try to get my mind right.

"You can count on bein' here 'bout thirty to ninety days. That's usually how long it takes to process your paperwork and find you the right home to do your time. You only have thirteen-and-a-half months, so you are considered a short timer. They won't send you to a fire camp or work camp because you are too short. You prob'ly aren't an escape threat, you're not a gang member, and you're prob'ly a level one security risk cause of your crime and you've never been in trouble before," Psycho went on willingly.

I got the distinct impression he was talkative by nature and he got a kick out of teaching naive peckerwoods the ropes just like he liked to order the messy hits. He attracted more new recruits that way, and he earned more respect from all the convicts overall. And, he knew it too.

"Do you think it might make a difference where they send me if they know I will be deported when I get released next year?" I asked Psycho enthusiastically. I was worried my imminent deportation would have a negative effect on where I would have to do my time. And, I was right.

"You're getting deported? Where you from?" Psycho asked energetically.

I was shocked by his question at first. I thought for sure he had done a thorough background check on me the first few days in his cell while I was feeling sorry for myself. I thought that is why he had so many kites flying in and out of our cell.

I thought he already knew everything about me because of the elaborate intelligence he had access to, but then I realized I hadn't discussed my citizenship or deportation with anyone since I was sentenced. So, I understood why he didn't know that part about me. That thought also triggered another even greater concern regarding the fact I used to be a cop. I knew if Psycho ever found out his greatest enemy inhabited the same home as he did, I would have accumulated enough frequent flyer miles for a one-way ticket flying solo like Ironman's goon did. Of course, I knew I would only be ready for take-off after a few dozen rapings and beatings first. I was sure of that.

"I'm a Canadian, born and raised. The judge told me the vehicular manslaughter charge is considered a violent felony, and because it is, I automatically get a strike in the three strikes law. And, when I get out, I will be deported. It's automatic. There is a legal recourse, in other words, I can fight it with an attorney, but there's not much chance to stop the deportation because of the violent felony part of the conviction," I responded willingly to Psycho's inquisition.

"That prob'ly changes everything for you then. If you're gonna be deported, you will be considered a flight risk. So, they will classify you prob'ly at a level two. That means you'll do harder time than if you were a one. One's get it easy," Psycho continued.

"What do you mean, harder time? Is it like this, worse, better, or what?" I asked Psycho, getting more worried by the minute that I was going to have to spend thirteen-and-a-half months locked down in a hellacious dungeon like we were in then.

"You'll probably stay here at DVI, or you will be shipped off to another maximum security prison somewhere in the state depending on the availability of beds when your paperwork is completed," he told me bluntly.

"You mean I might have to stay here?" I asked Psycho, utterly perturbed at the possibility of having to spend my thirteen-and-a-half months in this snake pit of poisonous vipers.

"It's a possibility. If you do, you won't have to stay in this cell. But, you might have ta stay in this prison somewhere on the other side of reception," he continued willingly.

Before I could quiz Psycho anymore, it was evening chow time. The guards came around to our cells with a pair of trustees on their coattails to divvy out the food trays, and I grabbed mine from the slot in the door about groin high like Psycho had done. I had hardly eaten at all since I was sentenced several days before, and I was so hungry, I would have taken on a pack of wolves bare-handed to get at some food. Although the slop looked like leftover vomit from someone's wedding party, I dug into the lettuce they called salad, the half-dry bread roll, and the crusty old refried beans and rice just like I dug for Sheryl a few months earlier.

When I finished the mess, I stuffed the tray back through the slot. I climbed back up on my bunk again and settled into the night totally exhausted from the marathon of unrelenting mental stress and lack of sleep. Somehow, I was able to block Sheryl's apparition from attacking me during the rest of the evening and night, and finally, I slept. The last five days had been like the sleep deprivation torture the Viet Cong practiced to extract information from our P.O.W. boys in Vietnam. But, when REM arrived, I slept like a dead man. Psycho's incessant pacing and yelling through the door for additional intelligence didn't even keep me awake. I fell asleep debating myself whether I was finally beginning to adjust to my new life, or I was just succumbing to that illusive magical healer—sleep.

I awoke at five the next morning to another chow delivery by the trustees and guards. There were no messengers allowed to fly their kites for the next two days though. Consequently, Psycho's screaming eighteen hours a day through the crack of the thick, steel door, and his efforts to communicate with friendlies down the cell block a piece, didn't help my sanity a lick. He wasn't allowed to receive any written kites, because the fog around the assassination the day before convinced the guards to ground the trustees and stop the daily morning and night flights.

Time was continuing its vicious onslaught, because the next two days felt like a year of drudgery. But, when the fog did lift, Psycho received the whole skinny about the killing from the dozens of kites flying in low under the door non-stop for the full hour in the morning and the hour at night. Apparently, the three guards watching the shower groups had momentarily taken their attention off the third tier's shower group just as the eight cons were approaching the shower stalls. There had been two active shower groups operating at the same time, one of which I wasn't aware of. I was too concerned about getting my shower within the time limit. According to Psycho, the H-wing guards personally witnessed the tail end of the execution when the hatchet men chucked the non-frequent flyer over the rail. But the minuscule cameras planted in the concrete walls all over the wing captured the whole dirty deed. When the horn blew, one of the cops reviewed the tape in a matter of seconds and identified the three culprits who tossed Ironman's lieutenant over the side of the third tier. Subsequently, the cop broadcast the information over the highly technological listening devices in the goon squad's helmets, so they knew which cons to grab as they were running as instructed up the stairs to tier three.

When I asked Psycho why the skinheads didn't know about the cameras, he was coolly unconcerned, and his calm reply shocked me a little.

"They did know. Two of 'em just caught their third strike recently, and they're headed to Soledad next week. So, they are already down for twenty-five to life. Another murder conviction won't do squat to them. They are way past the point of caring about human life, even their own. To them now, it's all about makin' a name for themselves, so they will become feared. Now they will command virtually unlimited privileges and power at Soledad, because most other cons will be scared of 'em. When they made the hit, they knew exactly what they were doin'," Psycho explained nonchalantly.

"What about the third guy? How much time does he have?" I asked Psycho inquisitively.

I completely understood the two-strike skinheads basically had nothing to lose, but I wondered why the other guy would commit a cold-blooded murder if he didn't have much time to do. It made sense to me to just lie low and do the hitch without attracting undue attention to himself. He would get home more quickly with that philosophy, I thought.

"He just picked up nine months for a parole violation. He's just a skinhead soldier told to help on the hit. He had no choice. When a con commits to a gang, he does what he's told when he's told, or he gets an attitude adjustment quick. Sometimes, I order hits and use low-level soldiers just to test 'em. My thinkin' is, if they don't wanna folla orders, they shouldn't have joined up to begin with," Psycho went on calmly.

"How much time do you have to do?" I asked Psycho curiously. He seemed to be in the mood to talk, and I was prying. The entire game the prison gangs played was intriguing to me.

"I caught two years this time for cookin' meth. I actually got one year cause they only found me with a smidgen of my batch, but because I had two strikes, my sentence was doubled automatically," he told me willingly.

"What did you get the two strikes for?" I asked Psycho. I wanted to know just how ruthless and vicious my cellie really was.

"I got my first strike right after the three strikes law passed about seven years ago now, I guess. Me and my homie did a home invasion and smashed the dad as soon as we crashed the door. Then, we took turns raping the college daughter and her mother, and then robbed all their money, jewelry, guns, stereos, and everything else we could find. We thought we got away, but my homie drove too fast and the cops stopped us a few miles away. We pleaded to home invasion and they dropped the rape, otherwise we both woulda caught another ten for sure. The second strike was when I did a robbery at a store. I nailed the storekeep with a bat and caught the second violent strike. Before that, I stole cars, did lottsa burglaries, and robbed a lotta people for money to support my drugs," he explained voluntarily.

Psycho seemed to be proud of his longevity and tenure in the prison system, and it was obvious he was bragging about the strikes he caught from his previous convictions. He also enjoyed telling me many of his war stories from the seventeen years he had been in the joint since he was eighteen years old. So, I seized the day. It was a perfect opportunity to continue my placating game; I could pass the time faster, and I could continue my prison education all in one swoop.

Psycho didn't disappoint his audience either. Psycho's willingness to yack was like a godsend to me, because in the next seven weeks as his cellie in the Gladiator School, he definitely became my favorite teacher. Although he was my only teacher at the time, and I didn't like him as a person because of his racist views and utter disregard for human life in general, I figured I might as well sift him and learn what I could. I knew that, the more intelligence I could usurp from the formidable supreme commander of the New Order White Supremist gang, the more likely I could use my newly gained expertise to stay alive and healthy until I could blow that pop-stand and go home.

However, I misinterpreted Psycho's interest in his wanting to talk all the time. Sometimes, between our marathon discussions, he would inform me quite bluntly that he was tired of conversation. He just wanted to sleep, read porno magazines and masturbate, or write letters to some girlfriends he had on the outside.

I still must have had more horseshoes hanging around, because those down times were like little blessings to me. I was never able to capture any internal peace, but I had plenty of time to contemplate my fate in prison. I was also able to strategize a plan to pass the time and imagine how my new life in Canada would play out. I realized sadly that Karyn wouldn't be able to pack up and leave her mother, friends, job, and life in California when I was eventually deported. But, I still prayed daily that God would help her make up her mind to move to Canada with me anyway. I loved her. Her loyalty and valiant heart had easily earned her that. I hoped that devotion would carry through the storm we were both trapped in.

The time factor set in well though during the regular reprieves from Psycho's discourse. Time stood on my neck and shoulders like a diehard Mack logging truck. It wormed inside my head like maggots on a fresh carcass. It grabbed at my heart and soul like a tentacled giant octopus. However, I fought them all off hard. In my blown mind, I became warrior-like. I could never really destroy or vanquish my monsters altogether, especially the monster called time, but I managed to survive somehow. I started by analyzing my physical well-being and how painful my back had been feeling since the accident. I came to the conclusion that I was in terrible physical condition. And I had taken my health and my past physical strength and athletic potency for granted for way too long. I had stopped running, riding my bike, and rollerblading every day in my regular cross training routine. I had spent too much time in the bar drinking and playing pool to escape my troubles in my marriage.

Even though I had been treated often by my favorite chiropractor, it seemed my back was deformed. It felt like it had been a constant target for a squad of medieval warriors' spears. Every time I moved, or when I just reclined on my bunk completely still, my back ached and throbbed like there were eight pumping diesel pistons pounding up and down on it. My body was weak, and my confidence level, because of it all, was lower than a snake's belly in a wagon rut.

Upon further reflection, I was annoyed when I realized my high level of personal conditioning had started deteriorating about five years before when I began my teaching career. I sat behind a desk during my tenure as a teacher, and I had let myself become a slacker and a sloth physically. Before I started teaching, I always worked very hard physically to make a living and support my family, and I was tenacious and relentless in keeping my body fit for high intensity athletic competition, like playing hockey, for example. But, the intellectual work demanded of teachers was quite a different type of work than I was used to my whole life, and I forgot very quickly what being in good physical shape was all about.

Like I said, when I became a teacher, my physical conditioning level suffered dramatically. That was why my back hadn't healed very well since the accident, and that was why I felt weak and decrepit lying on my bunk in my cell, day, after day, after day. So, I did something about my pathetic state of mind and body. I went to work again. Whenever Psycho was sleeping or just lying on his bunk, I took advantage of the breadbox's space we lived in.

In my pea-brain, I planned to begin a strict workout regimen immediately. The program dictated that I complete 100 push-ups, 100 squats, and 100 crunches seven days a week with a high level of intensity and enthusiasm. In my whacked out mental state, I envisioned myself as a lean mean fighting machine by the time I was moved to my destination prison a month or two later, and all the dumb gangsters infesting my new home and infringing on the little freedom available to me had better look out. I also thought that, although I had a bunch of frost on the old pumpkin, I wasn't ready to croak yet, and I was definitely not waiting for the shovel. At least, that is how my mind worked at the time in its demented state. You see, I had forgotten I was forty-four years old. My mind said I could do the 100, 100, and 100 no problem. But, my body screamed in agony when I struggled to reach 25, 25, and 25.

I was so weak, my ninety-six-year-old grandmother, God rest her soul, could have beaten me in Indian wrestling any day of the week and twice on Sundays. Kodi could have stuffed me in hoops, and the teenage-girl bullies in the neighborhood cul-de-sac could have used me as a whipping boy. That is how weak I was sitting in the joint at first. I was a disgrace to all of mankind.

Well, apparently, God stepped in again and helped me out. He gave me the mental strength, courage, fortitude, and tenacity to get up off the deck and go to work like there was no tomorrow. He also made me realize that my life probably depended on it too. Consequently, I fought to complete the 25, 25, and the 25 every day for about a week. By about the fifth day, it seemed I didn't struggle so much, and the level of difficulty seemed to be lowering rapidly. That was the signal to my pea brain to increase the dosage. So, I added 15, 15, and 15. I didn't do 40 push-ups at one time though, or either of the other sets all at one time. I split the whole program into two sets of twenty each. Three days later, I increased the dosage again to three sets of twenty. One week later, I increased to four sets of twenty. And, by the time I was moved to my destination prison, I was up to 200 push-ups, 200 squats, and 200 crunches each seven days a week.

I was truly amazed at my physical transformation after a month. One night, as I reflected on the drastic change in my body, I felt like I could do push-ups forever. My back felt strong as a mule pulling a plow, and my legs felt like massive pins powerful enough to lift a truck.

Suddenly though, at the precise instant I playfully jested in my mind about how strong my legs were, my mind raced once again back to that dark night in the country when I was too weak to lift the truck off Sheryl. Instantly, my mind dove back into its cave packed with guilt and remorse, and Sheryl's face appeared again. Her mouth seemed to plead with me insistently, "Get me outta here. I don't wanna die here," like she was still under the truck after all that time, and her big, brave husband still couldn't dig her out. That gruesome image and thought caused me to immediately break down into an uncontrollable crying jag. I had been bragging to myself again how powerful I was as a man, and how all the other convicts had better look out for Randy Wiens. But in my false bravado, I was totally useless to help Sheryl when it mattered the most.

However, I knew I was lucky in one sense. My sobbing spell happened to be in the middle of the night when the racist animal was tucked away snuggly in his little bunky pooh. He couldn't hear me sob. He couldn't see my anguish. He couldn't jam me for exhibiting my human weakness.

During the long and treacherous weeks locked down in Psycho's cell, I learned that in prison a single human is absolutely insignificant. I was only a number. I was without flesh or a brain. I simply existed as a body for my period of time. No one cared what I thought. No one was concerned with my well-being. And, for sure, no one was going to help me unless he was going to receive something more valuable in return. So, I waited for Psycho to drop the other shoe he was carrying. He had gone out on a limb for me, and he pulled the system's strings to help me out of the huge jam with Ironman. All I could do was wait for the call, and I knew I had to come running when the phone rang. Otherwise, I knew I would be picked cleaner than a turkey neck at Christmas.

Fortunately, several weeks into my stretch at the Gladiator School, I was finally able to communicate with the outside world. I was past the point of being desperate to contact a reasonable and sane human being on the outside of the prison walls. I was even ready to sell my soul to the devil for the opportunity. So, I decided to ask Psycho for help in the matter, even though he was adamant about not discussing the price at the time.

Surprisingly, Psycho was willing to help me out without flinching. He immediately flew a kite to one of his trustee comrades who had connections with another skinhead through the kite service he also had mastered like Psycho. In a matter of hours, I had three sheets of lined paper and a two-inch pencil delivered to our cell. When Psycho passed the materials to my hands, I tore into that paper so furiously; I was like a marooned sailor on an uninhabited island desperate to float off a bottle. I wrote to my kids in minuscule letters, barely large enough to make out on the other end so I could have more room to write. After so many days isolated from my loved ones and rest of the sane out in the free world, loneliness was a terrible monster like time was. I was desperate to make the most of what I had.

As far as Psycho was concerned, he couldn't write very well. Plus, he said he had burned most of his bridges with his loved ones on the outside, so he wasn't ever interested in writing anyone. His life was inside the prison walls, with a brief vacation on the outside from time to time whenever his current visit was terminated. He also told me he would always come back. It was the life he chose to lead. He had incredible power and an army of loyal soldiers to carry out his will, but most of all, prison was the only thing he was ever good at. Psycho told me one day that he wanted to do another violent crime so he would pick up his third strike the next time around the barn. That way, he wouldn't have to deal with the judicial system any more. To Psycho, all prosecutors and judges were the lowest scum on earth, and he wished he could blow them all up at once.

Psycho's attitude about life was acutely corrupted from spending so many years in the joint; I knew I could never change his brainwashed and hardhearted attitude. So, for my survival, I used him like he was using me. However, I was always afraid of him. I didn't know when my kick at the payback cat would come. Sooner or later, I knew I would have to repay him.

Well, the wolf came to the door before I could sneeze. And, of course, my big fat mouth gave me away like an abandoned kid. Mistakenly, I mentioned to Psycho that I had Karyn on the outside, and I was requesting her in my letter to send me some more materials, like stamps, paper, envelopes, and a better writing utensil. Instantly, Psycho jumped on me like a mountain lion on a wounded buck. He didn't ask me, he told me, to make sure Karyn sent a twenty-cent stamp booklet for every piece of paper he obtained for me, and two booklets for the pencil. He also wanted three more booklets for the single stamp and the envelope he would find for me to mail the letter off to begin with. After he completed his demands in his friendly, but obviously aggressive and serious tone, I smiled at him politely. I told him I would be happy to meet his bargain basement price.

According to Psycho, stamps were like real greenbacks and Franklins on the outside. The cops didn't allow us convicts to handle or circulate actual money at any time in the prison system, so stamps became the cons' money instead. Of course, almost everything in life is reduced to monetary value. Money talks. In prison, money talks really, really loud; if a con has some, or he has access to some, he is king of the world. Unless of course, that con is the enemy. Then, he is killed, and his stamps are plundered.

Consequently, Psycho's eyes lit up like two one hundred watt light bulbs fresh out of the pack when he realized I had Karyn. She had money to send me. She could buy stamps. She could send stamps. That was Psycho's only mentality and reason for living at that particular moment. He couldn't explain the process regarding the Gladiator School's United States mail procedure fast enough. He was falling all over himself in a hurry to tell me that the cops allowed stamps to be received from family. He was so excited, because he knew he had me over a barrel. I owed him, and the stamps were how he decided to collect.

Dumbfounded by my luck, and all the horseshoes and cat lives I had, I was totally willing and eager to have Karyn send me whatever stamps it took to pay Psycho off. That way, my debt would be paid and I wouldn't have to participate in a hit of some kind and risk a further conviction and catch more prison time. I had already had my fill up to my eyeballs. Also, Psycho would have plenty of the stamp-currency to purchase the tobacco he craved so desperately, and we both could afford some additional hygienic items. Psycho said everything we needed would be accessible, but it would be extremely expensive in the bargain. I told him I didn't care. Whatever the cost was for me to be able to hack off the layers of stench inhabiting my entire body, I was willing to pay it with open arms.

For the next two weeks, Psycho and I waited for Karyn's package as impatiently as a father-to-be waiting for his first kid to slide out of momma. He paced. I worked out even harder. We both stunk like rotten eggs at Halloween. Neither of us talked much, and there was no sign or indication the prison lockdown would terminate. To me though, I was extremely happy about the fact that my exposure to all the other convicts and gang members was paralyzed. I didn't want to have any contact at all with Ironman or any of his dog soldiers. I knew if lockdown ended, my ticket might be punched too. Locked down, I knew I had a fighting chance to make it out of there alive and physically healthy at least.

Karyn's package of writing materials and stamps finally arrived. Naturally, Psycho beat me to the punch from his bottom bunk when the mail guard made his daily 9 P.M. delivery. When he passed me my mail, he watched my hands nervously. I quickly ripped it open like a long-awaited Christmas present and handed Psycho his stamps. While he went off into his world of kites to scam some tobacco, I began to feverishly read Karyn's heart-warming and loving letter.

From Karyn's first sentence, the Rocky Mountains slowly began to lift from my head and shoulders. Her expressions of love and faithfulness and loyalty warmed my inner soul. She told me my kids were making out wonderfully, and that Mark and Tammy were doing an especially magnificent job with Logan. He was thriving, and Mark and Tammy were having fun with the entire adventure of taking care of their imprisoned friend's kid.

Karyn also explained that countless friends and relatives asked her about me daily. But, mostly, Karyn talked about God. She explained that, in my deepest despair and loneliness, God was always only a prayer away. He would never let me down, and if I asked him to forgive me with a sincere heart, he would. I had already heard that many times from Coach, Philip, and Lloyd, but it was a welcome and refreshing reminder. The bottom line was that I knew I wasn't alone after all. I had many people on the outside who loved me dearly. And, I had God right beside me, whom Karyn confirmed loved me most of all.

Right then, I knew I needed to start to get to know God much better. Although Karyn, Coach, Philip, Lloyd, and others had introduced me to God after the accident, he had been lost to me in the violence and the overall shuffle of prison life. However, I knew I was safe for the time being because of the lockdown. So, I proceeded to concentrate on God's Word. I managed to persuade Psycho to connive a Bible from one of the prison guards, and I began to read fervently. I read for hours every day until I was moved a few weeks later to Folsom, my destination prison. I would sleep, eat a little, work out, and I would read about God.

The more I learned about my heavenly Father, the more at peace I became. Reading about forgiveness, including the forgiveness of others as well as my own, I started to think that maybe I wasn't a lost cause. I thought that maybe, just maybe, my hard heart could be softened through God's grace and humility just like Karyn said it would if I wanted it badly enough.

Chapter 9

The Big House

Thankfully, my stretch at the Gladiator School housed with Ironman and Psycho ended after about two months. While the Gladiator School's correctional guards shackled me again and loaded me like an automatic hay baler onto the prison bus bound for Folsom, I began to reflect upon the time I had just finished at Tracy. In retrospect, the time seemed more like two years instead of two months.

As I hunkered into my window seat, the bus lurched forward. I realized how it was a supernatural phenomenon how any human being could physically and emotionally endure the vile and beastly existence at the Tracy Prison. I had always been a survivor, but engaging in life in that horrible place was way beyond anything I had ever experienced before. I had witnessed similar vulgarity and sheer disregard for human life when I worked for the sheriff's department years earlier. And, I occasioned to observe other fictionally created monstrous characters in the movies and other multi-media. But, to personally live with and experience the Ironmen and the Psycho's of the world was the nightmare of the century. It was the ultimate torture test just to stay alive and unmolested.

Finally, the bus pulled up at Folsom's main gate. After enduring the same personally intrusive and humiliating inspection procedure I experienced at the Gladiator School two months earlier, I found myself inside another holding cell inside Folsom's towering, concertina-wired concrete walls. I didn't talk to anyone, and no one bothered me. I just sat. I sat and waited for the next adventure in the brutal wonderland.

About an hour later, a Folsom guard instructed a dozen of us convicts in the holding cell to file out slowly down a narrow hallway. The tunnel-like pathway was dark and eerie, and it suddenly triggered the accident experience all over again in its surreal imagery like just about everything did during my prison experience. My mind was still not right, and I doubted if it would ever be healthy. I even began to doubt whether it had ever been healthy.

Anyway, we emerged out of the darkness, and we were all ordered brusquely to file methodically along a long brown counter to receive our prison issue of clothes and hygiene items. When we were finished with our gathering of essentials, we were called individually into the lieutenant's office for a one-on-one interview. It was the prison's policy to instruct each con regarding the rules and regulations and his acceptable behavior. Also, the boss cop would inquire as to the type of job we might be interested in during our stay at the Folsom Inn. It was mandatory for every convict to work at some job or another to help with the general labor needed to manage and maintain the prison's minimum standards of cleanliness, organization, and various inmate programs the inmates were privileged to have if they didn't cause any problems.

Depending on our qualifications, experience, and overall interests, we would be placed into a job mostly to satisfy the prison's needs. For example, there were several openings in laundry, in the kitchen as cooks, servers, or dishwashers, and in janitorial services. They were some of the least liked jobs, and most of the cons had to be volunteered by the lieutenant if his quotas for the jobs were to be filled at all.

Of course, the second I told the lieutenant I was a teacher on the outside, I was told I would volunteer to be the G.E.D. (General Education Degree) teacher for the entire prison. Obviously, the prison system didn't have many opportunities to incarcerate teachers in their ranks, and when they did, they made a point to waste no time in recruiting them. Many convicts were illiterate, and teachers were valuable commodities.

Within minutes of my interview, it seemed I had graduated to royalty status among the rest of the peasants. The boss trustee the lieutenant had handpicked as his right-hand man blabbed all over the reception area and yard that my name was Teacher. Teacher could help them all with their letter writing to their families and help them pass the G.E.D. test too. Teacher could help them write and file their appeals, and Teacher could help them write their complaints to the warden. I had no idea where my good fortune had crawled out from, but I didn't care. I was just grateful I didn't have to work in the laundry, wash dishes, or serve the other cons their food during chow times.

When I was escorted towards my new six-foot by eight-foot concrete home, the guards had to parade our nine-con covey through the exercise yard where half of the prison population was getting some fresh air or exercising. Apparently, the procession was part of the great ritual and initiation process into the prison system. Most of the convicts had been housed there for a long period of time, and it had become their home. I learned right away that it was vital they all learned about, or investigated, the new arrivals scrupulously and comprehensively. Potential enemies would be sought out methodically, and when they were detected, they were dealt with expeditiously and brutally. Absolutely no one would be allowed to violate or disrespect their home, their person, or any of their comrades or friends. Those that did failed to last a full sun. It was the lay of the land and way of the prison world.

To me, our procession seemed as if it were a routine inspection of the fresh new baby virgin chickens in the house. When I said new chicken, I actually meant young, fresh, and rookie meat. I am not trying to be facetious. I am as serious as a gangster burning my house down just for disrespecting his colors. We were highly analyzed and dissected minutely as potential sex toys, soldiers, runners, or for any other useful purpose the boss cons needed for their gangs to thrive within the prison walls.

As we trekked through the yard, 200 heads fish-eyed all of us. I had never felt so naked and vulnerable in my life. I felt their beady eyes undress me and their minds wonder what I could offer them in the way of booty, intelligence, or just for their personal gain. It seemed like darkness had set in, and my jungle was infested with malicious predators. Every con in the yard stopped in their tracks as we walked through the yard with our duffle bags draped over our shoulders. They honed in on their potential prizes. It was like we were the only girlies on a deserted island. It was like farmer's market on Saturday night. The gangs were scanning for enemies and for future queens they could molest freely. They searched our gaggle for fellow soldiers to beef up their ranks.

Whatever the reasons were, the new meat arrival was the signal that more new games were about to begin. The fresh chickens would be tested for texture immediately, and they would either be able to survive the harsh environment, or they would become punks at the mercy of whoever wanted to dominate them sexually or physically.

However, my new cellie turned out to be another godsend. I wondered how many horseshoes God had given me to begin my life, because the exorbitant number seemed quite skewed somehow compared to most people. Everywhere I looked around me, there were drug fiends, gangsters, murderers, rapists, and many other convicts who had violated society's laws in some way or another. However, Ben gave me new hope. He seemed to be a normal person. He didn't belong to any gang or practice the racist views running rampant in the entire prison system that most other white guys lived and died for. Although he was a habitual criminal, his example was incredibly encouraging. He respected me and all the other cons to the letter. But, he didn't take any nonsense or disrespect from anyone. And, he was willing to teach me how to survive. All he wanted in return was for me to help him learn how to read and write.

The next several months became a seemingly endless routine. The guards would open our cell doors at various times depending upon when our job required our presence. The guards would escort everyone who had a job to it. The convicts who hadn't been volunteered for a job yet, and those who weren't working at the time, would be allowed to exercise in the yard during the day or stay in their cells and read or whatever. There was a television in the main area where many of the older cons hung out. It was also used by the cons who didn't want to get caught up in the constant scams for human sex toys and objects, or drugs, or other paraphernalia, supplies or items that might make a con's prison stay a little more comfortable.

For me, I tried to fill my days by teaching the illiterate convicts how to read, write, and eventually pass the G.E.D. test. On the streets, most of the cons didn't graduate from high school. But, inside the prison walls, many of them desired to clean up their act, rehabilitate, and eventually contribute appropriately in society upon their release. Some of the cons were sincere about their work with me, and others only did it to get out of work at a daily prison job. When I did detect the scammers, my job was to inform the lieutenant so he could subsequently remove him from my classroom and assign him the dirtiest, filthiest job he could conjure up for him. However, I never did snitch on the work dodgers. I knew if I did, I could be murdered or seriously hurt for being a rat.

When my teaching job ended for the day, I would spend the rest of my allowed time in the yard working out and maintaining and continuing to improve my physical conditioning. I lost thirty pounds over the next few months due to the horrendous menu and the grueling workouts I forced myself to accomplish seven days a week. If we were locked down and unable to get out of our cells, I still completed my daily ritual of 300 push-ups, 400 squats, and 400 crunches. When I was permitted to go to the yard, I finished all of my exercises first, and then, I walked around the circumference of the exercise yard for an additional hour and a half. When I was finally released, I had attained my professional baseball playing weight and the same level of physical conditioning I had enjoyed twenty-three years earlier. I couldn't perform athletically like I did when I was twenty-two years old, but my old weight and strength sure felt good for a change. It was a shame my mind wasn't in the same virile spirit and condition. Basically, I was a mess. I tried to fantasize and think about some happy places, but mostly, I found myself looking over my shoulder for an attack of some sort.

During the days while I was teaching or working out, there seemed to be endless convict conspiracies inside Folsom prison. There seemed to be bloodshed around every corner. There was the real threat of bloodshed down every corridor. And, it seemed everyone was scamming or planning to scam someone else. The games were played to attain or maintain power over individuals or rival gangs, to find or create new meat for personal sexual pleasure, or just to antagonize the prison system in general.

174 • Now I Know Who I Am

During my stint at Folsom, there were many occasions when I would casually walk by another open cell and witness some of the most vile, despicable, and cruel scenes I never could have imagined until I actually saw them happen in front of me. The average human being would think of these horrible things as fictional or an exaggeration. To him or her, they would undoubtedly be too gross to think of as real in human society. However, those who are naive to some of the horrors in the real world, let me introduce you to some of the realities prison life has to offer. Pray that you never have to experience them first hand. A good start would be: to not drink and drive and kill your wife because of it.

Anyway, one particular day after my teaching shift and workout were completed, I walked down my tier corridor to the shower. About five cells down from my cell, I noticed a Norteno gang member propping himself up with one arm elevated casually on the upper doorframe of his cell door. He was facing me when I first caught sight of him. But warily, when I noticed him scoping me out as I approached, I became more than a little suspicious. I had learned at the Gladiator School that cons absolutely don't make eye contact with unfriendly or unknown cons for any reason. It is considered highly disrespectful. If it does occur, the aggressor in the staring contest will usually go Medieval on the other guy. If the aggressor figures he can't take care of the disrespector alone, he'll recruit as much help from his fellow gangsters as necessary for the maiming to follow.

Of course, I couldn't show weakness, so I eyeballed the Norteno just as hard. I simultaneously prepared myself for battle. I had learned to take nothing for granted in prison, and I had to be ready for anything this unpredictable idiot would bring me. In the prison life I was banished to because of my idiocy and blatant disrespect for Sheryl and society, preparation for battle was a constant process for survival. And, I couldn't ever forget it for a single minute even if I was the Teacher.

"Hold on there, peckerwood," the Northerner ordered insolently.

"For what?" I returned sarcastically.

Again, and forever in prison, I knew I couldn't show weakness. If I did, I knew I would be finished for sure.

"Pretend you're talkin' to me a sec, will ya? We're takin' care of some business in here, and we don't want any cops comin' around. If they see us talkin', they won't get suspicious," he explained, as he backed off his aggressiveness a little.

"Whaddaya mean?" I said stupidly as I approached him.

I quickly assumed something illegal or against the prison rules was taking place in the cell, but I had no idea five other Norteno gang members were taking turns raping a Border Brother repeatedly like wild animals. As I glanced over the spotter's shoulder easily with my height on him, I witnessed the ghastly spectacle in horror. There were four grown men holding an appendage each so the Mexican convict was completely helpless. The fifth violator seemed to be in his final lustful love throes as he pounded furiously at the Border Brother's hindquarters.

"Just stay here and talk to me for a few minutes like we are long-lost friends. This shouldn't take too much longer," he said more affably this time with a sly smirk on his evil mug.

Apparently, he figured I would automatically do what I was told due to what I was witnessing behind him at the particular time. However, he was wrong.

"I'm not interested in your games," I told the molester gruffly, and I casually continued on my way to the shower two more cells down from the detestable panorama.

"Wait a minute, peckerwood. Do you know who we are? All I've gotta do is say the word and you're next in here. You hear?" the scout spat after me insolently as if everyone had to bow down at his feet if he ordered it so. It was obvious he wasn't used to someone just saying no.

"Look pal. I don't care who you are, or who they are. Get lost and leave me alone," I hissed back at the gangster as I spun on my heel and stared him down.

Just then, my cellie came out of our cell towards us. He had heard my voice and perceived correctly that I might need some assistance. The scout didn't see or hear Ben come up from behind him because he was facing me. But, when Ben tapped the gangster on his shoulder blade, he jumped like a shot cat. When he whirled at the offender and saw that it was Ben, for whatever reason, the gangster didn't say another word. He averted his eyes from Ben instantaneously, and humbly, he seemed to slide back into the cell where his beast-like buddies were finishing. Ben instructed me to go ahead and finish my shower. In the same instant, he stuck his head in the cell and boldly told the Nortenos to break up their love fest before we were all locked down for six months.

Fortunately again for me, God had sent me another guardian angel. The Nortenos respected Ben, or feared him, I don't know which, and disembarked from their ride and dispersed peacefully. I didn't know until that moment that Ben had incredible clout and a following of his own like some of the other gangs.

However, the difference was that Ben's comrades were only other convicts like me who didn't want to take any nonsense, or become some gangster's punk-boy, or be disrespected in any way. Luckily, there were plenty of us to look out for each other too. Although we only had to support each other occasionally, when we did, we took care of business quickly with the least amount of damage inflicted. Although we had to get violent a few times, the battles didn't take long. And somehow, we were able to stay away from being thrown in the hole. We were never hurt. I was able to shower somewhat peacefully, and thankfully, I maintained my virginity.

Ben was the only fellow convict I formed a bond with. Some of the others were useful at times for information regarding our survival in the joint, but most of them were people to be avoided if at all possible. Ben respected me, and I respected him. We backed each other without hesitation, and we talked about our lives out in the real world away from the prison insanity.

I was grateful and fortunate to be able to spend several months with Ben as my cellie. It was obvious from the beginning that no one willingly messed with him, so I felt a little safer. At the same time though, there was always a vicious storm of trouble brewing in prison. It was a harsh daily reality. Like the millions of cows, chickens, and pigs housed and fattened throughout the country for slaughtering, they, and we, didn't know when the knife was coming to cut our throats. Some freak was always wielding the knife in the prison system. We just didn't know exactly when it would slash our way.

One day, Ben was working at his job in the commissary when I was faced with a serious dilemma. When it happened, it blatantly reaffirmed my determination to change my ways so I would never have to experience that filthy place ever again.

It began in mid-January. The winter rains were dumping buckets on a few of us who didn't allow a little water to dampen our workout spirits and regimen. Anyway, I had just finished my exercises, and I had jogged about thirty laps around the yard. When I pulled up close to the parallel bars in the corner of the yard just below the guard towers, I became more than a little suspicious. Two convicts I didn't know approached me rather slyly. One of them was really fidgety, and he looked behind him and all around constantly as if some private dick was on his tail. He was a slender six-footer, and he was obviously soft. The other was even more feminine, but he didn't bat an eyelash when I confronted them on their unusual approach.

The peculiar part was that one of them was black and the other was white. Both of them together didn't present a physically threatening capability, or an aggressive demeanor to me, but the fact that two different races had integrated for anything was a blood-red flag to me.

"Whattaya want?" I asked the two guys sternly as they walked within six feet from where I was bent over with my hands on my knees resting.

"What's up, Teacher? I'm Deek, and this is Smoothy. Sorry ta bother ya while yer workin' out, but my homey needs your help," the bolder black guy told me straight up with a slight pleading tone adding to his request.

"Whatever it is, make it quick. We aren't playin' tiddly winks out here," I said back to him, but a little softer this time.

I knew I could handle them if their approach happened to be a ploy and they went off on me. So, I began to relax a little. But, I also knew my current habitat was in a dangerous jungle of vipers and merciless animals. So, I tried to expedite the conversation to minimize my exposure to the hunters. They were only staying out of the rain for the time being.

"We heard the G.E.D. lieutenant likes you a lot. Zat right?" the black guy asked me questioningly.

"You might say that. Why do ya wanna know?" I returned apprehensively.

I was impatient. And, I was scared. The whole conversation was already too long. I even started to look around a little myself just in case a jungle animal had decided to brave the weather.

"Straight up, Teacher, Smoothy has to get moved right away. The Surenos are rapin' him reg'lar, and he's goin' nuts. He can't defend himself, and none of the guards care if they're getting him or not," Deek explained honestly.

I didn't know their connection, or why the black guy was trying to help his white friend. I thought they might have known each other from the street, because Deek called Smoothy his homey. But, that didn't mean squat in prison. Races just didn't mix. They didn't talk. They didn't hang out. If they were caught doing it, members of their own race would educate them very, very quickly.

However, I knew what they wanted from me right away. They wanted me to speak to the lieutenant and convince him that Smoothy had to be moved to another prison. I also knew that, what I did or didn't do at that point, might ultimately determine whether Smoothy lived, died, or continued to be a pleasure-punk for the Surenos gang. But, most of all, if any of the gangs found out I helped the salt and pepper collaborators, I was dead, cut, or raped for sure. Even Ben wouldn't be able to help me.

"Do you know what you're askin' me?" I asked the two guys concernedly, as I took turns staring directly into their eyes.

"Yes. And, we're sorry we have to come at you like this, but we got no choice. Can you help him?" Deek asked me pleadingly, while Smoothy kept looking around restlessly.

"I'll see what I can do when I go to work in the mornin'. But for now, don't approach me anymore for anythin'. You'll know if I was able to help you or not if they move you," I told Deek and Smoothy calmly, as I turned on my heels away from them.

"Thanks, Teacher. I knew you would help. Tell him Smoothy's in 304 at the end of tier three," Deek said, friendly-like to my back.

Then, they were gone. I continued to walk around the exercise yard in the rain to try to figure out what I had just gotten myself into. I realized that Smoothy needed my help, and I had a choice to make. I could try to help him, or I could leave Smoothy to the sex cannibals and mind my own business.

My intuition told my brain in the rain to forget about Deek and Smoothy like they were just a couple of bad cheeseburgers I had eaten one time in the free world. However, it also dawned on me that I needed to help this guy—for me. I had looked the other way too often in my life. It was time to do something for someone else.

I flagged the lieutenant down the next morning as we walked through the full exercise yard towards the education building. I didn't want anyone to get suspicious about me talking to the cops, so I kept it all business until I got him alone.

"Lieutenant. I need to talk to you about some problems with the testing procedures. Can you come to the G.E.D. room so I can show what's goin' on?" I asked the lieutenant boldly.

"What kinda problems?" he demanded, with his usual crass tone when he was around a group of cons.

The lieutenant knew the prison game as well as anyone. All cops were every con's enemy, and he knew that talking to me friendly-like was a no-no. He knew that, if he was cordial to me, the other cons might figure I was getting special treatment somehow. And, if they perceived I was, someone would be finding the shovel for me.

"The state's G.E.D. paperwork is in the room. Can I show you? It's hard to explain," I asked diplomatically, without making eye contact out of respect for him.

"OK. I'll meet you there in a few minutes," he grunted, as if I aggravated him.

He showed up an hour later. But, I had nowhere to go anyway, so I continued my work, grading all the tests from the previous day.

"Teacher, what did you wanna talk to me about?" the lieutenant asked me a lot more affably this time as he squeezed his large frame through the half-open door. There were no other cons around.

"I couldn't talk to you out there, but I need your help on somethin'. The Surenos are molesting a skinny white guy in 304 on tier three. His name is Smoothy. That's all I know about him. He said none of the other guards wanna do anything about it, so he asked me to ask you if there is any way you can move him. He knows he's gonna die, or he's gonna kill someone if somethin' isn't done now," I explained quickly, hoping that he would take me seriously.

"I know the guy. He's a popular queen. But, it sounds to me like he's had enough. I'll take care of it," the lieutenant told me matter-of-factly, as if the situation regarding Smoothy was an everyday occurrence.

When I finished my shift that day, I went back to my cell feeling pretty good about myself. I had grabbed the bull by the horns for someone else's benefit. And, when I told Ben what I had done, he praised my efforts and told me he would have done the same thing. I believed him too, and that made me feel even better. There was honor among thieves.

Sadly though. Smoothy wasn't moved to another prison as promptly as he needed to be. When I walked out to the yard for my daily workout the next morning after chow, I noticed a pair of EMT's carting him off on a stretcher. A crew of guards escorted them out of the yard down the long corridor leading to the prison gates. I assumed they were taking Smoothy to the hospital for something. I thought maybe he had been raped again, or stabbed, beaten up, or hurt in some other way because I was too late. And, that bothered me. If I would have sought out help immediately, I thought, when Deek and Smoothy first approached me, Smoothy would still be healthy.

About the regular occurrence of stretchers and EMT's, they were normal happenings around Folsom. No one was safe from their death wagon waiting for yet another victim outside the concertina-wired cement walls. Smoothy was just . . . another one. It turned out he almost bled to death from major damage to his rectum. I never saw him again. Deek never came around anymore either. He probably thought I just blew him off when they asked me for help. I never did find out for sure.

The word around the yard was that Smoothy had stuck a three-inch pencil up through the end of his penis into his bladder. He believed that by hurting himself badly enough to have to go to the prison hospital, he could escape the Surenos and their molestations. Barbarically for Smoothy though, when he did the dirty deed with the pencil, a regular rapist from the Surenos crew came by Smoothy's cell for some action. When he witnessed Smoothy finishing the pencil thing, he whistled for a few of his Surenos boys to come and join in on some fun. They all proceeded to rape him repeatedly and viciously. He didn't stand a chance. At the time, I supposed the Surenos wanted to enjoy Smoothy one last time and give him a send-off he would remember. They also knew the pencil thing would get him out of there to the hospital and probably keep him from coming back to the same prison.

When I heard the story, I believed it. It was obvious Smoothy was desperate when he and Deek approached me in the yard. I also knew that people like him, and the Surenos gangsters, were capable of anything—even sticking-the-pencil-through-the-penis-into-the-bladder thing, and raping-a-guy-hard-and-long-enough-to-cause-near-death-from-excessive-bleeding thing. For me, I just felt guilty that I couldn't get Smoothy help soon enough.

CHAPTER 10

Nature vs. Nurture

During my prison term at Folsom, I had an incredible amount of time to kill. My teaching job took up several hours, and my work outs burned a few more every day. The rest of the time, I stayed inside my cell to try to escape the endless games, abuse, and carnage outside. Usually, I sat or reclined on my bunk. I read the Bible. I wrote letters to my friends and family. I even initiated a successful Bible study group. Most of the time though, I found myself deep in thought, analyzing my life. Why? Because I was totally lost. I didn't know who I was. And, I figured I needed to find for myself if anything good in life would ever come my way again.

Strangely though, it seemed that every time I dove into my own psychoanalysis, I became even more desperate to figure out where I went wrong, and why. I had to find the origin of my monsters and kill them before I went insane.

I started by delving heavily into my past I went deeper than I had ever gone before. However, I couldn't reflect with a clear and reasonable mind. A monster loomed. It was the great battle of guilt and remorse and disgrace raging in my head. The people I had hurt haunted me every second. The vivid images of all of them, especially the ones carrying my wife and kids, flashed repeatedly inside my head as constant reminders to what I did to them. I could see them all very clearly. They were all shaking their heads in shame—at me. At the same time, they were confused. They couldn't understand how I, Randy Wiens, was so selfish and despicable. "You destroyed our family. We could have had it all if you weren't so arrogant and stubborn and prideful" is what they all echoed in unison over and over and over again. It seemed their voices would never stop, even when I finally slept.

That's when a miracle happened in my life. It began after I turned to prayer. I had done a lot of praying before then, but I hadn't completely surrendered to God yet. I thought I had after the accident before I was sentenced, but I really didn't. I only prayed when things became un-bearable and I slid to the edge of insanity. But, that all changed pretty fast when I started to realize the only path to inner peace was through God. I finally figured out I had to pray all the time—during the storms and the kinder emotional weather. I had to pray when I felt bad and when I felt good. That was the only way I would ever find the necessary peaceful frame of mind to dive deep into the recesses of my life and figure out who I was. So I did. In fact, praying to the Lord and reading about him in the Bible saved me from myself.

I began by spending countless hours on my knees on my top prison bunk. I no longer cared if anyone saw me pray either. I was no longer embarrassed to show my love for the Lord. Why? Because I finally real-ized I was weak. I was frail. Only God was strong. He was invincible. He was my only weapon against my monsters.

I didn't fully understand it at the time, but God had always been around waiting for me to ask him for help. He was always ready and willing, but I wasn't—for forty-four years. However, when I surrendered to Him, the Lord jumped in with all guns blazing. He answered my prayers. He granted me the strength I had been begging for. He gave me the strength to get up off the deck, to begin the marathon and lifelong walk with Him, and to engage in my own forgiveness and happiness. And finally, he allowed me to dive back to my past freely and with a clear head. I was shocked and angry at first because of the monsters I conjured up. But eventually, in my new frame of mind, I knew I had to relive it all many times in order for me to be able to put it away forever. Only then could my inner peace have a chance to prevail.

I can't pinpoint the exact moment it all seemed to come together in my mind. But, somewhere between the thoughts of bashing my head against my cement cell wall, and hearing the words of forgiveness spoken mercifully from my children's lips, made me want to become a better person. And, that is what drove me back to my past so passionately. In fact, I stayed in reflection whenever I wasn't just trying to stay alive or maintain my virginity.

I began my own recovery by starting from scratch. I began by reflecting back to my childhood. I believed that, in order to cover all the bases, I had to first identify where I came from, what perpetuated my malformed behavior to begin with, and what really caused me to end up in prison. Only then could I figure out how I was going to fix my angry and broken mind.

Reflections in Folsom Prison:

I was born Randy Roy Wiens on March 6, 1957 in Kamloops, British Columbia, Canada. At my birth, my mom and dad and my two-year-old sister lived in Chase, a small town of about fifteen hundred people, thirty miles from Kamloops. We lived in a tiny garage for a few years while my dad built a small house for us on the same property we lived on. The building went quite slowly, because my dad was a truck driver who worked twelve to sixteen hours a day to bring home the bacon. My mom also worked long hours as a telephone operator initially, and a few years later, as a waitress and a cook. Although I don't remember anything of my life up to about the age of five years old, my mom and dad both have filled in the blanks over the years quite well regarding what life was like for me during those younger years.

Mom told me I was an extremely active baby who always pushed the envelope in everything I did. When I finally slid out of Mom after a forty-hour labor marathon, I was a whopping 21-inches long and 9 pounds 3 ounces. I pulled myself up to a standing position by my crib's rails at five months. I started running, not walking, at nine months. I was potty-trained many months earlier than normal because of my dad's impatience. Basically, Dad told Mom he would kill her if I filled my diapers anymore. And above all else, I had a profound knack and determination to throw every potential projectile that I could launch with either arm. By the time my second spring rolled around just after I turned one, my frisky nature had put a lot of extra mileage on my mom's body and brain with premature aging and gray hair to boot. She quickly got into racing shape chasing me everywhere. She tried constantly to keep me out of the mischief I would always seem to find when I wasn't held by someone or tied down.

One day, my mom was more tired than I was around noon, and to take a mental and physical break, Mom decided it was naptime for me. Well, she slept. I didn't. While she slept, I crawled off the bed beside her. Like I was on a mission of dark conspiracy, I picked up my dad's clean work shirt off the kitchen table, and I walked outside where Buddy, our black Labrador, was panting happily because he finally had a playmate. I proceeded to walk straight out to the gravel road in front of our house. But, I guess that spot wasn't good enough. I ended up down the road about a block. I sat in the middle of the road on my duff and repeatedly scooped gravel into my dad's shirt and dumped it back on the road.

The story has it that Mom awakened and panicked because I was nowhere to be found in the house. When she ran outside hysterically to look in the yard, one of the neighbor ladies was screeching at Mom from her porch down the block. In her hysteria, she screamed to Mom that I was sitting on the road down by the Reardons and I was gonna be killed by a logging truck. Of course, in a full sprint in two strides, Mom ran down the road in a panic and crying at the same time.

However, Mom didn't know that I had been in the best hands possible during the whole playful experience. Buddy had been watching me like a hawk. I sat in the road playing as happily as a grizzly snarfing a salmon, and Buddy sat right beside me ready to protect me from anything or anyone traveling on the gravel road. When my mom reached me and I was safe in her eyes, the neighbor lady yelled over to Mom from her porch that I had followed Buddy down the road holding on to his tail. Apparently, that relieved my mom's rant for a moment, because she was the one who trained Buddy. She taught him to pull me around the house slowly so I could learn how to walk.

Unfortunately for my mom, she told my dad about my escapade when he came home from work that night. According to my mom, Dad started beating her senseless as soon as he realized I may have been in some danger. He slapped her at first. He turned it up a notch and began punching her with a closed fist as his anger grew. Then, he finished off his tirade by putting the boots to her a few times before he came to his senses. He blamed my mom for sleeping on the job and said she was useless.

Although my mom's story has always been that Dad was always quick to anger, and he became extremely violent and mean when he did, she stayed with him through all of his physical abuse because of her upbringing. She said she was taught that when you make your bed, you have to lie in it. She did.

Anyway, I am the oldest son, of the oldest son, of the oldest son. And, to my dad, I was his pride and joy. Consequently, he was naturally energetic in his unyielding determination to bring me up right and raise me to be tough no matter what. Dad told me many times that my grandpa Jake molded him in the same manner. So as you would expect, making me sturdy and resilient was Dad's main obligation and reason for living as a father. And he didn't care what anyone else thought either, especially my mom.

When I started walking, Dad took Mom and me along with him in his big-rig lumber truck if she had a day off. Whether we went along or not though, Mom would always get up with Dad at three or four on his working days that she wasn't working the night shift at the telephone office. She always made sure Dad had a good hearty breakfast, another mountain of food packed into his lunch-kit, plenty of coffee in a huge thermos, and a jug of ice water to last him through the day.

When Dad took me with him on the truck, Mom made sure Dad had plenty of diapers and warm clothes for me and food and drinks for both of us. Dad's rig was always parked outside the garage in the yard, and as soon as he plunked me onto the passenger seat of his truck, I would always fall back asleep hunched against the locked door and window on a huge pillow. However, I would always wake up around 6 A.M. when we reached the screaming sawmill up Chase Creek. By then, the sawmill was in high gear pumping out studs, beams, or whatever else had been ordered by Nakamota's customers.

My mom said that in my younger years before kindergarten started, Dad took me with him at least two or three times a week. Although I was always awake when we hit the mill, he would always leave me inside the truck. Too many loaders, forklifts, and other trucks bombed around the mill yard helter-skelter, and it was too dangerous for me outside the truck while Dad conducted the loading of his lumber truck.

When I was old enough to ask questions, Dad told me that, besides the heavy equipment, there was just as much danger from wolves, black bears, and even the odd grizzly bear. Dad said the wild animals were attracted to the massive garbage pile the mill workers produced during the week. He said that, at least once a week, Mr. Nakamota had to torch the garbage pile. Otherwise, there would be so many animals gathering for a feast and fighting for the easy pickings, he could start his own zoo. Besides that, Nakamota's sawmill crew, including my dad sometimes, would blast away at the bears with their high-powered rifles, and Nakamota didn't want a stray bullet to kill someone by mistake.

According to Mom, Dad was a fairly normal father during the first years of my life. He would work extremely hard, sometimes too hard, but he always tried to spend time with his family. Mom and Dad had little or no money for entertainment, so Dad tried to create some of his own. Mom said Dad would always carry us on his shoulders for our excitement and enjoyment. He would wrestle with us on the floor in front of the television. He would tow us behind our 56 Plymouth on his homemade sleigh in the winter. And, he would take us all to the Shuswap Lake, just out of Chase where we lived, on the Sundays when the weather was good enough in the summer.

On one occasion at the lake, Mom said Dad decided it was time for me to learn how to swim. I had just turned two the previous March, and Mom said Dad was brought up to believe that two-year old sons were old enough to experience their first rite of passage. This first one turned out to be a humdinger. Mom's story has it that, one day, a group of our friends and neighbors had gathered with our family at the lake like we always did whenever possible in the summer. We all ate heartily. I ran around naked on the beach or the wharf while they jumped through some old rubber skidder tubes my dad salvaged from Nakamota's. Even us little kids participated in rock skipping contests on the glassy water, and generally, we all just had a wonderful time.

Sometime that day, Dad hoisted me up onto his muscularly toned 6'1" frame like always to give me a thrill, and also, to continue my manly molding to make sure I would never be a wimp in my life. He carried me, and we both laughed all the way up the steps of the high diving board on the wharf we had been playing on as a large group. My mom didn't know at the time if Dad's joyfulness was part of his game to distract me, or he was just kidding around like he always did to try to get attention. Either way, my mom was furious that Dad would carry me up those extremely high steps—on his shoulders no less. She began to yell and scream at my dad for his ignorance and stupidity. In front of everyone there, whom were all concentrating intently on the scene unfolding by that time, she swore and cursed at my dad. She shouted that his ego would end up killing his own son.

However, obstinately disregarding my mom's pleading and cussing, my dad didn't hesitate a second when he reached the end of the high diving board. He simply walked to the end of the high board. He calmly lifted me off his shoulders. He grabbed a strong hold around my chest under my armpits with one hand and under my butt with the other. And then, he chucked me into the 100-feet deep water with a broad and beaming smile on his face the whole time. I guess my mom freaked out, because as I was flying through the air, she ran. Clothes and all, she hit the water less than a second after I did. She said she covered the fifty feet between the wharf and where I entered the water in about four strokes. Of course, by the time she got to me, I had surfaced; I naturally floated on my back with my head above the water.

My mom did get to me quickly, but she was in a complete state of panic the entire time. I suppose her motherly instincts had kicked in as she saw her two year old in mid flight. She was afraid her son was facing imminent death while her careless and egotistical husband didn't think it was any big deal in the slightest. She grabbed me and towed me back to the wharf with one hand holding my head up, while she thrashed the other hand through the water for all she was worth so neither of us would drown.

In the meantime, my dad had dived into the water beside my mom and me at about the same time my mom reached me. When he surfaced, he swam alongside us still laughing and bragging to everyone eagerly watching the spectacle on how well I did. Most of the men and children laughed right along with him. But, my mom said that not one of the other mothers would speak to my dad for months. Apparently, they thought he was an idiot, just like my mom did. She said she wouldn't give him sex for a week because he scared her so badly.

Another time, my mom said my dad taught me to shoot a gun at the age of five. His culture and traditions nurtured him to believe that it was absolutely mandatory that every Wiens knew how to handle a gun and how to shoot properly. Guns put food on the table, and all Wiens' had to be good providers. My dad's oldest son, me, was no exception. So, to educate me properly, Dad always took his hunting rifle and a shotgun with him to work in his big truck. He never knew when he was going to spot a deer, moose, or a grouse or two. And, he wanted me to see him shoot one when he did. Why? Because back in the early sixties, wild game was a vital food source. Store-bought food was rare—other than milk, flour for Mom's homemade bread, and a few other main items like salt, pepper, and butter. And, Dad wanted to make sure I learned all about it early in life.

Anyway, ten miles into the bush one day, Dad hit the binders hard on his empty lumber truck. He shook me awake rather rudely as the trailer slid to a halt on the gravel road. He calmly ordered me to grab the 4-10 shotgun from the gun rack behind us and blast the dumb, unsuspecting grouse strutting down the middle of the road twenty feet in front of the truck. To my dad, it didn't matter if I was only five. Learning to shoot was another rite of passage. It was a perfect opportunity for me to learn how to shoot to kill for food.

Of course though, by the time my dad helped me get the heavy 4-10 shotgun off the rack, load it with the single shell, cock it for me, and help me aim it out my window, the grouse was too far away for a kill shot. But, Dad didn't pass up on the opportunity anyway. He quickly ordered me to pull the stock up tight to my shoulder and then shoot anyway. So, I did. I pulled it up and yanked on the trigger hard. The blast shattered the air. The recoil threw me backwards violently. And, my head bounced off the back of the steel cab like a beach ball a few times before I realized what happened. Naturally, the dumb grouse proceeded to walk off the road into the bush as calm as you please.

Dad told my mom later at the dinner table that the look on my face was priceless. I didn't know if I was hurt, dead, or what after I yanked on the trigger and everything settled down. Dad also said I had the wildest deer in the headlights look he had ever seen. After I shot the gun, Dad went on about how I didn't stop talking about the experience all day until he finally told Mom at the dinner table. He guffawed all night about it. The bottom line was that he was proud of me and that I had shot my first gun at age five. Of course, Dad and I were proud as punch as my mom listened in horror to all the details. But, Mom swore up and down for years that she almost killed Dad with a frying pan for his stupidity while he slept.

I don't remember it, but Mom told me that when I was in grade one, the first really bad experience I had was in regards to my dog. Strangely, Buddy didn't show up at our regular meeting place after school like usual. I looked all around and scanned up and down the block. I searched behind all the neighboring houses. I knocked on all the neighbors' doors to see if they had noticed him running around. And, I hollered for him at least a hundred times. But, no luck. Buddy was gone. I would never see his beautiful hairy face light up again as he picked me out of the group I always walked home with. I would never again watch him bound over to me drooling and yapping crazily and jump up at my chest in utter glee. I would never again see him swim like a fish and snag every stick or can I threw out on the lake as far as I could.

Mom said that when I walked into the house panic-stricken and totally confused about Buddy not showing up, Dad was sitting at the kitchen table.

"Hey Dad. You seen Buddy around? I looked all over and can't find 'im," I said pleadingly, as I leaned on the table close to him hoping beyond hope he had a clue.

"Look, dammit! I lost my job at Nakamota's today. I ain't worried about your stupid mutt," Dad snapped back at me as if I was the one who had canned him.

I was confused about Dad's foul mood, and I didn't like him very much right then. He had just blown off my best friend's disappearance like he was an insignificant scrap of garbage we tossed into the stinky can out on the back porch. To him, Buddy was nothing. To me, my friend was everything.

"But, Dad. What am I gonna do? I hafta find 'im," I pleaded with Dad boldly. I was in a daze, and I really didn't hear what he was really telling me.

"Look. I told you. Don't bug me. Buddy's gone, and that's all there is to it. Now, git! You can get another dog sometime," he yelled at me angrily, as I cringed at the thought of Buddy really being gone forever.

Just then, Mom walked into the room yelling and screaming and cursing at my dad about something I didn't understand right away. She had been listening to Dad and me talking around the corner to the front room. She knew there was going to be trouble when she witnessed my frantic search around the neighborhood for Buddy from the front room window.

"You bastard. You tell 'im what you did. You tell 'im you killed him. Go ahead. Tell him like a man," Mom screamed at my dad, as if he had killed her young.

However, Mom said Dad didn't look at either of us. The cat got his tongue. He simply stood up and left the house. He drove off in a cloud of dust half way down the street. Mom gave me the bad news.

"Your father killed Buddy today. He was fired from his job. He said Buddy was sick and he had to shoot him. But, I don't think there was anything wrong with him. He just did it out of meanness," Mom said she explained to me in tears, as she held me tightly to her breast. I cried for hours, and I had a great contempt for my dad.

Although I don't really remember the details about the Buddy incident because I was still pretty young back then, that is what Mom had made me believe for many years after that. To this day, I still don't know for sure if Dad really did kill my dog out of meanness, or Buddy was really sick and Dad just did the humane thing by putting him down. Mom wasn't very happy with my dad for most of my life, and it wouldn't surprise me a bit if somewhere along the line, she fabricated the story to build herself up and to knock Dad down. My mom had a habit of doing that. I realized that after I got older. But, that still didn't change what I grew up to believe. I believed for many years that my dad murdered my dog in cold blood. He got mad at somebody else at work and took his anger out on my dog. That is what I believed as a kid.

After the Buddy episode, my own memories kick in. My mom and dad filled in some details over the years, but mostly, the childhood reflections I analyzed in prison were from my own memory banks.

I remember distinctly when I went to schoolin my early years. I helped the other kids with their numbers, and I always teased the girls. Basically, I had boundless energy, and I seemed to be in trouble with my teachers most of the time. I played baseball and hockey a little later on. I teased Connie, my two-years-older sister, constantly. I spent countless weekends at my Uncle Hank's and Auntie Babe's house. I threw everything I could get my hands on. And, I rode with my dad in his truck whenever he let me skip school.

During my early childhood, I embarked upon countless excursions with my Uncle Hank and Auntie Babe. They took me hunting and fishing regularly, and I always enjoyed staying with them. They taught me a lot about life and being a man, and I will forever be beholden to them for loving and caring for me the way they have done my entire life. Although they were strict, I always loved them both dearly. I will always be loyal to them for what they have done for me throughout my life.

Unfortunately though, my dad always took great offense to Hank and Babe's special connection they developed with me. It seemed to my dad that I would rather spend time with them than him. That made Dad very angry and envious, and it all caused a great feud between Dad and Hank over the years. To me at the time though, when I was a young boy, my dad was always working. Or, when he was off from work, he didn't seem to want to play ball or do much with me. He wasn't interested in taking me hunting or fishing. He didn't want to watch me play baseball or hockey or do anything else with me that I craved to share with my dad. The only quality time I remember spending with Dad as a kid after I was about seven years old was helping him on his truck. Hank and

Babe simply filled the great void in my heart at the time. My dad wasn't there for me much. Hank and Babe were.

On the other hand, I have to say honestly that Dad was my hero when it came to the trucks and working. It seemed I was in constant awe of his physical abilities and incredible resilience. He drove his trucks six days a week, twelve to sixteen hours a day. And, he attacked his work with a great passion to be the best at what he did. That's what he pounded into me too. He always told me it didn't matter what job you had, if you do your best, you will always put food on the table. And, his philosophy really stuck with me too. In every job I've ever had, I have never been satisfied until I was recognized as a top man for the job. To this day, I am very proud to have garnered that trait from my dad.

Dad was flat out tough too. When it came to work, he'd chew nails and spit out tacks. He was like the Paul Bunyan of the freight truck world. He could be dying from pneumonia, but he showed up for work every day. If he got cut or hurt doing his job, he would suck it up and finish the job anyway. He wasn't about to let anyone say he wasn't tough enough to work through a little bout of sickness or a little scratch of any kind. Many times, he was hobbled or weakened by a flu bug or something, but he'd still force himself to go to work. Sick or not, he staggered under the heavy loads on his hand truck. Sometimes, I would even see huge gashes in his hands from the sharp objects he wrestled off the trucks. But to him, they were always only little scratches. That was Dad. That was his great physical and mental toughness. I respected him because of it.

Dad worked almost all the time. But, I remember studying my dad's every move when I was a kid, especially when I rode with him and helped him on his freight trucks. In particular, I liked going with him when he let me skip school. I would rather work like a fool for a month than sit in a boring classroom for one day. I'd rather get up at three in the morning, brave forty below zero winter weather, and bust my tail all day fighting the snow and ice with Dad than rub shoulders with all the pansies at school. I was a truck driver's son. I was a Wiens. I didn't want to go to school. I wanted to work and be tough like Dad.

Watching my dad work was like the best entertainment you ever saw. It was like watching a maniac and a magician all at the same time.

He was so fast and masterful with his freight hand truck that I had to run to keep up with him. He maneuvered and shuttled loads on that thing like greased lightning. It didn't matter if it was raining buckets or snowing blizzards. My dad was like the proverbial mailman when it came to his freight delivery job. He always got his loads through and on time. Even if he had a monstrous fridge to get off the truck by himself, he would get it into the customer's house or warehouse unscratched every time. Back then, there were no hydraulic lifts on the back of the trucks either. It was all manual labor. How he wrestled and manhandled those fridges, and every other piece of freight big and small, off the back of his huge semi-trailer, I will never know. It was like a super-human thing.

On one special trip with my dad on his truck when I was about seven, I found a new friend and loyal companion. It had just broken daylight when I awakened to the bright sun stabbing my eyes through the huge semi's windshield. Dad was shifting down on a long graveled grade coming up and out of Chase Creek. I had slept through it, but Dad had just finished loading a gargantuan load of fir 2x4s at Nakamota's sawmill when he started the steep climb out of the mill. It was a long pull, and we were approaching the crest of the hill when I thought I saw a little animal. The sun was blinding, but I was sure I saw it moving in the bushes in front of the truck off to the right of the front fender of the Cornbinder. Without hesitating a lick, I bolted straight up, so I could see what it was. But, I lost sight of it momentarily. It disappeared behind the front corner of the truck. Instinctively, I smashed my nose against my passenger window quickly, and luckily, the steep grade had slowed the truck to a crawl enough to where I could see her plain as day. It was a baby cocker spaniel. I didn't know the difference at the time though. All I saw was a little puppy in the bush in the middle of nowhere who needed a big person to help it.

"Dad! Ya gotta stop! There's a puppy on the side of the road back there!" I yelled at my dad excitedly.

"Where? I didn't see nothin'," he said back, doubting my young judgment.

"In the bushes! I saw 'im plain as day! You gotta stop ta help 'im!" I begged, and I hoped at the same time that Dad would believe me.

"Alright. Let's take a gander," Dad said playfully all of a sudden. I remember thinking his goofiness was a little out of character, but I didn't care at the time.

Dad finished the hard pull about a hundred feet later and hit the binders in a massive cloud of dust. I tried my best to keep my eyeballs glued on the area where I saw the cocker in the big mirror hanging outside my door. But, I was like a desperate blind kid groping for the Holy Grail. I couldn't see squat. All I could think of to do then was to get out and go find him as fast as I could. But, Dad must have detected my over excitement, because he put the skids on it right away.

"Holder there, Rand. Go slow. There's other animals out there too. You need ta wait for me," Dad explained to me caringly, although I didn't care about taking it easy. I wanted that dog. Not now, but right now.

While I chomped at the bit waiting for Dad to take his big hunting rifle off the gun rack behind the seat over the window and shove its clip in, I opened my door and stood on the running board. I held onto the handle on the side of the cab. I leaned out as far as I could to see if I could see some sign that the puppy was all right. As I craned my neck around the side of the load of lumber, I worried that maybe the truck had squished him. By then though, Dad had gotten around to my side. He gave the okay. I jumped off the truck, and I stayed tight on Dad's heels. Every step or so, I would peek around Dad's huge frame and try to see the cocker.

The dust had settled by the time we cleared the back of the truck. Dad saw her first. She was about a hundred feet or so behind the rig trying hard to crawl onto the road on her wobbly little legs. When I saw her, I couldn't control my excitement any longer. I took off. I ran faster than the speed of light. Dad didn't say anything either. In fact, when I got to the puppy and picked her up gingerly, and then I looked at Dad proudly beaming from ear to ear, I could see dad's huge smile plastered all over his face. Right away, he threw the strap of the big gun over his shoulder and grabbed her from me to check her out. I was in love immediately. The cocker was so beautiful and furry. I just hoped Dad would let me keep her, I thought.

Sadly though, just after Dad reached us, it wasn't all peaches and cream.

"It's a little bitch," Dad said to me, as he took her from me gently.

"What's zat mean?" I asked Dad inquisitively, with my cheeks starting to hurt from my hard smile.

"It just means she's a girl," he continued his lesson on dogs jovially.

However, just then, Dad heard the bushes shuffle a little from where the puppy had emerged. I didn't hear anything except for the cocker's panting in my ear as I held her up for a big hug. Without saying anything to me, he stepped over to the side of the road. He hesitated for a split second to ready his gun again before he parted a big patch of bush. When he did and he saw what was behind the thick overgrowth, he relaxed the big gun and let out an empathetic groan. It seemed as if he was suddenly saddened by something.

"The momma's dead. There's some more dead pups too. Looks like this little tyke is the only one left," Dad told me sorrowfully, as he closed up the bushes and turned back to me.

"Whattaya mean? What happened?" I asked Dad dejectedly.

"Some jerk prob'ly dumped the mother off out here. Prob'ly didn't want to take care of the litter. Looks to me like the coyotes killed her. They ate some of her and some of the other pups. I'm surprised they left a live one. Maybe they heard us comin' and took off. I think that's what I heard a minute ago," Dad told me insightfully.

I was sad for the momma and the other puppies, but it didn't last very long. All I could think of was my new pal.

"Hey Dad! Can we keep her?" I asked him optimistically, as I stared right into his eyes, kind of daring him to say no.

"Sure. I think we need a mutt around the house," he granted, with a huge smile plastered all over his face.

The next thing I knew, Sandy and I were inseparable. It was like it was supposed to be. She whimpered when I took off for school. I ran home from school every day so I could see her sooner. She rode in the car with us. She rode in Dad's truck with us. And, she always sat on my feet under the supper table so I could sneak her the delicious scraps from Mom's awesome cooking. Mom and Dad always knew Sandy was under there, but they didn't say much—unless I gave her all my liver.

My life with Sandy was heavenly until Darryl was a fresh bun in mom's oven when I was about eight years old. Until then, I had no clue that my Mom and Dad were on a one-way road to marital destruction. I remember the day specifically when my mom told my dad she was pregnant with my brother. We had moved to Kamloops by that time because Dad had lost his job with Nakamota's. He wasn't fired. They just had to lay him off because their business was slow. The only place he could find work driving a truck was in Kamloops.

The house we moved to was old and always cold. It was the middle of winter, and I remember chucking wood into the big furnace in the basement early that morning. While the furnace heated up and gradually began to heat the house upstairs where we lived, our whole family hunkered around the stove to keep warm until the furnace's heat kicked in. It must have been a rare romantic time for my mom and dad, because I vividly remember them hugging and kissing a lot. Just then, my mom took the opportunity to inform Dad, Connie, and me that she was pregnant. I remember watching my mom and dad at that precise second, and I will never forget my dad's reaction as long as I live.

He transformed from his moment of softness and kindness to a mean, angry, and cruel man. He pushed Mom away from him aggressively. He swore and cursed at her in front of us that the baby wasn't his and that she had cheated on him. He called her a whore. Then, he slowly, and eerily, looked at all of us in the room one by one like we were ugly strangers who suddenly crashed his party. When he finished making his rounds, he stormed out of the house without another word.

As kids, Connie and I didn't understand the seriousness of Mom and Dad's problems. Basically, we were too young to comprehend most of the adult world. So, in our untainted minds, we went about our own lives unperplexed. I continued going to school. I spent countless hours playing with Sandy and playing hockey and baseball. And, whenever time allowed, I went back out to Chase to spend weekends with Hank and Babe. I don't know what Connie did, because at eight years old, I was still oblivious to anyone's world except for my own. However, later in my life, I realized she was more of a mother to Darryl in his younger years than Mom was. Mom and Dad both worked all hours of the day and night. I played. Connie took care of my brother and everything else around the house for the most part.

After Darryl was born, Dad continued to deny that Darryl was his child. He continued to accuse my mom of cheating on him, although Mom said he was the one who was promiscuous throughout their marriage. Mom said Dad cheated on her often, and naturally, because of all the financial and marital problems, their fantasy of having a happy, harmonious, and fruitful marriage was forever cursed. Ultimately, their divorce became inevitable to everyone who knew them except to us kids.

After Darryl was born, I became aware of a serious change in my dad's attitude towards all of us in the house. Naturally, I took it personally. I blamed myself for Dad's mean attitude to me, and I started to get scared of him a little. For example, one night for some reason, he ordered my mom to set up the dinner table so that I would sit immediately on my dad's right. He and my mom sat on the ends of the table, my sister sat on Dad's left, and I sat on his right against the wall, kind of hemmed in. I didn't realize it until much later in my life that he positioned me there purposefully because he was right handed and he had poorer dexterity with his left.

Anyway, I learned why Dad made the new seating arrangements pretty quickly. Dad knew we were having fried liver and onions with mashed potatoes and a veggie. He also knew I hated liver. So, when Mom plopped a huge, mounded plate of fresh deer liver in the middle of the table, I saw it immediately and cringed. Of course, my dad had been studying me intently as to what my reaction would be when I saw the foreboding meat. To my dad, I was old enough and ready to experience another rite of passage. In other words, I was a Wiens, and I would learn to eat the food placed in front of me without complaint or bad attitude about it. Eating was a privilege in my dad's mind and not a right.

Of course, at eight years old, I cringed again. And then, I complained that I didn't like liver. Instantly, my dad backhanded my face with his closed right fist. My head bounced off the wall directly behind my chair, and as I reeled forward from the nasty blow, Dad smashed my face again maliciously. According to my mom, she flew over the top of the table and attacked my dad's face with her fists and nails. Like two wolverines battling for their own territory, they tore at each other sadistically. They swore and cursed and screamed obscenities at each other all the while.

And, that was the first time I remembered my dad hitting me. Before that moment, he had yelled or screamed or broke something in anger from time to time, but I couldn't recall he ever laid a hand on me.

The liver beating was really the first time I realized Dad was angry and frustrated all the time. I didn't know it then, but he was discouraged with life in general. And another kid on the way was the straw that broke the camel's back. He lashed out at his loved ones in the process. Psychologically, he was totally messed up from his own cruel, and sometimes brutal, upbringing; his dream-life wasn't being realized no matter how hard he tried. He had to work too hard all the time for the pittance truck driving paid him, and he could never seem to make ends meet or get ahead financially. Plus, he fought the whole idea about whether Darryl was even his kid or not. Consequently, it was natural for depression and frustration to drive him into ugly mood swings. His meanness was the result. All we could do was look out for it and stay away from him if we sensed he was going to snap.

In today's society, I believe it is more common for men and women to seek professional help during such serious emotional times like Dad was experiencing. But sadly back then, Dad was always too proud to consider alternative therapy or other possibilities about much of anything. He was a man. He was a Wiens. To Dad, it naturally followed that men, especially Wiens', take care of their own problems when they have them. However, the real problem to begin with was that Dad didn't think he had a problem with anger. So he continued to go down with his own ship.

It was right after that when Dad killed Sandy. When I ran home from school, Sandy wasn't in the front yard waiting patiently where she was supposed to be. I searched for her frantically. I worried myself sick. When I went into the house this time, I was deathly afraid. I didn't know why exactly. But, I had a sick feeling in the pit of my guts.

"Mom! You seen Sandy? I can't find her!" I yelled at her as I rampaged through the front door. Mom was in the kitchen, and as I ran into her rounding the hall-kitchen corner, I knew there was big trouble when I looked up into her mortified face.

"Sandy's gone, Rand. She had a huge lump on her neck. It didn't look good. So, Dad had to shoot her," Mom informed me, as she fought back the tears welling in her eyes.

Her soft voice didn't help though. I went nuts. I ran back out of the house bawling and yelling—at nothing—at the world. I hated everything just then. And, I didn't trust Dad either. I didn't know if he had killed Sandy out of his meanness, or if she really was sick. I didn't know if Mom was just covering for Dad either. Mom was trying everything in her power to hold their marriage together, and I was more than a little suspicious. I thought maybe she didn't want to rock their weary ship over a dumb animal.

Strangely, Dad never talked to me about my dead friend. Mom or Dad never mentioned Sandy again to me. We never had another dog in our family after that either. And, for a long time, my mind was trashed. I just couldn't understand any of it. I hated them both for a long time after that because of the injustice of it all.

Understandably, the sadness I felt wrenched at my guts in other places besides home. My stomach was a constant mess, like fried liver and bad cottage cheese had teamed up against me. I couldn't pay attention in school at all, and it seemed my only sanity came from my sports and out in Chase with my aunt and uncle. All I could think of doing was to dive into baseball and hockey and go hunting and fishing with Hank and Babe whenever I was allowed.

On another occasion shortly after the liver bashing and the probable murder of my best friend in the whole world, Mom bought me an old used bike for my birthday. Mom said some neighbor had put it out in the alley for the garbage man to pick up. But, she salvaged it. She blew up the tires. She oiled up the gears and chain. And then, she happily gave it to me after supper one evening. She couldn't afford a new one. But for me, I was just proud as punch. To me, it was a very special gift, and I wanted to show the world what my wonderful mom got for me.

Before it got too dark, I proceeded to ride it down to the end of my block to show my friend. However, on the way to my friend's house, he and another friend of his I didn't know started throwing rocks at my new bike from behind an old clunker parked on the street. Of course, I took offense immediately. My dad always told me to never start trouble, but if it came, he told me to finish it quickly. So, I did. I proceeded to jump off my bike. I chased my friend down like a wolf on a cottontail. I caught him in about fifty feet, and I proceeded to pummel him until he ran away crying to his momma. Proudly, I got back on my new wheels and rode it home. I wanted to tell my dad how well I did before he went to bed. He went to bed at about seven or eight because he had to get up at three or four to head out on his freight truck run. And, I wanted to make sure he knew I didn't start the fight, but I finished it quickly like he taught me to do.

However, it didn't go according to my simple plan. When I opened the front door to our old duplex, Dad met me with a fist to the side of my head. My head bounced off the end of the open door. It ricocheted off the hallway wall, and my body dropped limply to the floor in a heap. I felt like I was a hundred pound sack of spuds being dropped from the back of Dad's big truck. I guess my mom heard the ruckus when I hit the floor, because when I came to my senses, she was airborne in the middle of jumping onto my dad's back. Her method of operation was to keep Dad from pounding on me some more. Somehow, she dragged him away from me. But then, he turned his fury on her. The next thing I knew, my mom was crying. My dad was swearing and cursing like a madman and trying to explain to Mom that I had kicked my friend in the groin area for no reason at the same time. I was bleeding profusely from my nose and right ear in the meantime.

A few seconds later, my dad calmed down enough to explain to my mom more clearly that my friend's mom had just called him. She said I beat her son up for no reason and kicked him in the groin. Well, of course I denied the sacking. Why? Because I was innocent of the charge. I didn't do what he said I did. I admitted to Mom and Dad that I gave my friend a few good smacks in the head because he was throwing rocks at my bike. But, I didn't start it. I told them I finished it quickly like Dad said to do. But, I didn't start any of it.

When I explained, my dad averted his eyes immediately. Surprisingly, he showed little remorse for smashing my face in before he found out what really happened first. Then, my mom took over. She marched me right down to the neighbor and confronted the mom and the son. It was all so peculiar and surreal to me. Mom walked right into the lady's house without knocking and started interrogating the son on the facts regarding the one-sided scrap we had. He fessed up right away after his dad told him he would kill him if he lied about it. My mom said thank you very much to the lady for almost getting her son killed over her son's lies and her panic, and she marched me right back home and told my dad that she hoped he was proud of what he did to me. She yelled at him that I was totally justified in whooping on my friend. I was only acting on what Dad taught me to do anyway: don't start anything, but finish it good and proper if it comes my way.

Mom and Dad both didn't spare the horses when it came to punishing our childish or irresponsible behavior as kids. In fact, when I reflected on it in prison, it was definitely child abuse. We didn't know the difference. We even learned to believe we deserved the harsh treatment most of the time.

We were normal kids, as normal as any. We got into mischief often like every other human kid. But, like most parents, ours felt they had to teach us right from wrong too. I just didn't understand my parents' methods back then.

Dad had several lessons for me when I was around eight or nine or so. Like I said earlier, I loved to throw things. So, whenever winter rolled around, I threw snowballs at everyone and everything. Of course, my throwing habit rubbed my teachers and my principal the wrong way too. At recess, at lunch, while walking to school, or while walking from school, no moving mammal or vehicle was safe from my best fastball. Whenever there were no live ones or cars within range, I nailed signs or walls or even the vacant house's windows from time to time. And, whenever I unleashed one, I dreamed about being a big league pitcher some day. I wanted to be rich and famous and take care of Mom and Dad and Connie and Darryl. We were poor then, but I was going to fix all that, I thought. When it all boiled down, I only stopped pegging snowballs when my hands froze up or the snow wasn't wet enough to pack a good hard one. Oh yeah, it really bugged me back then when mother nature gave me the fluffy stuff too. You can't make a good snowball unless there is a little wet in it.

Anyways, I got home from school one day, and nature happened to start a good dump for quality snowballs. I didn't have a hockey practice that day. I figured Connie could do all my chores. And, I knew Dad was sleeping. Mom told me in the morning that he had to go out on an all-nighter on the truck, and he had to sleep until about eight. So, I decided to make a snow fort up behind our house on the side of our hill. The location of my fort was perfect too. Our house was built on a steep side hill, and when I looked over the wall of my fort, I could see over the top of the house down to the busy road. And man, it was target rich too. I hit the mother lode. I couldn't pack and chuck my snowballs fast enough. Logging trucks, cars, and pickups, came out of the woodwork. They all passed our house on the busy road from the pulp mill a few miles down towards the river. I guess it was quitting time, because I couldn't reload fast enough. None of them were safe from the great snow warrior either. He was bound and determined to vanquish the mighty evil machines—or die trying.

After awhile, I calmed down a little from all the excitement. I figured I only had a short window of time before my hands would be too cold to do my work. So, I became selective in my targeting. From then on, I tried to cream the front windshields and side mirrors on the moving cars and trucks. I tried to nail the side windows of the moving chip trucks and logging rigs. I don't know what my ending tally was, but I know I scored countless direct hits on the targets I was gunning for.

My fun ended a little differently than I expected though. As I launched a good hard one, I saw my packed ice missile splat heavily against the side of a Volkswagen. When I heard the dull thud through the cloud of snow coming down, I had a bad feeling. My fastball had hit something too hard.

In about two shakes of a lamb's tail, I knew I was in big trouble. I had missed my target ugly and beaned the passenger door of a lady's green bug by mistake. She slid to a halt. She stopped all the traffic behind her. She took her sweet time to find a clear place to pull off the road while a dozen loaded big rigs air-horned her. She calmly got out of her car. She walked down the side of the road about 200 feet to the walkway in front of our house. She halted briefly as she scanned our house, then proceeded to walk casually towards our front door. When she disappeared behind the house, I freaked. I knew right then the bug-lady was going to snitch me off. She was going to sell me out. Nooo! She was going to get me killed. That is what I really thought.

About two minutes later, although it seemed like a month, a familiar voice ripped through the brisk air out of the snowy dusk from the side of our house. It was Dad.

"Randy! Get down here, now!!" he growled up at me from the side porch.

Mortified beyond my wildest young imagination, I suddenly realized the lady had awakened Dad from his much-needed sleep. He had a sixteen-hour shift ahead of him, and a mean old blizzard was brewing up fast. I also knew Dad was going to have to do battle against it in a few more hours. By that time though, I knew I was in deep trouble for sure. That was automatic as breathing. I hadn't figured on anyone calling me to justice for pegging snowballs. To me, it was all harmless fun. But apparently, the big dent in the side door of the lady's green bug proved my reasoning wrong.

On my way down the hill slipping and sliding on the fresh white blanket, I thought seriously about running somewhere. But, I had nowhere to go in the heat of the moment. Plus, I knew if I did run, when Dad caught me, he wouldn't leave enough of my dead carcass for the coyotes denned up behind our place. So, with my tail between my legs, I faced the music.

"What the hell are you doin?" Dad screamed at me, as I walked up the porch like a whipped puppy.

"I made a fort, and I was practicin' my fastball," I stammered with my head hung lower than a double chin on an old bulldog.

"Get up here! Now! A lady's at the front door and said you put a big dent in her new car. Zat right!?" Dad continued to yell at me.

"Yes. But, I didn't mean to do it. I didn't think I'd hurt anythin'," I tried to explain as calmly as I could as I walked up the porch stairs tentatively towards Dad standing half-naked in the doorway. I was definitely in no hurry to meet my maker at my age.

When the first open-handed roundhouse crashed into the side of my face, I knew Dad's wrath was only in the baby stages. He never saw any problem as being small since Darryl was born. It was the end of the world when something took him out of the little box he lived in.

"You go to that lady right now and tell her you'll pay for any repairs from your paper route money. Tell her you don't care if it takes forever," Dad continued his scathing, as I cowered in front of him waiting for more blows.

But, he stopped for the moment. I walked through the house to the front door on pins and needles. I was careful to take off my boots first though. I didn't want to add fuel to Dad's fire. Naturally, like death and taxes, Dad was tailing me like a hide on a moose.

"Are you the boy who hit my car?" the bug lady asked me in a soft voice when I reached her.

"Yes. I did it. Uhh . . . I'm really sorry though. I'll pay for it. I have a paper route," I told the lady shyly.

"Well. I'm not very happy about what you did, but I suppose no one was hurt. Don't worry about paying for the dent. My husband can fix it up. Just don't throw anything at cars anymore. You could cause an accident and someone could get hurt," she explained to me in a friendly tone as she glanced up at the fury in my dad's face.

"I'll be glad to pay for it if you change your mind," I told the lady again, as I looked right into her eyes this time. She had shown me some mercy, and I sure didn't expect it. However, I did know it would be different in a minute when the lady left.

"No. It's okay. Bye," she told me kindly. I guess she realized Dad would take care of me when she left. Then, she was gone. I never saw her again.

When I turned towards Dad after I closed the door, I still didn't look at him, because I knew the lady was right on the money. All I could do was to brace for what was coming next.

"Get in your room! Now! Take your pants down and bend over the bed! I'll be there in a minute!" he bellowed so loudly, I could almost feel his hot air on my cold face.

I followed orders like I was always told to do. I knew if I ran away and hitchhiked to Hank and Babe's, Dad would come after me for sure. That was a no-brainer. I had nowhere else to go either. I had no choice but to drop my drawers.

I was scared out of my wits the whole time I waited. About ten minutes later, Dad came into my room frothing at the mouth. He was swearing and cursing obscenities I was accustomed to by that age, and he was carrying a two-foot long piece of rubber hose. While he made me wait, he had gone out to our old shed and cut off a hunk of old garden hose. It was still frozen when he started whacking me with it all over my legs, bum, and back. Of course, every time the weapon cut the air wickedly and landed somewhere on my cold, naked flesh, I screamed in agony.

Luckily for me, Mom came to my rescue again just in time. She had come in from work and heard the ruckus in my room. She thought I was dying and came running. She was getting used to diving onto Dad's back in Connie's and my defense. Her intervening had become a regular occurrence since Darryl was born, so it didn't bother her in the slightest to fly through the air and tackle him again. But, when she yanked on his neck, he stopped whacking me. That was all I cared about.

The next thing I knew, Mom and Dad were yelling and screaming at each other about the whole mess for an hour until Dad had to leave for work and go brave the blizzard. All I could do was to try to find a comfortable position to sit or stand or lie in. But, that was impossible. Although I hadn't seen Roots yet back then, now I would equate the hosing I received that day to Kunta Kinte's whipping. It was harsh. Just then though, the real reality set in. I had a hockey game the next day. I was the best player on the team and we were in the playoffs against a nasty team. The coach needed me to have my best game. Somehow, I knew I wouldn't be able to give it to him like he wanted. I just had my hide tanned, and I figured it would take a week at least for the welts and stinging to subside.

We lost the championship game two to zip. I could barely skate because of the pain on my back and legs, and the coach was all over me for playing with no heart. I couldn't bring myself to tell him Dad had whipped me pretty good the day before. So, I just hung my head in shame and took the beating from the coach too.

The threat of the rubber hose was a pretty good deterrent, until spring rolled around anyway. When the snow melted, and the ground dried out, my old pitching arm was soft. It was weak because I wouldn't dare to throw anything after the snowball-denting-the-green-bug-from-my-fort incident. And, with Little League only weeks away, I knew I wasn't ready to go out there and mow them down. So, I started to figure out some ways to get my arm in shape.

When I walked around the yard one day looking for a good rock to throw at a tree or something, a brilliant idea hit me right between the horns. On one side of the house, our old dilapidated shed where Dad stored his tools looked like a perfect target. Leading up to one of the sidewalls of the old building, there was a stretch of grass about twenty feet wide and sixty feet long. The long part led up to the shed. I figured, if I put a strike-zone-like target on the side of the wall, I could throw my ball at it all day if I wanted to. Dad surely wouldn't get mad at that. I wouldn't be bothering anybody, and no one would get hurt. Plus, my arm would get stronger and my control would get better too.

The first thing I did was to find some old white chalk in the shed. I knew Dad had some in there, because he always used it to mark his boards when he sawed them for something. When I found a good sturdy chunk in an old can on the side window ledge, I proceeded to mark some thick lines. I made sure they replicated the strike zone for eight-year-old guys like me, because they were whom I was going to be pitching against shortly.

I was satisfied with my job after about ten minutes. I was really anxious to get started, so I raced into my bedroom and retrieved my one and only old baseball stashed in my closet. I sprinted back to the shed and paced off about forty-five feet, the distance of Little League mounds. When I stepped off the last stride, I flipped around to face the wall. And, it was magnificent. A rush went through me like you wouldn't believe. I found myself dreaming it was the mound at Yankee Stadium I had seen on TV. I was a big league pitcher facing down the Yank's best hitter. I was going to strike him out.

I threw my bullets at the wall for hours. Each time I threw one, it would crash against the side of the wall and plop back onto the grass in front of me. I missed the target most of the time, but I chalked that up to my arm being out of shape. It wasn't long before I started hitting the target pretty regularly though. By the third day, although my arm was sore, I realized I was hitting the target almost every time. Fantasizing about the Bigs every day helped me take my mind off Dad too. Usually, I worried every time I came home from school or hockey or baseball. I never knew if I had done something bad enough to cause Dad to bring on the hose.

Unfortunately, by the fifth day, another real problem began to loom like a wild thunderhead coming my way. The shed was disintegrating before my eyes. Every time I threw another fastball, pieces of the shed splintered off the wall like it had been shot with Dad's high-powered moose rifle. After a few more, the ball penetrated all the way through the wall into the shed. Of course, that was annoying in itself, because it took too long to walk all the way up to the shed, around the side wall to the door to get inside, then hunt the ball down amongst all the junk Dad stored in there. I was saddened mostly though, because I knew Dad would be mad at me again. He didn't disappoint me either.

"Randy! Get out here!" he yelled through the house for me when he came home for dinner that night.

I was kind of hiding in my room after I busted the garage wall that day, because I knew Dad had to walk by the shed to get into the house. That was where he parked his pickup when he didn't drive his rig home.

"Hi, Dad. How's work?" I asked inquisitively, and trying to appease the situation any way I could at the same time.

"Don't give me that. I see you busted the wall on the shed all to hell," he growled his conviction at me. Next was the execution. I was sure of it.

"I was practicin' Dad. And, there's nowhere else to throw. I didn't mean to break it." I tried to explain my side to Dad politely, but he wasn't buying the cow.

"I hafta work all hours of the day and night, and then I hafta come home and fix stuff too. Besides all that, do you know how much lumber costs these days?" Dad raked me over the coals pretty good.

But, I knew that was only the beginning. My rubber hosing was literally right around the corner, right around the corner in the hall closet waiting to strike like a mean old monster.

When Dad whipped me that time though, I don't think I cried at all. As a matter of fact, I know I didn't. I knew from experience that the more I cried or whined about anything, the harder he lit into me. So, I laid there, bare butt cheeks pointing up in the air and all, waiting for the next hot one. And, like I suspected, he stopped after a few of his best. He stopped and told me to wash my hands for dinner. Mom was not home yet, and Connie, my 10-year-old sister, had macaroni and cheese and wieners on the go.

There were several hose-jobs from Mom and Dad over the next six years or so, but my favorite came a short time before Mom split the sheets with Dad for good. Connie and I had been fighting over what I always thought to be nothing like we always did back then. Connie beat on me because I would always stick her with the dishes and all the other chores while I went out to play with my buddies. I fought to defend myself over the injustice of having to do dishes or anything else other than playing a sport of some kind.

However, our battle that day turned out to be pretty gruesome. When Mom came home from an all-nighter at her waitressing job, her frustration became instant, horrible anger when she walked in on Connie pounding away on my back she was sitting on. It seemed that is where she always ended up when I purposefully pushed her over the edge. She was a tough little honker for a girl when I riled her.

Anyway, Mom decided we needed to learn a lesson about fighting. So, she ordered us to sit on the couch in the front room until she returned. When she left, Connie and I looked at each other in horror. We were scared to death. We knew what Mom was like when she got mad at us. And, it was never pretty. Of course, a minute later, Mom returned with the rubber hose. She told us to stand up in the middle of the floor while she sat on the edge of the couch and gave us her motherly spiel.

"You wanna fight? Okay. Start fightin'. And, don't stop fightin' till I tell you to stop," she hissed at both of us in her rage.

Naturally, Connie and I started to beat on each other like amateur boxers vying for a gold medal in the Olympics. We didn't have a choice. Every time Mom noticed we weren't trying to hit each other with our fists as hard as we could, she would whack us somewhere on our bodies with the rubber hose. The more haymakers we landed on each other, the less we had to endure the whipping. It didn't take very long before we both got tired of swinging though. In short order, it got to the point where neither of us could lift our arms up from our sides, let alone punch each other in the face anymore. Blood had splattered everywhere, and both our faces were a bloody pulp. But, Mom kept whacking us with the hose if we stopped anyway. It didn't matter how much we cried or sobbed. She rained her blows on us like a windmill.

Mom's fury kept coming until Connie and I just stopped. We looked at each other's messed up face, and somehow, we both understood that there was no point in fighting. We were being beaten up whether we fought or just let Mom wail away at us. So, we ended it. Without discussing it, we both decided to just let Mom finish her madness when she was ready. We had learned our lesson. And, after Mom did stop, Connie and I never fought again. We knew what was good for us if we did. The hose had become our instant cure.

CHAPTER 11

The Hoser

From the time Darryl was born until I was about thirteen, I don't remember Dad and I doing much together for fun at home. However, I do recollect that many times, he would have me skip school so I could ride with him on his freight truck. That was about the only time he was nice to me. Actually, he was a different man altogether when I went with him. He was as polite and kind as can be to all his customers, bosses, and fellow workers, and he never raised a hand or said a harsh word to me at all. In fact, he treated me like a king on the truck, and I gave him everything I had in my appreciation.

Dad was also the best teacher I have ever seen. He taught me everything about driving a rig. He taught me about all the different cars and trucks on the roads we traveled on. He taught me everything about how to use a hand truck most effectively. He taught me about warehousing and loading the trucks with the correct weight distribution. He taught me about the wild game we saw every day on the road. He taught me all about logging and lumber and sawmills. He taught me how to work hard and smart. And in the hot summertime, he would always stop at a lake on the side of the road so we could take a quick dip and cool off from the scorchers. When we finished swimming, he bought us a cold pop, usually a monster-sized 16-ounce bottle of Coke, to put a great finish on the productive long days.

Unfortunately, life became an extremely cold and desolate place for me at home though. My excursions with Dad on the trucks got to be less and less too. It got to the point where my parents would be willing to fight to the death every time they walked into the same room or breathed the same air. Home seemed to become a constant horrible nightmare and the last place I wanted to be. Dad was mean and angry with everyone and everything, and Mom withdrew into a shell. Neither of them had any time or patience at all with Connie or me in the slightest. Darryl was still too young to get any of their wrath and frustration. So, Connie and I got it all. We were in the way and became a major burden. Our feelings became expendable. Consequently, Dad and Mom ordered us to be seen and not heard, to disappear altogether, or Dad would start swinging and ask questions later. I hated those mean streaks Dad seemed to get into more often, and I forgot how kind and generous he could be when his Mr. Hyde came out. I really loved his Jekyl. But the Hyde guy I could do without.

On one occasion, I was memorizing my lines for a play in my bedroom one afternoon. I was the lead actor in my school's Thanksgiving performance, and our first presentation was that particular night. My character was Zanthas Amanthas from the planet Radamanthus in the constellation Orion. My nickname was Buck. The bottom line was that I was really excited about the whole deal, because Dad and Mom had decided to come to the play and watch me. It was a real shocker when Mom gave me the news that morning about coming to watch. But, I jumped for joy just the same.

However, Dad's decision to get off work early and go to a stupid play wasn't his idea. He had to be manipulated by mom. He said he would come only after Mom's tirade the night before regarding the fact he never spent any quality time with the kids.

Naturally, the family thing didn't turn out the way it was planned. After supper, Connie cleaned up the dishes while I practiced my lines some more in my room. I only had an hour before I had to leave, and I was nervous. Meanwhile, Mom and Dad were off in their room getting showered and dressed for the gig.

The next thing I knew, all hell broke loose. Dad started screaming at Mom, and Mom yelled back at Dad. Worriedly, Connie and I ran down the hall to see who had died. We halted in the open doorway to watch and hear the rest of the war.

"You stupid bitch," Dad snarled at Mom, as he stood in front of the mirror hanging in their tiny closet checking himself out.

When Dad snapped, Mom was standing by their creaky old double bed buttoning her only good blouse. It hadn't dawned on her, but Dad had just stuck his arms in his only good shirt and threw it over his shoulders when he realized the unthinkable had just happened.

"What did I do now?" Mom replied timidly to dad's caustic tone, as she struggled to look up at Dad in the face.

"My shirt's not ironed! I can't go to no #@%$#@ play or anythin' else with a wrinkled shirt. Why didn't you get off your fat ass and iron today?" Dad continued his attack.

However, by that time in their relationship, Mom wasn't about to lie down and take Dad's abuse for all the tea in China. It sort of reminded me of a mother grizzly I had seen on TV protecting her young with all her teeth and claws hell bent for election to kill the aggressor.

"What the hell you talkin' about? I work all night and day too. The only difference is, you drive a truck, and I'm a waitress. That's it. You don't work any harder than I do. And Mister Big Important Jake Wiens— you can iron your own shirt. How 'bout that?" Mom tore into Dad like there was no tomorrow. Then, she just stared at him, waiting for his next round of ugliness.

"Well, then! How 'bout this?" Dad said creepily, as he grabbed his shirt viciously with both hands and ripped it apart.

Naturally, the shirt disintegrated, and buttons flew everywhere. When they clicked onto the linoleum and scattered like magic jumping beans, I thought it was pretty funny for a second too. But, then I figured it was a little strange. Dad, a grown man, had flipped out over a shirt not being ironed. I didn't understand it. To me, it was simple. Get the ironing board out, plug the iron in, and voila, a pretty ironed shirt in two minutes.

To make a long story short, Dad or Mom didn't come to my play performance. They stayed home and argued all night. In fact, Mom called my buddy's mom on the horn. Mom knew she and her husband were taking their son to the theatre to watch him perform. He was my sidekick in the play. We were supposed to save our planet Radamanthus from the evil earthlings by stealing all their horses and six-guns. With the earthlings weaponless, we could return home. Our children would be safe forever. When my friend's mom picked up the phone, Mom asked her if she could pick me up. She did.

After the play fiasco, my mom and dad seemed to hate the sight of each other. They would avoid each other like the plague, and nothing kind came out of their mouths. Until then, suppertime had been the only brief lull from the storms always brewing. But, they were dumped along the wayside like the rest of the happy family times around there. In fact, like the last few soldiers defending the motherland, peaceful suppers were annihilated too.

One cold afternoon after hockey practice, I came home to the most delicious, tantalizing aroma a young kid could ever imagine. At first, I thought I was in the wrong house. It had been such a long time since Mom was in a good enough mood to bake anything. But, when I realized I had the right place, a huge smile gaped all over my face like a kid in the candy store. Immediately, mom's homemade cinnamon buns and pies tickled my nose hairs and made my mouth water all the way to the kitchen. I didn't even take off my shoes like I was supposed to. It was like I had a massive bullring in my nose, and I was out of control, being pulled toward the heavenly smells. My sore groin from hockey disappeared the closer I got to the kitchen. I just couldn't wait to tie into the fresh batch of my favorite goodies.

Mom didn't have to work that particular day, and for some reason, she was going all out for supper. I guessed Mom was trying really hard to make Dad happy, but I didn't care what the reason was. I knew we would be having a great feast that night of some kind. And as usual, she didn't disappoint my pleasure center. She boiled up a heaping pile of mashed spuds, a gargantuan moose roast with dark gravy, and we had a can of hot niblets on the side. I kept a monster-sized glass of icy cold milk handy to wash it all down.

Pathetically though, Dad wasn't a happy camper like the rest of us, readying for the tantalizing morsels about to glorify our taste buds. As soon as he sat down and heaped his plate high with all the fixings, the meal was no longer a pleasure. It was no longer the fun family feast fit for kings.

"Where's the homemade bread?" Dad snapped at Mom, like making homemade bread for the master was the only thing in Mom's life besides breathing.

"I ran out of ingredients. I bought Randy a stick with my tips, and I ran out of money to buy more," she explained lovingly, trying to appease Dad's meanness.

"You mean to tell me you spent all the money on a #@$%@ hockey stick instead of stuff for bread? Haven't I told you a million times I want homemade bread every day?" Dad fumed at mom, but he looked at me like he was going to kill me later for sure because I needed a hockey stick.

"Come on. I made you a beautiful moose roast and gravy and potatoes just like you like it. The kids are enjoyin' it. How 'bout we do too?" Mom said to Dad affectionately, as she reached over and put her hand on his arm, trying desperately to keep his wheels from flying off.

"Woman. Don't give me that!. What's the point of makin' a good meal without homemade bread? I don't understand you!" Dad went on, oblivious to anything in his world except for the stupid bread.

"Wait a second, honey. I just remembered. We have some bread. Lemme get it," Mom told Dad suddenly, out of the blue. Then, she got up and went to the fridge.

While Dad glared after Mom like she was a brave Saint Bernard sniffing after some life-saving medicine of some kind, Connie and I stayed quiet. We knew better than to yap about anything when they were in the middle of a good one. Me, I just kept digging into my feast. Connie just sat and watched Mom fetch the bread.

Mom reached the fridge in a few steps, grabbed the bread like a good little wifey, and spun around towards all of us at the table. However, she didn't have a chance to take two steps before Dad snapped. He bolted up out of his chair like a charging rhino was attacking him. Naturally, in the same breath, Mom froze. She stopped faster than a bug splattin' the windshield at sixty miles an hour. She knew exactly what was up though. She also knew what she was doing. She knew the store-bought bread would rile Dad and cause his lightning to strike.

Mom wasn't mistaken either. Dad never said a word this time though. He just stormed over to where Mom had halted. He ripped the plastic-covered bread out of her hands as if he were snatching an old lady's purse. Then, the funniest thing happened. Dad threw the store-bought bread down onto the linoleum kitchen floor and proceeded to stomp it to death. He jumped up and down on it at least twenty times before he got tired. He had made a new meal too. Road pizza. The bread loaf was flatter than a squished momma raccoon on the highway.

While Mom and Dad continued their battle down the hall and into their bedroom, I successfully completed my feast. I had two heaping helpings and wished I had room for more. When I finished, Connie and I did all the dishes without arguing to see who would wash or dry. Actually, we never talked at all. We knew the score around there, and we were both very, very worried about it. But, at the same time, we both knew we couldn't do anything. So, what was the point of discussing it?

Our family jumped from the frying pan into the fire when I came home from school one day. I had just turned thirteen a few months earlier, and it was a cool spring day. Walking the mile and a half home from school, I was calculating how much time I would have to eat, gather my hockey gear, and tape my stick before I had to leave for my hockey practice across town. I had to hurry to catch the bus to get there. But, my thoughts quickly changed to horror when I reached home a few minutes later. As I approached our duplex, I noticed our old red van had been backed up to the front steps. This seemed a little odd to me, because I knew Dad had left at three that morning on a long trip delivering freight, and I knew he wouldn't be home until late that night like usual. I also knew that Mom didn't like to back up when she drove. So, I became a little suspicious.

About a minute later, my whole life shattered into a million pieces. As I walked up the stairs to the duplex, a man I didn't know came out of the front door carrying our black and white television. He didn't acknowledge me in the slightest, and I continued on up the stairs. My mom met me just then at the front door carrying a box of dishes, and when she noticed me, she didn't even say hi. She just ordered me to go sit in the front room. She had to talk to me about something. When I reached the front room, I noticed Connie was holding Darryl on her hip in her usual babysitting posture. When she noticed me, she began to cry. She appeared to be so sad, she couldn't even look at me. She could only stare at the ground while Mom spilled the beans.

"Connie, Darryl, and I are leaving with Kane. Are you comin?" Mom asked me matter-of-factly, as I sat on the edge of one of our old ratty chairs. It was the only piece of furniture left in the entire front room.

Mom looked haggard and dreadfully saddened as she asked me the question. She was utterly broken. At the same time, I was confused about everything that was happening around me. I couldn't understand what Mom was telling me and asking me at the same time.

"Whattaya mean, you're leavin'? Where's Dad?" I blurted anxiously.

"I can't live with your dad any more. Kane and I are gonna be to-gether, and Connie and Darryl are comin' with us. You need ta decide if you're comin or not. Kane's gotta job in the bush up in the Kootenays, and we're ready to go." Mom spit the bad news out through the few tears trickling down her cheeks.

"I'm not goin' anywhere. I'm staying with Dad. Besides, I've gotta game tonight, and my team's countin' on me to be there," I told Mom in my confusion.

In my young mind, I just couldn't see how I could leave Dad by himself while Mom took off with this guy I didn't even know, with all the furniture to boot. Plus, I didn't know where exactly Mom, Connie, and Darryl were going with this moron. The Kootenay Mountains were a long way from Kamloops, and I wasn't about to give up hockey or baseball for anybody if I had a choice in the matter. And apparently, Mom gave me the choice as clear as a bull moose had horns.

After a few minutes of sobbing and tearful goodbye hugs and kisses, I remember waving to my mom, sister, and brother out of our wall-sized front room window as they pulled out of the driveway onto the road. For some reason, I stood at the window and kept waving after our old red van until it disappeared from my sight altogether. Then, I sat. I sat down on the empty carpet in the empty room. My heart was broken and empty too, and as I stared out of the window hoping and praying and crying they would come back, I suddenly realized it wasn't all just a bad dream. I was alone. My mom had left me.

It dawned on me after a few minutes that I only had about twenty minutes to gather my hockey gear and get to the bus stop a block away. I figured there was no point in missing my game, because Dad wasn't going to be home until later that night anyway. So, I hustled and got to the game on time. I scored two goals and had three assists that night. I will never forget it. For some reason, I skated faster and better and passed the puck and shot better than I had ever done before. It was many years later before I realized the added enthusiasm and passion that night was probably caused by my fear. I was running—no skating—scared all night until I got home. I didn't know what Dad would do about Mom taking off with a stranger and taking Connie and Darryl too. But, I did know whatever he did wouldn't be pretty. I just hoped he wouldn't use the hose on me or use me as a punching bag in his rage.

As the bus pulled up a block from our house, I tried to bow my neck into a position where I could see out of my window if Dad's pickup was home yet. It wasn't. I felt a huge sigh of relief escape my throat and lips, and I trudged home quickly with my heavy hockey bag hanging on my shoulder. I dropped the gear up in my room on the second floor of the duplex, and that is when I heard the unmistakable chug of Dad's truck pulling into the driveway.

When Dad walked up the duplex's stairs and filled the doorway, I met him with a dismal and disheartened look on my face. As he stepped towards me, I was standing several feet away blocking the doorway that led into our empty front room. Dad looked weary from the fifteen hours he had just driven in his truck, and his two-day growth of beard made his face seem like it was permanently fixed into a scowl he had no physical control over. He definitely didn't seem happy, and I couldn't imagine what he would do, say, or think when I told him the ugly story. However, I forgot the front room was empty except for the single old chair in one corner. When I backed up into the front room, Dad noticed its emptiness immediately.

"What in the hell is goin' on here?" Dad spat at me confusedly, like I had something to do with the empty room.

"Mom said she left you. She took Connie and Darryl and most of the furniture in the van and went with some guy," I answered as fast as I could. I didn't want to give my dad any more excuse to get mad at me.

"Whaddaya mean she left with another guy?" Dad turned to me, and he looked like he was going to kill me right then and there.

But, the fury and wrath I expected from Dad never materialized. It was a miracle, but he just sat on the empty chair in the corner and started crying.

"Mom asked me if I wanted to go too, but I said I wanted to stay with you," I told my dad straight out.

With tears in his eyes, Dad looked up at me and managed a paltry smile.

"Thanks Rand. Did she say where they were goin?" he asked me calmly. I could see plainly that Dad was trying to keep his composure and change the subject. He had never let me see him cry before, because he was a man. He was a Wiens.

"She said they were headed for the Kootenays. The guy's name is Kane, and he's got a job up in the bush somewhere around there," I responded, with my voice starting to crack.

Then, I broke down completely. I started sobbing uncontrollably, even though I knew Dad would probably jump in my face for crying. I couldn't help it. I tried to be tough like Dad told me I had to be always, no matter what happened in my life. But, the tears just kept gushing like a busted dam.

In the meantime, Dad got up and walked right past me to the front door. I sort of expected him to tell me to stop crying, or hug me, one or the other. But, but he didn't.

"Have you eaten?" he asked me calmly, as he turned and faced me from the doorway.

"No," I responded, trying to get a hold of myself. I figured there was no use in crying any more. I just wanted to know what was going to happen next.

"Let's go get somethin'. Looks like the cook quit," Dad told me plainly, and I followed eagerly.

I was really hungry, because I hadn't eaten since lunchtime at school, and the melee when I got home distracted me from eating before my hockey game. However, the main reason I rushed after my dad was because I didn't want to be left alone. It was already too scary that Mom was gone, and it didn't look like she would be back any time soon, if ever.

Within two weeks, Dad and I moved to a basement suite. It was a dump, but it was the only thing Dad could afford due to all the bills Mom left for him to pay. Basically, Mom turned her back on her entire life to start over. I didn't know until much later that she felt she had no choice though. Dad and Mom didn't get along at all, and their constant battles and bickering were destroying them both emotionally and psychologically. To Mom, in her mind at the time, her escape was absolutely necessary for her sanity and maybe even for her physical survival. She couldn't handle the fact that the fantasy life she had always dreamed of since she was a young child would never be realized with my dad. She had made a terrible mistake in marrying Dad in the first place. And, after seventeen years of Dad's verbal and physical abuse, she couldn't withstand the onslaught any longer. So, she ran away from her detestable life.

In the meantime, I assumed Mom's role in the kitchen and the house. I didn't know how to cook very many different dishes, but Dad expected me to have a hot meal ready for him when he got home just the same. So, I learned to cook real fast. I also cleaned the house, washed dishes every day, and I washed our dirty clothes at the Laundromat down the road about a half a mile a couple of times a week.

I also got a job packing groceries right away. I was thirteen years old. I felt I was old enough to get a job. So, I took the chance that, because I was already a six-footer, I might be able to pass for sixteen. My Uncle Hank told me the owner of the grocery store might hire me because I was big. Luckily for me, he did. And, although he never let on that he knew my real age, he knew the real scoop about me from the get-go. However, to him, I was an excellent worker. I was responsible, reliable, and completely honest, and when he called me to come to work on my days off, I never said no. He liked that about me. So, he kept me on.

A few months after I started working, I started to think of something special I could buy for my dad's birthday coming up. Immediately, I thought about the .308 Savage hunting rifle he was always pining for and wished he could afford. He told me a million times about his dream gun, and I knew it would be the perfect gift if I could swing it. I started the ball rolling by going to the neighborhood sports shop close to where I worked. When I first walked in and noticed the gun Dad craved was hanging directly in front of me in a long gun rack behind the counter, my eyes almost bugged out of my cranium. However, immediately, I became totally intimidated. I realized I was probably dreaming too big, and I almost turned around right then and there. I knew my mind was writing checks my wallet couldn't cash. I was under age first of all. I only had the $40 that I had saved for some new skates and a stick I needed for hockey. And, I knew the gun cost a whole lot more dough than I had to my name. So, all I could think of was to stand there in the store dreaming of that beauty of a gun that Dad had wanted forever. I just stood and stared at the grand prize hanging so majestically behind the counter only a few feet from my trigger finger.

Amidst my growing depression, I somehow conjured up the courage to shoot from the hip anyway. When the owner of the shop noticed me eyeballing the Savage, he walked over and struck up a friendly conversation with me about hunting in general. When I expressed my interest regarding the possible purchase of the high-powered rifle, he unlocked the chain securing the massive row of guns on the wall. Then, he handed the .308 rifle to me with the breach open. I must have been really nervous, because my face felt hot, and I was jittery.

"How much ya askin' for this?" I asked the shop owner maturely, trying to conceal my angst and act like an adult would in a similar situation at the same time.

"With tax, it'll come to about $180," he returned casually, while he studied me closely the whole time to see if I was really serious about buying the gun or not. To me, it sounded like a million, but I didn't let on how ugly the amount was in my young mind.

"How much if you put a four-power Bushnell scope on it too?" I asked the guy plainly. If I was going to try to buy the gun, I thought I would try for the whole enchilada. I knew Dad couldn't even afford the scope, let alone the gun and the scope.

"About $240," the shop owner replied quickly. It was obvious he knew his business and his merchandise well enough to rattle off prices like he did, I thought, as the huge numbers he spoke at me registered in my thirteen-year-old brain. It was more money than I had ever seen before, let alone have all of it to buy the rifle.

"Is that the best you can do? I'm trying to figure out a way to get this gun for my dad's birthday," I explained to the owner.

I was trying to negotiate a little like my dad always told me to do. Dad said if you were sincere with the person when you try to buy something, he would usually dicker with you at least a little.

"It depends. How do you plan to pay for it?" he inquired affably.

"I have $40 cash now for a down payment. I also work at the Safety Mart after school and weekends packin' groceries when I'm not playin' hockey. I get about fifteen or twenty hours a week, depending if my game's outta town on the weekend or not. But, at least fifteen. You can call the owner of the store if you wanna check," I suggested. By this time though, I was starting to get more than a little excited. The storekeeper seemed to be getting interested in my plan.

"Well. I don't usually let my stuff go like that without some sort of collateral. Do you have anything I can hold until you pay it off?" he asked openly in his friendly, businesslike manner.

"Why can't you just keep the gun till I pay it off? Huntin' season's still a long ways away, and I can pay it all before he needs it," I asked excitedly.

To me, it was a no-brainer. Dad wouldn't have the gun for his birthday, but at least it was better late than never, I thought. I figured he more than deserved it. He worked so hard all of the time, he rarely had any time at all for the simple pleasures, like hunting on rare occasions.

"Sounds pretty reasonable to me. You sure that's what you wanna do?" he asked me frankly.

Of course, I jumped at telling the gun shop owner yes, and as I began to fill out the paperwork, I started to get goose bumps all over.

Dad was going to get the surprise of his life in a few months. The only problem was that I still hadn't solved the birthday present issue, and I didn't want to go home empty handed if it killed me. But, that little matter didn't take me long to figure out either. I thought I would just buy Dad a new hunting vest. His old one had more holes in it than a hockey net.

While I worked on the multitude of pages of ownership and responsibility for the new .308 rifle, my mind halted in mid-thought. I glanced around the room before asking the owner how much his hunting vests cost. And, as my good fortune had it, my eagle eye caught a rack of vests and other hunting gear to my left in front of the long gun rack counter. On top of the rack, there was a large sign that said: Sale. All items. $9.

"I still need to get somethin' for my dad's birthday after all. Any chance you'll take $31 for the down payment, so I can get Dad one of those vests?" I asked the shopkeeper frankly, pointing at the sale rack at the same time. He was hunkered across the counter supervising me at the same time he was writing on the provincial gun documents that were mandatory in British Columbia.

"I can do better than that for ya. Just pay me a fin. You're already payin' a lot of dough for the rifle, so I can cut four bucks off the vest," the owner offered.

"Thanks mister. I appreciate that very much," I told the guy with a huge grin pasted all over my face.

I strutted out of the store beaming with pride from ear to ear. I was so pleased with myself for being able to take care of business on my own like that. But, before I closed the door behind me, I turned and looked back towards the gun rack one last time to see if I could catch a glimpse of Dad's new gun. Like it was all meant to be, I immediately noticed the gun owner chaining Dad's present back up on the wall. I smiled again, and when I finally closed the door, I rode my bike home like a maniac. My powerful hockey legs shot my bike down the sidewalk like a rocket. I pedaled so fast I thought I might be breaking the speed limit. I was definitely on an incredible adrenaline rush from my recent experience, and besides that, I knew Dad would be home for dinner soon. I wanted to make sure I had a hot meal ready for him. He was on another marathon freight run.

Unfortunately though, life chucked another monstrous screw into my psyche's motor when Dad came home that night. Of course, I was so incredibly happy because of what I was able to do for my dad, I felt like I was floating carefree on cloud nine. And, I also had my favorite meal prepared for Dad and me. It consisted of my awesome meatloaf, mashed spuds, and the gravy I saw Mom cook a million times. I even had a loaf of fresh bread left over from when my Auntie Babe stopped by for a visit a few days before.

However, when Dad walked in, my cheerful spirit was atomic bombed within minutes.

"Whattaya so geared up about?" Dad asked me coarsely, as I almost ran to meet him at the door with his hunting vest hidden behind my back.

I was chomping at the bit to give him his present, even though it wasn't his birthday yet. But, at the same time, I also knew he was impatient because of the severe frustrations he had to deal with at his work for so many hours, six days a week.

"I got somethin' for your birthday comin' up," I informed Dad, as I yanked it out from behind my back and thrust it at him. My jubilation was bubbling out of me like one of Mom's boiling-over pot of spuds.

"Thanks, Rand. But, I got somethin' more important to talk to ya about," he said flatly, dismissing the vest like it was just another dirty rag or something.

"Whattaya mean?" I asked Dad as my eyes hit the floor like some soldier telling his comrade to hit the deck in an air raid. I was instantly dejected. I didn't think there could be anything as important as Dad's present to talk about at that moment. Wow! I couldn't have been more mistaken. I had taken the whole birthday thing for granted. I was so far off base, a ninety-five-year-old, almost-dead granny could have Indian wrestled me and won easily without breaking a sweat.

"I'm movin' in with Alice, and you're gonna have ta find another place to live. There's no room for you at her house," he told me matter-of-factly, although his eyes avoided mine. It was obvious he felt guilty about telling me his news.

The horrible revelation slammed into me like a humungous D9 bull-dozer plowing over one of my old tinker toys. I felt like a red-hot brand-ing iron had just branded my ears.

"Whaddaya mean I hafta find another place to live? Where am I gonna go?" I blurted out, with tears welling in my eyes like a fast-rising dam in spring run-off. I had already forgotten about the vest, and the gun.

"Call Uncle Hank. You spend all your time out there anyway," he said strangely, as if he already had my whole assassination plot planned to the letter before he got home.

I figured in my tortured brain he had probably thought about it all day, or even longer since he started dating Alice about a month before. The only thing I knew for sure was that my mom had left me stranded, and now Dad didn't want me either. I just couldn't figure out why.

CHAPTER 12

The Gypsy

I did end up moving in with Hank and Babe. I stayed with them for a while until we all realized it wasn't practical to transport me back and forth to Kamloops for school and my sports every day including weekends. They had jobs they had to work every day. Hank was a faller in the bush, and his logging work kept him going really hard and long hours. Babe cooked and toiled long and erratic hours in the Chase hotel. Plus, Kamloops was thirty-two miles one way. Winter conditions up north in British Columbia were brutal. Besides all that, I wanted to continue playing hockey and baseball. Kamloops was the only place around that provided those opportunities. It turned out that living with Hank and Babe forever, like I really craved desperately to do in my heart, was just not in the stars. And, I understood completely when I ended up moving again to another relatives' house right away. They lived in Kamloops, and they were willing to give me a shot too. But, that didn't last long either. Dad or Mom didn't offer any of them compensation or child support to help with my voracious appetite and all the school stuff and hockey and baseball gear I needed regularly. They simply couldn't afford me. Consequently, I felt even more like no one cared about me. I was alone. I was like a beached whale. I had no one to dig a channel so I could float off safely once again. I was like a forgotten prisoner of war. Actually, it was the exact opposite, because many people loved and cared about me, but that's how I felt. I didn't know any better. My mommy and daddy left me. What else was a kid supposed to think?

Just when my life seemed utterly hopeless, I decided I had better start thinking of how I was going to survive physically and financially. I knew I would end up being completely homeless and an orphan otherwise. A short thought later though, my future seemed to thrust itself into my brain. It was abrupt, like a mortar shell hitting the ground in front of me. In another second, it became a no-brainer. I began to contemplate the brilliant idea to quit school, quit hockey, and quit baseball, so I could work full time to support myself. Simply, I would be able to take care of myself. I wouldn't be a burden on anyone.

Fortunately, I had a turn of luck before I was able to follow through with my erroneous plan of self-destruction, I found out I had some guardian angels out there who did love me and who desperately wanted to pick up the ball my mom and dad had dropped off a cliff. First, my Auntie Babe started the ball rolling. She took the bull by the horns out of her disgust for my dad. She orchestrated the plan for me to move in with the parents of my dear friend Larry, with whom I grew up in Chase. Auntie Babe contacted the Kamloops welfare department and arranged for a monthly allowance to be paid directly to Larry's folks. Because of Auntie Babe's love for me and her interest in my welfare, they would be compensated somewhat for my bottomless stomach and for the expensive sports and school.

I felt so lucky. I felt like I had just won the lottery. They all treated me like a king, and Larry and I became closer than ever. I continued to go to school and play hockey and baseball. I was happy as a clam most of the time. I was even able to pay off Dad's .308 Savage hunting rifle before the hunting season began. I missed several weekly payments due to the fact I needed to use some of the intended money for new baseball cleats and a new glove. But, the gun shop owner didn't worry because he still held the gun as collateral. The bottom line was that I was proud of myself for paying the gun off and being able to give it to my dad even though he had tossed me out on my can and left me for the vultures in life.

I gave Dad's gun to him on one of the rare occasions I saw him after he moved in with Alice. He was quite shocked and taken aback when I handed it to him, but he didn't say much. I could see plainly that he felt guilty about the entire mess, but that was as far as it got. He didn't feel responsible for me enough to keep in contact much either, or to support me financially. Nor was he interested in watching me play hockey or baseball. As a matter of fact, I don't remember Dad ever seeing me play in a baseball game of any kind. And I have played at every level of baseball there is—from T-ball all the way to the professional level.

Similarly, he had almost the same lack of interest regarding my hockey, except I do remember Dad watching one game when I was about fifteen years old. I scored two goals for him that night. I remember I was so proud that my dad had taken the time to come and watch me play. I skated so fast that night no one could catch me. And, when I scored both times, the first thing I did when I scored was to look for Dad. I needed him to see the goals I scored for him.

Horrifically, my good fortune ran out a little more than a year later. It turned out that I was eating Larry's family out of house and home too. I was almost sixteen by then, and I was pushing 6'4" and 180 pounds of hollow legs and a bottomless cavern for a stomach. Also, my skates, sticks, and other hockey and baseball equipment overburdened them. The pittance the welfare paid them didn't even scratch the surface of what it really cost to support my school, my sports, and me. Of course, Dad was nowhere to be found to cough up some dough to help out financially. Dad didn't even bother to call me. He was mad at Babe for putting the welfare on him, and he was mad at me for causing him so much grief. I guess he had enough grief without me in his life. Anyway, I was destined to be homeless and destitute once again. At least, that is what my young mind was pounding anyway.

However, another guardian angel had been hovering around my life the whole time. His name is Craig Sturgeon. To say this guy is a hero and a godsend would never come close to describing how generous, completely selfless, and loyal he is. Not only was he an awesome coach of young men, he was, is, and always will be, my closest friend. When I was down for the count and wondering if I could conjure up the strength to get up off the mat again, he offered to take me into his home and his life unconditionally. His incredibly gracious and loving wife, Monica, went along with Craig's plan to make me a part of their family. And the Sturgeon's became more like parents than my own were. They took me under their wing. They flat out took care of me. They treated me like royalty. They provided me with my own room and spending money just so I didn't have to go anywhere with an empty wallet. They spent countless dollars in supporting me in everything I aspired to do in sports or anything else. And because of the Sturgeons, my life prospered.

By the time the Sturgeons got a hold of me though, I was already quite sick psychologically. Many neglected emotional issues caused by my dysfunctional family life had really screwed me up. I had defined my own life in my head by my sports, but I really had no clue or upbringing to know about relationships and regard for other people in general. Hockey and baseball had become my main reason for living, not other people's feelings or problems. Sure, I attended school and earned good grades. I carried out the necessary day-to-day functions in life. However, I was in survival mode only. I didn't have the time or energy to care about other people. I was having a tough enough time keeping the monsters away.

Usually, a brief stint or weekend out in Chase with Hank and Babe helped maintain some of my sanity, but my hectic sports schedule seemed to throw a big cog in that wheel more than I cared for. So I turned to sports to medicate and counsel my ravaged psyche. I needed to be seen. I needed to be noticed. I needed to feel like I existed in the world.

Expectedly after awhile, even sports didn't fill the great void in my heart for a sense of belonging. I felt very, very poor. I felt like I was a burden on the Sturgeons. And I felt ashamed of my parents for leaving someone else to hold the bag. They both left me. Sink or swim or let someone else take care of me was their motto at the time. In other words, I was an extremely angry young man who was in desperate need of love, affection, loyalty, and a sense of belonging in the world as a human. But by then, my mom had left me and all but disappeared from my world. Dad thought I was old enough to take care of myself like he had to do at my age. He cut the apron strings, tossed me to the curb, and went about his own life. And I didn't understand any of it. My brain was in a constant state of loneliness and upheaval. Monsters were constantly ravaging my cognitive gates, and even the Sturgeon's powerful love could not break the walls I had erected around me.

Somehow though, a miracle had been playing itself out in my life at the same time I was feeling sorry for myself in my dementia. The miracle turned out to be that I was blessed with above-average athletic ability. Consequently, because of a subconscious and innate defense mechanism I was blessed with, I turned to sports for my emotional and psychological survival. I dove into hockey and baseball voraciously just to burn up the vast frustration and anger pent up inside me and to escape the monsters on my heels. Basically, I competed and lived. In other words, I skated and survived. I spent the vast majority of my time and energy thinking about and participating in my sports. They provided me with camaraderie, respect, and loyalty; I even found an acceptable form of the sense of belonging I craved so desperately.

Before I met the Sturgeons, my hockey and baseball ability had earned me the grand opportunity to play on many elite teams, including a hockey team that toured Europe. On that particular team, I was fortunate to be one the all-star players picked to represent Canada against several French, German and Dutch hockey teams. When I returned from Europe, I continued to play on a Kamloops all-star team, and we traveled throughout British Columbia to compete. Our opponents across the river were our best competition locally, but we always seemed to handle whatever they brought to the rink when we locked horns.

During one hockey game against our cross-river rivals, I had the pleasure of meeting and getting to know a highly renowned oral surgeon in Kamloops. The meeting came about shortly after the beginning of the second period. I was in hot pursuit of a defenseman on the other team who had just taken a pass off an elbowing penalty face-off. As I bore down on him in full stride to knock him into the middle of next week and take the puck away from him, he cut loose with a 100 mph slap shot. His shot was an attempt to shoot the puck deep into our end of the ice. But unfortunately for me though, the defenseman miscalculated the timing on his shot. Instead of blasting the puck into our end, his stick struck the puck a hair too much out in front of him. The puck shot straight up and smashed into my face. My front teeth disintegrated on impact. My head snapped back viciously like it had just been struck by a sniper's bullet, and my left glove came up to my mouth instinctively all at the same instant. The wicked slap shot didn't knock me down, but it caused me to stagger and wobble like a drunk after a long binge.

Immediately, the referee blew his whistle for an injury timeout while I managed to skate over to the bench in a daze. When I reached it, I started to regain my faculties somewhat. I lowered my glove from my mouth and noticed it was covered in blood. Stuck in the blood was about a half dozen pieces or so of my broken teeth. My coach eyeballed my glove too. Then, he lifted my crushed upper lip up to observe the real damage underneath. His tortured facial expression told me the whole story. Three of my front teeth were shattered at the gum line. I was bleeding profusely from several different areas inside and outside of my mouth. My top lip had split like a solid ice flow breaking up in the spring thaw.

The coach motioned our trainer to quickly escort me off the ice. That is when I was taken to meet my new oral surgeon friend. It took him a while to slice and dice the remaining chunks of teeth out of my upper gums. But, after he stitched me up, I felt as good as new. I didn't make it back in time to finish the game, but I was right back in there the next day. It was a three-game series, and I wasn't about to miss the next game over a few missing teeth.

When Sturge came into my life, he was coaching an elite hockey team that I had been too young to play for until then. Fortunately, he recruited me as soon as I was eligible. And besides the great fortune I experienced in the Sturgeon's home, I learned to love and respect Sturge as an awesome hockey coach as well. However, under his tutelage and tough style, I learned even more that the world was no place for wimps.

To Sturge, hockey was analogous to life in general. He taught his players regularly that a hockey player sometimes finds himself skating powerfully and effortlessly down the ice. He has the puck on his stick. Sometimes, the winds of freedom even brush across his face on his way to the net on a wide-open breakaway. And, when things are going well, he shoots the puck like a laser into the top corner. And naturally, the goalie can't compete. The shot is too pure, and good, and flawless. The goal wins the game for the player's team. And, he is the hero in the eyes of his teammates, his family, and all of the fans.

On the other hand, Sturge taught us that hockey, like life, isn't always that easy. Sometimes, when the player is skating purely and effortlessly and flawlessly, he is smashed into the boards by a vicious defenseman who has no personal regard for the player in the slightest. To the defenseman, the player is just another insignificant bug to squash. The defenseman simply doesn't care if he is dead, dying, or damaged in the slightest.

After his analogical story, the questions Sturge always put to us then were: What should the player do now that he has been crushed like a logging truck had just run over him? Does he just lie on the ice and bleed? Does he snivel and whine until his mommy comes to his rescue? Does he feel sorry for himself and blame everyone else around him for his misery? Or, does he pick his rear end up off the ice, whether he is missing a bunch of teeth and bleeding or not, and skate back into the game with courage and confidence?

Sturge's wisdom and keen insight forced us to be resilient. He didn't accept anything short of it. That is because he was orphaned liked I was abandoned. He was discarded like dirty underwear too. However, he learned to survive in spite of the countless hits below the belt. And, that's how he coached all of us. Life's monsters may have slowed him down from time to time, but Sturge always got back up on the wild broncos whenever they bucked him off. He simply refused to let the old plugs stomp him. That's how Sturge coached us. That's how he still lives.

At seventeen, I was too old to play for Sturge's team. However, a much larger door of opportunity raised its majestically beautiful head. Fortunately, I was good enough athletically to be recruited to play junior hockey, the equivalent to the minor leagues of professional hockey. Unfortunately though, it was time to pack my bags once again.

"I was just starting to feel like I was part of a family," I told Craig and Monica emotionally on their doorstep, while their two daughters stood beside them.

I towered above all of them. Subtly, while we exchanged an array of departing endearments, I stepped down to the next step so I had to look up at all of them slightly. It was my way of showing my respect for them.

I was ready to hit the road running. I already had my old Dodge Dart loaded to the gills with my clothes, hockey gear, and of course, a mountain of Monica's awesome grub. She was always worried if I was hungry, and she always made sure I had a full stomach. I was headed to Vancouver, a large metropolitan city several hundred miles away from Kamloops, and she knew how hollow my legs were.

"You are family, Wiener. Always remember that. This'll always be your home. The door's always open for you whenever you come back," Sturge told me affectionately.

"There are no words to describe my gratitude for what you've done for me. I will never forget it," I told my friends, as I fought back a flood of tears.

"Don't worry so much about what we've done. Maybe you can do the same for some other kid someday. Your life is just beginning. You have the whole world to look forward to. Just go out and do the best you can, no matter what. The rest will take care of itself," Sturge told me as we embraced in friendship. I was extremely emotional, and I tried to express my gratitude for what he and his wife had graciously done for me in an extra hard hug.

"Thanks for everything anyway. I'll miss you," I told the Sturgeons as I walked away.

"Don't forget our number. We wanna hear from you often. Call collect if you hafta," Sturge yelled after me.

Then, I was gone. I was seventeen, and I was embarking on the biggest adventure of my life. I was going to a strange city to play hockey and to go to school hundreds of miles away. And, I was alone. I had the Sturgeons and Hank and Babe back home, but I was flying solo.

I reached the hockey rink in Langley, British Columbia, a suburb of Vancouver later that afternoon. It was prearranged to meet my hockey coach there. When I arrived, he called my new host family, the folks who agreed to billet me for my senior year in high school and the hockey season. The Langley Lords hockey team paid them for all of my room and board. By the end of the hockey season, they turned out to be my greatest fans and my dear friends.

When I laced my blades up for the first practice with my new team, I was one hundred percent intimidated. Every other player on the team had incredible skating, passing, and shooting skills, and a level of anger and aggressiveness that rivaled my own. Consequently, I started to wonder if I was way out over my head in the ocean of sharks I was swimming with. I also learned by the end of the first practice that, in order for a rookie to be permitted to survive at that level of hockey, he had to earn his teammates' respect. And, it was definitely not freely or easily given.

The first thing a rook had to undergo, and successfully endure to earn that respect, was the hockey initiation process. It was traditional and cultural for hockey players to welcome the new guy by testing him. Only in that way could the new guy be assessed properly regarding his unconditional character, toughness, and loyalty to his team's cause. The weakling who whined or complained or showed less than appropriate attitudes toward the initiation would be dealt with unmercifully. In other words, the wimp would be automatically targeted by every teammate during practice, on road trips, and even outright spurned from team activities and functions. The bottom line was that, if the rook couldn't hang, his coach and teammates would weed him out without hesitation. If he couldn't skate with the big dogs, he was banished to spend his eternity with the rest of the poodles in human society.

My initiation was no less than brutal, to say the least. It started when I naively threw my hockey gear off at the end of the first practice and hustled to shower up. Our locker room only had three showerheads, so I figured I would be little Mr. Smarty Pants and beat everyone. I was really geared up because of all the excitement from my first skate with my new team, and I wanted to be ready to go out with the boys and celebrate.

Anyway, my first junior hockey shower turned out to be a horrible nightmare. As soon as I lathered my head, six of my new teammates gang-tackled me while the soap flowed over my eyes. I was totally blinded. Two of them grabbed an arm each, while two others snagged a leg each at the same time. The other two were right there just in case their partners in crime couldn't hold me. But, they could. Like a well-oiled machine with copious experience in such necessary matters, they proceeded to heave me out of the shower. They forcibly plopped me down on my back on the team's training table in the middle of the locker room so everyone could enjoy the show easily from their individual lockers encompassing the room.

While the four goons held me down, the other two spotters went to work. One of them swiped most of the soap and wetness from my eyes, while the other one tightly tied a noose around my penis. The noose was on one end of several long hockey laces tied together. The noose-goon threw the other end over the oblong light stand bolted to the ceiling and pulled up all the slack in the penis-line. My eyes burned from the shampoo like my buddies had just stuck hot pokers in them, but they didn't care. They wanted to know if I could hang, or not. They just stood calmly and continued to administer my agony, while the rest of the audience busted up like wild hyenas.

When the noose-goon thought he had me under total control a few seconds later, he tugged on the line viciously to give me the clear message that he was in complete control. When he was satisfied with his handiwork, he nodded to the other henchmen to release my appendages. Of course, I didn't move. The noose-goon told me if I did, I would become penis-less instantly. So, I just took my medicine and patiently waited for my day of reckoning.

They continued by shaving every hair off my body except for one eyebrow. They reshampooed my hair with a large jar of Vaseline. They covered my entire body with black shoe polish. When they all finished their dirty deed, the noose-goon released the penis line. Simultaneously, all of them retreated. By that time, I had forgotten the burning in my eyes, and they all saw quite plainly that I wasn't a happy camper. Warily, they awaited my reaction.

My reaction did come. However, it was definitely not what they had in mind before they started their grand perniciousness. I raised myself up slowly and methodically, and I casually walked back to the shower. I had formulated in my little rookie brain that I couldn't take them all on. Plus, I suspected the initiation was only a test of my character, toughness, and will to begin with. So, I calculated my next moves while they stewed about my reluctance to rip their heads off. Oh, I knew what I was going to do, to all of them.

But, it didn't come just then. I was too busy rubbing myself raw to rid myself of the disgusting materials blanketing my body from head to toe. As a matter of fact, it took me several hours to clean up enough to put my clothes on comfortably. In the meantime, all the other players went along on their merry little ways. I went home to eat a cold dinner, and I went to bed conspiring my revenge. By morning, it was all pretty clear in my brain.

I got up early for school and finished the homework I failed to complete the night before. Then, I drove my old Dodge Dart to school like usual. I ignored the merciless teasing and mockery from my fellow teammates and from all the other students and teachers in my classes. They saw endless humor in my hairless body and one eye-browed face. But, I didn't care. I knew my kick at the ugly cat was coming really soon.

When I laced my blades up for hockey practice after school, I noticed that everyone in the locker room was walking on eggshells around me. However, I didn't eyeball any of them, and I pretended I had forgotten about their little game the day before. I just calmly suited up and hit the ice. For what I had in mind, I knew I was going to need a good warm-up before the rest of the team came out and the coach blew his whistle to start practice.

Practice did start a few minutes later. As a team, we all completed a series of skating maneuvers, shooting drills, and line-rushes. That took up about half the practice, and the entire time, the initiation goons were very careful not to come around me too closely. They had accurately perceived that too, because my lust for vengeance was pasted all over my face by that point. They knew I had blood on my mind.

The last half of the practice was taken up by a team scrimmage. In other words, out of the four lines, eight defensemen, and two goalies we fielded for our team, the coach split us all up into two equal teams to give us additional game-speed experience.

However, what the rest of the team didn't know was that I had arrived at the rink earlier than any of the other players to talk to the coach. When I arrived, I explained my plan to him. He agreed immediately, and he told me straight out that he would make sure none of the initiation goons would be on my team during scrimmage. Although he agreed willingly, he made me promise that I wouldn't hurt anyone. At the same time, he hinted quite strongly that it was necessary for me to confront my aggressors effectively. He had already heard some grumblings of doubt from a few other players. Their reservations were in regards to my toughness compared to the team's high standards. Because I didn't retaliate right away, some of my teammates had labeled and judged me as a weakling.

But, the coach wanted me to stick. He said he liked my style of play. During the team scrimmage, I crushed every perpetrator that moved on the ice. I bowled them over at mid-ice like a wrecking ball. I crushed them into the boards like splattering eggs against a cement wall. And, my elbows flew at their faces like heavy clubs every time I skated into a corner with them. If any of them even looked like they wanted to drop them, I looked at them, raised my solo eyebrow, and said with a wry, little smile on my face, "Let's go." And, you can believe I meant it.

It didn't take me long to make my intended impression either. In about ten minutes, no one would even skate close to me. Even the spectators at my initiation who had such a hilarious time at my expense skated wide of my under-control, but rather thorough brutality. The coach finally had to blow the whistle and call us all together and publicly tell them, and me, it was all over. It was obvious to him that I wouldn't stop my onslaught until he did, and he wanted all of us healthy for the game the next night.

By the time practice was over and everyone had showered, every one of my teammates shook my hand apologetically. They all accepted me. I had passed the rookie test. After my initiation, it didn't take long before my competitive nature took over in all aspects of my game. I wasn't only able to compete adequately; I developed into an excellent player at the junior hockey level very quickly.

By the time my initiation and my rebuking of it was over, I appreciated Sturge and all my other hockey coaches a lot more than I had previously. They had predicted that, because of my ideal size and extraordinary aggressiveness, I would undoubtedly become a quality left-winger in junior hockey and maybe even pro hockey later on. That position maximized my physical and mental tools. There, I could usually manhandle the other team's players in the corners, manipulate the puck from them, and pass it to the front of the net so one of our guys could score. They were right too.

Sturge also had forewarned me that I would have to scrap a lot in junior hockey too. Of course, he was right again like everything else he told me and taught me. I had to drop my gloves often. I had proven myself as a hockey player who was fearless in the corners or when it came time to duke it out. Consequently, I became a regular target. Everyone seemed to want a piece of me. I was like a gunslinger everyone wanted to send to Boot Hill. However, the state of mind I had developed in my life eagerly welcomed any and all challengers. You see, taking on all comers and doing battle was my favorite way to release the anger and frustrations that dominated my mind. My nurtured anger about life in general drove me maniacally at times, and because it co-existed so perfectly with my natural size and strength, I became a formidable adversary. My new coach really liked that about me.

During the season, I also had several bouts with injuries. During one major bare-fisted encounter, I took my competition too lightly. In other words, I had developed a really big head, and I felt like I was invincible. This short little dude was like a killer wolverine determined to rip out my throat. Before I could tap him with one of my hammers, he smashed me in my face so many times that I felt like my head was Rocky's speed-bag. I was able to finally catch up to the little rascal, but by the time I tagged him good and cut him really badly over his left eye, I was missing another front tooth. I was bleeding profusely from my upper lip where a tooth had busted through, and I needed a half dozen stitches or so over the bridge of my nose.

On a different occasion a few games later, I was still on the mend from the Tasmanian Devil's attack on my face, but I still skated into the corners aggressively. However, one of their beefy defensemen decided he was going to try me. When he did, I took a little frustration out on his body as I smashed him into the boards. It felt really good to be giving instead of getting, and as he crashed to the ice all elbows and knee-caps, I was proud of myself. Well, the guy must have thought I was too mean, because he proceeded to skate after me and challenge me further at center ice. Of course, I obliged him without thinking about it twice. I gave him two good rights before he was able to grab on to my uniform in self-defense. Apparently, he figured if he could get in close on me, I couldn't tag him anymore. Well, he was right about that, but I took him down to the ice in my anger.

Unfortunately though, as I fell on him with all of my body weight, my bare right hand braced for my fall instinctively. Consequently, the instant my hand made flat contact with the ice, the referee who was trying to break us up skated right over the top of it. His skate was like a size twelve razor blade too. In an instant, the white ice became red with my blood pouring out of my hand like a stuck hog. The team doc sewed me up right away, but it took a dozen stitches to do it. The ref apologized to me later in the dressing room, but right then, I used one of Dad's old expressions when he took a whack somewhere on his freight truck deliveries. I told him not to worry about the little scratch he gave me. I told him I was just upset the doc didn't use a bigger needle to administer the freezing solution. The one he stuck me with was only about a six-inger.

On yet another occasion, the opposing coach of one of our arch rival teams sent one of his lackeys after me. Apparently, the coach had decided that I needed to be taken down a few notches. So, he ordered the hit. Unwittingly, I didn't notice the assailant line up across from me at the center ice face off circle after I had just assisted on our first goal. When the linesman dropped the puck, the attacker brought his stick straight up and gave me a two-hander with it across my left ear and temple area. Luckily, my helmet softened the devastating blow enough so my cranium wasn't crushed on the spot. When I collapsed like a demolished building, I swallowed my tongue and crumpled to the ice out cold. And, I don't remember any of it. Our trainer told me later that my eyes were open through the entire incident, but I was unconscious just the same. They hauled my carcass off the ice on a stretcher. The team doctor examined me thoroughly. But, the next thing I remembered after the ref dropped the puck just before the hit was when I stepped naked into the shower.

Another shocker hit me like a hammer a few weeks later. I thought my girlfriend had an unwanted bun in the oven. She had guaranteed me when we first met that she would take the pill regularly, but guess what? Naturally, after a game one night, she informed me quite casually that she had forgotten to take it a few times and she had missed her period, which was unusual for her. Of course, in my selfish and independent world at that time in my life, I blamed her for the whole mess. To me, it was obviously her fault. It definitely wasn't my fault. I had told her many times not to take any chances. Neither one of us could afford to have a kid right then.

Anyway, our team went on the road for the next ten days, and I stewed the whole time. Why? Because, I am a stewer. I worried so much that I got a bleeding ulcer after a game one night. I had just finished eating a spicy pizza, and then I hit the sack. It was already late, and we had a back-to-back game the next night. Sometime during the night, I had this terrific urge to perform a number two. But, when I tried to get up off my bed in the hotel room, I fell down. I was incredibly dizzy. I could hardly function at all. Somehow though, I managed to drag myself to the toilet without waking my roommate. I hauled myself up onto the pot. And by then, I knew there was something seriously wrong with me.

Naturally, just like most other serious situations I had already experienced in my life, I thought I could handle the problem alone. I had it in my head that I didn't need help from my roommate sleeping in the bed beside mine when all I had to do was to yell at him. I was Randy Wiens. I was tough. But, the next thing I remember was an ugly nurse and her huge breasts hovering over my face. I was in a stinky hospital room, and she was hooking up my IV line to a portable drip stand. Apparently, I had collapsed unconscious off the toilet from loss of blood. My roommate heard my head crash into the tub in front of the toilet, and he came running. He called the ambulance, and I was rushed to the hospital where I was laid up for a week.

When I got out of the hospital, all I could do was watch our last road game from the bench. I was too weak to skate, let alone be effective out on the ice. Then we headed back home to Langley. My girlfriend picked me up at the rink where the team bus delivered us. Although she had a dumb-looking grin pasted all over her mug as I approached her, I was madder than a hornet at her for getting pregnant. Naturally, I blamed her. And, in my ten-day stewing psychosis, I had assumed the worst. I thought I was going to have to quit hockey just when I was starting to prove to be a potential professional prospect. I believed I would have to get a job to support a wife and kid and all the rest that comes with it.

Fortunately though, she didn't drop the bomb. And, when she told me she wasn't pregnant, I almost jumped out of my skin in relief.

Speaking of girls, sex, and affection, before I moved to Vancouver to play hockey for the Langley Lords, I was deathly afraid of the entire female gender. From the time I was thirteen when my mommy left me, I began to have a strange and powerful sense of pleasure in my groin area whenever I saw a cute girl. But I would always be embarrassed at those new feelings and thoughts. And, I was confused about how to deal with them. Consequently, if I noticed an attractive girl approaching me in the hallway at school, I would turn around and walk the other way, regardless of the fact that I might be late for my next class. When one of them tried to talk to me for any reason, I would feel my face turn red instantly. My tongue would be tied tighter than a hangman's noose.

However, by the time I finished my hockey season and graduated at eighteen, I began to develop into a girl chaser. Back then though, I figured it was just my virility and natural instincts kicking in. And to me, it was quite simple. Lust, sex, and the hunt in general, were all perfectly normal and acceptable in the society I knew. I was a big man on campus because of my athletic talents, and the girls swarmed all over me. It was natural for me to try to get all the phone numbers I could manage in my hectic schedule with school and hockey. At least that is what I thought then.

CHAPTER 13

On the Road Again

I was completely surprised when my mom showed up at my graduation. She and Kane, the man with whom she all but disappeared from my life with, along with Darryl, drove several hundred miles to celebrate my big day with me.

Before they blessed me with their presence though, I had rarely seen hide or hair of them. From the day Mom left me with Dad, until my graduation, I had taken the initiative to visit all of them periodically. I looked them up whenever I was in their neighborhood, because I still loved my mom and brother desperately. Even though Mom left me, I tried everything I could think of to maintain some kind of connection with her and my brother. But, they were rarely in a financial position to visit me. From what I perceived in the limited personal contact I had with my mom's situation, it seemed Kane was fired from his jobs regularly. Or, he would just quit because he simply didn't want to work. He banked on Mom supporting his loathsome laziness. He freeloaded off Mom, and he sucked her into his various schemes with his lies and his charm. And, Mom fell for his performance hook, line, and sinker. At least, that is what I believed to be the truth back then.

Whenever I did catch up with them, it was always obvious my mom loved me and had been pining for me the whole time I was gone. Sadly though, I couldn't trust her anymore. I kept her at a far distance emotionally because of what I believed in my heart to be her betrayal. I was hesitant to share my real love and emotions for, and to, her, even though I still loved her desperately. I just couldn't stand to be hurt by her again.

Naturally, my attitude and spurning of her affections destroyed her even further, and it was obvious to me that my rejections ripped several more pieces from her heart. But, I had become hardened. Over the five years since Mom first left me, I had built up an unbreakable barrier of mental toughness. I became infinitely stubborn and bull-headed. I became so cynical in all aspects of my life, that hardness was the only way I could handle the anguish and discontent running rampant in my heart, mind, body, and soul. I couldn't fully trust anyone. During that incredibly fragile time in my life emotionally, I believed that I was truly alone. Of course, I knew I had Hank and Babe and Craig and Monica as my friends and as people who cared about me unconditionally. But, my family had discarded me. And, they were the ones I thought I needed. The others were infinitely gracious and incredible people. But in my tainted and perverted perception of the world in general, the wrong people cared for me. I needed my own family back then. I needed my own family's hugs and kisses and love and support and interest in me as Randy Wiens.

Turning eighteen and graduating from high school was an enormous accomplishment for me. Shortly after that, I also went to truck driver training school. I took the Class A test with air brakes. I passed it all with flying colors, and I earned the privilege to drive the big boys. I had learned a great deal about trucks and driving from my dad, and I figured the Class A license would come in handy if I needed a job wherever my travels took me. I figured if I didn't make it in hockey or baseball, I could at least get a good driving job to earn a living. College was nowhere in my vocabulary at the time, and so working for the rest of my life like everyone else on the planet was my only other option if sports didn't work out.

Ultimately, I felt quite proud of myself for everything I was able to do on my own, and my confidence level grew exponentially. I was finally an adult, I was a better than average athlete, and I had skills that were marketable in the working world. Mostly though, I didn't have to put up with the nonsense of school anymore. There had been thousands of times since my mom left me that I wanted to quit school and get a real job. I wanted to get on with some sort of real life. But, Canadian society required that I couldn't participate in sports without going to school. So, I put up with the thorn called school like a good little boy until I could legally fly the coop.

During the eighteen years before my graduation day, I had moved at least a dozen times. Mom and Dad had moved our family many times because of money problems. I had moved many times after Mom and Dad split up because they didn't want the responsibility of supporting me. Many strangers had opened their doors and their hearts and taken me in, and I endured an immeasurable loneliness the whole time. It was natural that I was lost in my own mind.

Consequently, I desperately needed some sort of direction and security in my life by the time I reached graduation and adult status. I was good in hockey and baseball, but a secure future in that whole mess seemed like it was only a wild fantasy or dream that I could never seem to capture. In fact, every dream or fantasy I had ever imagined had been blown to bits by life. It naturally followed that I didn't take any stock in dreaming or fantasizing anymore. I just lived day to day. I just tried to survive whatever monsters came my way.

I was also sick of just barely making ends meet with the low paying labor jobs I was constantly mired in. Between the grocery packing, shoveling grain out of massive train cars, digging ditches for sprinklers, shoveling snow, throwing hay bales, tying steel for reinforcing concrete, falling and bucking trees with chainsaws and other logging stints, and driving delivery trucks, I knew I wanted something more. Although I had, and still have, an infinite respect for every hard-labor worker on the planet, I sincerely believed that I could do more. Consequently, I was in terrible trouble in my mind. I was confused at the brutality life seemed to be sideswiping me with regularly, and I wondered if life would always be that depressing.

Emotionally and psychologically, I was a mess. I floundered around pathetically like a fish out of water flopping around in the bottom of a boat somewhere. I had no real sense of belonging anywhere. I didn't know who I was. The only thing I was really able to identify myself as was as an athlete. In all other arenas like family, a secure home and career, and unconditional love, loyalty, and respect, I was lost in outer space. They were all just fantasies in my mind, and that lack of belonging turned me into a slave of selfishness and pessimism.

In my utter confusion, I took the bull by the horns out of desperation, just like I had grown accustomed to do a million times in my young life already for survival purposes. I decided to make a move. And, it turned out to be one of the best decisions I have made in my entire life. When I finished my hockey season and graduated from high school, my mom left me again after my graduation. And I decided to stay in Vancouver, British Columbia to find a decent truck-driving job and to play senior baseball. Vancouver offered opportunities for both.

I did find a good driving job, working mostly at night hauling grain to the ships on the waterfront. The ships in turn delivered the grain all over the world from the Vancouver port. The senior league consisted of ex-professional players, ex-college players, and the best baseball talent in the entire metropolitan area of Vancouver. Vancouver's baseball opportunities provided a vast array of higher competition, and I knew I needed to go through Vancouver if I wanted to pursue my real, and true, love of baseball. Although I had developed into a pretty good hockey player, and professional hockey was a real possibility if I continued down the hockey road, I decided that summer I was just as good in baseball. So, I stayed in Vancouver and played.

About a month later, I pitched an awesome game against a highly renowned senior team in the province of British Columbia. I threw a gem. I gave up only two hits, one being a dinker over the second baseman's head, and the other a swinging bunt down the third baseline. I struck out twenty-one of twenty-seven hitters, and we won 3-0. After the game, a major league baseball scout approached me.

"Hey, Randy. Hold on a sec. I'd like to talk to you," the scout hailed me as I was daydreaming about the game on my way to my old Dodge Dart. I didn't know the guy from Adam, but I stopped in my tracks and politely waited for him to get closer.

"How's it goin'? I said to the guy friendly-like, and then waited for him to tell me why he wanted to talk to me.

"My name's Morlan. I scout for the Yankees," he explained, as he held out his hand.

I was shocked at first, but I shook the scout's hand strongly. A million thoughts flashed through my mind simultaneously, and I tried to conceal my excitement as well as I could.

"Nice meetin' ya," I sputtered, and stared at him eyeball to eyeball at the same time wondering what he wanted with me.

"I was very impressed with what I saw today. I was wondering if you'd be interested in playing college baseball in the States?" the scout asked me inquisitively.

It took a few seconds for the question to register. I was all ears when it finally did.

"Whaddaya mean?" I asked the scout excitedly and a little suspicious at the same time. I had experienced a lot of letdowns in my life, and I had learned I couldn't really count on most people in my life. But, I was game with this guy anyway. He was a major league baseball scout for the New York Yankees for heaven's sake. So naturally, I was keen to hear him out.

"I think you can compete at the college level right now and possibly play professionally after you develop a little more. I know a college coach in California who I'm sure would take you in a heartbeat. His name is Butch Hughes. He's the best in the business. Would you consider playing for him down there?" he asked me straight out, while he studied my reactions the entire time he talked.

"I sure would. When do I leave?" I offered quickly.

However, just then, I realized that maybe I shouldn't appear to be too eager, or seem desperate, to jump into something so big so fast, even though I was willing to pack my bags right then and there and hit the road for California.

"Are you sure? I want to make sure you are serious before I call the coach and set this up. I need a firm commitment. Do you have parents you want to consult with before you make up your mind? This is a huge move in your life," he asked me in a serious businesslike tone.

"My folks are out of the picture. I'm ready to roll right now. All I've gotta do is go pack a few things and buy a case of oil for my car," I confirmed maturely. Somehow, my jitters had vanished somewhere in the short conversation, and I was able to confer with the Yankees' scout prudently.

"Sounds good to me. Let's make the call," he told me eagerly, as he beckoned me to follow him to the pay phone about twenty feet away by my Dodge.

After he dialed a bunch of numbers, the Yankees' scout started talking to Butch on the other end of the line in California. I perceived immediately that they were close friends, and they respected each other's judgment. In less than a minute, the scout convinced Butch that I would definitely be a valuable asset as a pitcher on his team. Within three minutes, the scout had introduced me to the coach. I talked to him and agreed to play for him. The scout and I shook hands. He gave me a bunch of numbers and addresses for contacting him and my new coach when I got to California, and I thanked him for the awesome opportunity. A minute later, I climbed into my old Dodge and went home to pack. I called my boss and quit my job. I hauled up anchor and shipped out the next day.

I was stoked. I drove hard the whole way to the Golden State. I only stopped for gas, to drop some oil in my engine, and to swallow a burger once in awhile. It took me eighteen hours with the pedal to the metal, but I got to California safe and sound. I didn't know it then, but California would end up being my home for the next twenty-eight years at least.

I lived with some other baseball players in one of my coach's rental houses for the two years I played college ball. However, I was basically on my own financially. I was dead broke. My wallet was dry as a dead bone in a remote desert somewhere. Consequently, I decided to sell my baby and buy an old pick-up. I wasn't eligible for financial aid because I was a foreigner, nor did my mom or dad contribute anything financially as usual. Although I had a British Columbia Class A license, it wasn't accepted in California. I couldn't drive a big rig truck part time like I really wanted to do. Beside, truck-driving jobs were scarce. So I cut firewood instead. Because I had grown up around loggers and chainsaws all my life, it naturally followed that my chainsaw skills could support me.

I was right too. I got up before daylight five days a week. I drove forty miles one way to get to the oak trees I was cutting. I cut and split a half a cord of wood a day. I loaded it. And I delivered it to pre-arranged customers. My wood business wasn't lucrative by any stretch of the imagination, and I struggled to make ends meet from day to day. But I did it anyway. I was too stubborn not to. I was a Wiens. A Wiens wasn't permitted to shy away from anything with their tails between their legs. A Wiens could never go back home unless they were able to fend for themselves. That was a Wiens custom. Great success wasn't mandatory, but they had better work hard and not ever milk off another family member or anyone else. If they did, they were considered bums. I didn't figure that little gem out until much later in my life, but that is why Dad never gave me anything after he told me to find another place to live. He believed in his mind that teenagers were old enough to work and take care of themselves. That was the way he was brought up. And what was natural for him was natural for me.

I had also learned that there were very few people I could count on. I knew I could count on the Sturgeons and my Aunt Babe and Uncle Hank for anything I asked of them. But I was too proud to ask them for money unless I was desperate. Even then I always hesitated. They had already given me the world. I was ashamed to ask them for more. I was an adult in college. In my mind, I had to stand on my own two feet.

So, I kept on going to school, working, and playing college baseball. I wanted to prove to everyone that I could do it all myself. I convinced myself that I didn't need help. And, it didn't matter if no one called me, wrote me, or came to visit; I was going to make it in professional baseball on my own anyway. I was a big boy. I could handle it. And when I did make it to the show, I'd go back home and take care of all the people who took care of me, and my family too. Consequently, I became possessed by the success monster. And it is what drove me so hard.

When I met Coach the first time, he made some phone calls right away to organize a bullpen for me. He called one of his veteran catchers to help out and a couple of other sophomore hitters to observe my practice pitching performance. At nine the next morning, I found myself stretching, playing some warm-up catch, then standing on a pitching mound for the first time in California. Coach had heard about the potential I had from the Yankees' scout, and he was chomping at the bit to find out if I was for real or not.

I gazed towards home plate sixty feet away from where I stood on the hill in complete and utter amazement. I was in total awe because of where I was. I was in California. I was going to be a college pitcher and then play in the big leagues. I also was never more nervous in my entire life. I had played hockey a hundred times in front of thousands of fans. But standing there on that college mound, I had butterflies in my stomach like you wouldn't believe. It felt like I had just packed my guts with a massive plate of rotten cabbage. My mind raced like it had a flock of pigeons flapping their wings inside my cranium. And I felt stiff as aboard. I almost seized up solid. I felt as if my skin had just transformed into Lancelot's armor.

You see, I knew my future was at hand. It was all happening right then. I knew my performance that day would undoubtedly determine if I would play in the big leagues someday or I would have to go back home a defeated warrior and work a real job like everyone else. In my mind, I had to prove myself right then and there, or I would be heading home the next day. Of course though, I would have to borrow gas money from Coach first and hate doing it.

As I fixed the dirt around the pitching rubber, Coach told me what he wanted.

"Throw all fastballs. I wanna check your mechanics out. Don't throw too hard yet. Get real loose first," he instructed me casually. He had been eyeballing my style and mannerisms the whole time, and he could see my nervousness plastered all over my face.

After a few of my good fastballs, I started to loosen up pretty good. By the sixth or seventh pitch, I was loose as a goose and not nervous anymore at all. By the eighth pitch, I felt like I was throwing harder than I had ever done before in my life. I was so geared up and confident, I felt like I was Nolan Ryan throwing 100 mph. However, my big head busted like an exploded water balloon after my tenth pitch.

"You can stop throwin' now. I've seen enough," Coach told me matter-of-factly.

"Whattaya mean?" I asked Coach, completely surprised.

I just stood gaping at him when he spoke the words. They were totally unexpected. They seemed like Greek. They didn't follow my reasoning at all. I had figured I would throw some of my blazing fastballs for a while, then I would show Coach my curve. I wanted to make sure he saw all of my stuff. And, when I got done, I figured he would be greatly impressed. There was no doubt in my Canadian-backwoods mind that I would be his, go-to, type of guy. I would be the one he could always count on in a big game or to gut out a nail-biter in the ninth—every time.

"I've seen enough. I figure you'll be my eighth guy," he told me frankly, as he drilled his eyes into my face to observe my reaction and my competitive spirit.

"How many pitchers do ya have on the team?" I stammered.

I was in complete shock. I had been considered a professional baseball and hockey prospect up in Canada. I started to wonder if this coaching dude there in that no-name dump in Californy, the place ya oughta be, knew anything at all about baseball in the first place. In the second place, my name was Randy Wiens. Didn't he know who I was, I thought?

"I carry eight. And, you'll hafta work real hard to make the eighth spot. I'll hafta red-shirt ya if ya don't beat out my eighth guy now," he continued candidly.

As my eyes hit the dirt in front of me, I wanted to scream the injustice. I couldn't even look at this no-name coach who had brought me all the way down from Canada. I spited him. I had given up hockey for this, I thought. I just couldn't believe it. I was completely dejected and discouraged. My world had just collapsed around me once again. I felt like a booted dog cowering from my master's blows. All I could do was to just stare at the ground in desperation and think of what I was going to do.

As an emotional defense mechanism, I got mad. I didn't just get a little mad. I got furious. The hair on my neck stood straight up, and I thought about decking Coach like I had done so many times to my evil enemies in hockey. Thankfully though, my conscience kicked in just in time. I was able to control my temper, because I didn't want to disrespect Coach. He had given me a once-in-a-lifetime opportunity to make something out of myself. Besides that, he and his beautiful wife had been gracious hosts. They put me up, fed me, and they offered their house to me for free until I moved into a rental house.

So, I turned my anger on myself. This time, I was mad for being so ignorant. I should have realized that California was a supreme paradise for baseball talent. It rivaled every other area in the world when it came to spawning big league caliber players. They had the population density and the weather to play baseball year round just like I played hockey back in Canada. And, it was common sense that the best Canadian talent would be flat out mediocre in California. I just couldn't believe I was so dumb.

My mind was spinning in a million different directions, when suddenly, my competitiveness took over just as I kicked myself in the face one last time for being so stupid. I started thinking, then believing in about two seconds, that there was no way I was going to be number eight at anything. I was convinced I would prove to Coach and the whole world that I couldn't only get off the porch and run with the big dogs, I would lead the pack before long. Plus, I knew I couldn't quit and go home anyway. That would be unacceptable to my people. I knew I would never be able to show my face around Kamloops, Chase, or at any of my friends' or relatives' houses ever again if I quit. They all would think I was a quitter and a failure. Quitters weren't respected back home, and the fact that Randy Wiens couldn't compete against the big boys down in California would make him a laughing stock of the Canadian world. That wasn't really true, but that's what I believed at the time.

With a new energy and fresh burst of confidence, I responded to Coach's revelation regarding where I fit into his precious pitching rotation.

"The cream always rises to the top. It won't take me long to be number one," I told Coach enthusiastically, as I stared back up into his eyes. It had been several seconds since he had verbalized his assessment, and he was waiting for my reaction.

"That's what I wanted to hear. The Yankees' guy said you were tough," Coach told me as he turned towards the catcher and the other players and chuckled.

To make a long story short, Coach almost choked when it only took me about four months to become Merced College's number one pitcher. I attained that status by refusing to allow any other pitcher or player on our team to outwork me. I would have rather died first than let them beat me at anything when we ran drills, practiced, conditioned, or did anything else for that matter.

By the end of the season, we were California state champions. I was 16-1 as a starter, including the two games I pitched in the state championship tournament that year. The record still stands today, twenty-eight years later.

I was drafted a week later. The St. Louis Cardinals selected me as their fifth round draft pick. As luck would have it though, I wasn't allowed to go through the draft. I was a Canadian citizen, and unfortunately in 1976, Canadians weren't eligible for the American baseball draft yet. I could have signed as a free agent, but I would have had to sign for next to nothing. Undrafted players like me didn't command much respect or money in professional baseball. That meant I would have to agree to play for peanuts, especially when I was a no-name player before ever I hit Merced. If I had been a proven high school and college pitcher the scouts had been following over a period of years, then I had an awesome season like I had my freshman year in college that year, then the pros would be justified to invest in me. But unfortunately, that wasn't the case.

I was blown away by the Cardinals' bad news, to say the least. I was sad and dejected, and I felt let down again. I fell into a formidable funk that I couldn't shake no matter how hard and mentally strong I had become. I thought I had made it big when the Cardinals drafted me. But, I didn't. I was going to have to continue my struggle and toil on and off the field to survive. I was going to have to do it all again if I wanted another kick at the professional baseball cat. It all seemed so hopeless that I began to wonder if I should just quit and go back home to Canada and get a regular truck-driving job. I figured at least that way I would have a regular income and some security. I could build my own house, drive a better car, and I would be able to have a little cash in my pocket instead of being so morbidly poor all the time. I even thought about settling down, getting married, and spawning a few Randys somewhere down the line. Just being a regular guy all sounded so much more appealing than beating my head against a seemingly unbreakable wall. But, of course, I couldn't do that. I was too prideful. I couldn't take the embarrassment.

When I told Coach what the Cardinals scout said, he advised me to return to play baseball at Merced in my sophomore year and to do my best to repeat my record performance. He said, if I did both, he would build me up like a king. By the end of the year, the pros would have no choice but to offer me a wad of cash, free agent or no free agent.

So, I heeded Coach's advice. And by then, I was a little more encouraged by Coach's push to convince me that it was in my best interests to return to play for him another year. So, I committed to Coach that I would return. However, I told him that I had to go home and work for the summer so I could afford to live in Merced the following year. Coach told me he had many connections for work for me in Merced, but I told him I already had a logging job lined up that would provide much higher pay. Coach understood completely. We shook hands, and he wished me well. He also thanked me for working so hard and for leading his team to a state championship.

I headed back to Canada for the summer at break-neck speed. It was June 1976 by that time, and I only had about two months to work and visit my family and friends. At the end of August, the rigors of college and baseball started all over again. I had garnered an incredible respect for Coach and my baseball team, and I was chomping at the bit to continue my quest for the Holy Grail of professional baseball. But, I knew I would just have to be tolerant and patient, which were powerfully elusive attributes in my personality. I knew I had to take care of business first.

First, my mind battled itself constantly over my hurriedness to skip the rest of college and play pro ball sooner rather than later. But, I was determined to make a bunch of money logging so I wouldn't have to struggle so hard the following year. Second, I was flat out lonely. I ached and yearned to be back home in British Columbia, the only real place where those needs could be satisfied. I hadn't made any real friends during the first year I lived in California due to my tenacious and selfish campaign to be the best at everything. My cynical and competitive attitude sort of isolated me from most people. I also felt like I couldn't afford to let anyone into my life emotionally. If I did, I believed they might hurt me somehow like Mom and Dad had done. I didn't trust anyone. So, I lived in my own mind. I fantasized about the big leagues and taking care of everyone I knew financially.

When I first planned to go home, I decided to visit my mom and the rest of my family and friends. Although I still harbored a powerful grudge against Mom for leaving me, I still loved her. I figured I only had one of them, and somewhere in my dilapidated and stubborn mind, I still held a little hope that I could forgive her someday.

I flew home—not in a plane, but in my old wood truck. I ran old Betsy into the ground. I showed her no respect. I flat out forgot what she had done for me financially and how she enabled my stay in California to attend college and to play baseball to begin with. I drove her hard and unmercifully. I was like a horse at the end of the trail. No one or no thing was going to stop me. And luckily, the old girl made it home safely. She purred like a kitten the entire 1400 miles up to where my mom and brother were living with Kane, Mom's new man. The cops didn't bother me either, and even though I had to throw in as much oil as I did gas to keep old Betsy's beautiful engine up to snuff, she stayed loyal and true. She didn't let me down.

I worked like a dog that summer in a logging camp back in the bush about 100 miles. There were no roads where the logging camp was, so my crew had to fly in on pontoon planes. I worked for ten days, and then I flew back out of the bush for four days. I kept the same schedule for about ten weeks.

During my four-day weekend every two weeks, I lived with my mom. Although, in my supreme stubbornness, I kept her constant attempts to show her affections for me at bay. But, it was wonderful to be able to spend time with my brother. We seemed to eat up the four days fast every time by playing road hockey, going to the lake for a dip, or just catching up on old news. Darryl was my biggest fan too. I remember he always stared at me when I told my war stories of hockey and baseball. I can still picture his eyes as big as saucers, and his mouth gaping open when I described all the places my sports had taken me. And, he was always fascinated that his older brother had accomplished so much. He was proud of me, and we loved each other unconditionally. To this day, we are very, very close.

By the time the middle of August hit, I had to head south again to Merced College and another baseball season. I had made some pretty good green during the summer, and I was relieved when I counted my bank and realized I would be able to hack my woodcutting in half. That in itself inspired me to do my best at repeating my record performance.

Unfortunately, my sophomore season was a disaster. I did end up 9-3, but I definitely didn't dominate like the year before by any stretch of the imagination. All I could figure out was that it was the sophomore jinx, whatever that is. Later, I was able to nail my downfall down to my poor attitude. I felt sorry for myself all year for not having family interested enough in my great accomplishments or the incredible opportunity I was experiencing. I was in college and had a decent shot at the pros, but it didn't seem to matter to my family back home. Except for my brother, they seemed oblivious to my life altogether.

My bad attitude transferred on to the field too. I didn't work nearly as hard, and my statistics showed it all plainly. By the end of the year, there were no professional scouts to be seen. Their interest had waned. They concluded I was just another flash in the pan.

However, out of loyalty, Coach called the Montreal Expos' and the Toronto Blue Jays' scouts for me. Coach called them, because I was a Canadian. They listened, because they respected his superior coaching skills, knowledge, and record. He knew from his long experience in the game that they would be the most likely candidates to offer me a minor league contract, even though I didn't command any sort of a lucrative signing bonus as a free agent. I had dropped the ball by not repeating my freshman performance. Thus, I was forced to accept a Blue Jays' offer of thirty-five hundred dollars for my signing bonus. Of course I jumped at it like a starving lion, and voila, I was a professional baseball pitcher. Thirty-five hundred big ones were still like a million to me.

Instead of trucking back home that summer, the Blue Jays flew me to Utica, New York. Utica hosted a professional rookie league team affiliated with the Blue Jays in the New York-Penn League. I ended up playing the rest of the summer there, and I dominated the league just like I had done in my record year at Merced. I was inspired to work extremely hard once again, because in my mind, there was no doubt the major leagues were within my grasp. It seemed that my lifelong dream of making it big as a professional athlete was going to come true after all. Although I knew I had to perform at my best every day just to compete with the higher competition, the grueling work and the enormous pressure I put on myself to maximize my pitching abilities and performance daily were all easy for me. Playing in the Bigs was my dream. No one was going to stop me.

After my rookie season in September of 1977, I flew back to Canada again. I was very fortunate to be able to find another well-paying logging job right away, and I was able to save some cash for the upcoming pro season. I needed the money badly, because in rookie ball, I only earned $500 a month. My signing bonus was already gone. I had chalked up a lot of debt trying to make ends meet, and I ended up paying a big chunk of my bonus to get out of hawk. Coach had financed me when I was in the greatest need, and I was grateful to him for helping me so willingly. It was a mountain off my shoulders when I was finally able to pay him off.

I also visited my mom and brother in my off-season. Nothing had changed between Mom and me though. She would never talk about what she had done or why, and because of my limited communicational skills and my lack of courage to confront my mom directly at the time, I was never able to ask the appropriate questions. Consequently, I continued to stew about the whole mess. I still held a great contempt for Mom, and it worsened every time I thought about how she left me.

I also dated a young lady while I was home for the off-season. I had been having great difficulty in maintaining a serious relationship with women during my stint in California, because I was selfish. I was so focused on performing and competing on the baseball field, that my consideration of others was almost nil. I just wouldn't allow anyone to distract my raging quest to make it to the majors. The same situation occurred that winter. The lady and I were intimate, but being a rutting buck in my prime, I didn't respect the young lady like I should have. Back then, it was no big deal if I hurt people emotionally or not. I was Randy Wiens. I was going to play in the Bigs. No one was going to keep that from happening, no matter what. So, I ended our winter fling and left her hanging. I took off for another pro minor league season.

When I left Canada to begin my second professional baseball season, Toronto had promoted me to Dunedin, Florida, a team in the Florida State League. My new team was one step up from the rookie league I played in back in New York, and it was considered to be a top Single-A league in professional baseball at the time. Toronto also gave me a raise. Instead of $500 a month, they offered me $750 a month in my new contract. Although the additional money helped a great deal, I still had to dip into my savings for rent, food, utilities, and everything else I had to pay to maintain an apartment. Toronto paid for all of my expenses when we traveled, but I still had to maintain a residence at home in Dunedin.

I don't know what got into me regarding inspiration, but I completely dominated the new league. It seemed, the better the competition I had to face, the better I pitched. Simply put, I could see the end of the rainbow. I was in the finishing stretch. The oasis of succulent, life-giving water was within my grasp. Playing in the show was getting closer. It was about to quench the desert dictating my life.

Because I was getting everybody out, Toronto only kept me in Dunedin for half the season. It was obvious to them I no longer belonged in the Florida State Single A League. The hitters on the other teams, whether they were first round draft picks or free agent no-names, took their hacks against me in vain. My fastball sunk hard on two planes, my slider bit hard on two planes in the opposite direction from my fastball, and my internal anger fuelled my insatiable passion to conquer them all. And, at 6'4" and 210 pounds of lean and mean, I commanded a huge respect from everyone in the baseball world around me. Coaches and players alike gawked at my nasty tenaciousness and my sinker and slider.

I felt indestructible in the midst of all of it. When I got the call to perform, I stood atop my mountain like a king and stared all the opposing hitters down as they strolled or styled up to the plate to take their whacks at my stuff. I dared anyone to knock me off my throne. And, in the end, few of them were able to handle my stuff with any regularity or authority. They would step into the batter's box, then the next thing they knew, they would ground out weakly, pop up, strike out, or loft a lazy fly into the outfield. Rarely would they hit a ball hard, and I basked in the glorious sunshine of the media's accolades and positive ink.

I wasn't surprised when the Toronto Blue Jays promoted me to Triple AAA at Syracuse, New York in the International League. As a matter of fact, I couldn't believe they took so long to make the move in the first place. There was no doubt in my mind that I would dominate in the big leagues if they gave me a shot, let alone Triple AAA. But, I was content for the moment to have skipped Double AA altogether, because I thought it was one step in the minor league ladder I wouldn't have to conquer to get to the show.

When I reached Syracuse, I believed my time in Triple AAA would be short too. Actually, I really thought: Why are they wasting time and money on a plane ticket to Syracuse? I belong in Toronto. Couldn't they see that? At least, that is where my arrogant mindset was at the time anyway.

I ended up finishing the season in Triple AAA. I pitched very well, but I didn't dominate like I did in the other pro minor leagues and college. However, I pitched well enough to play in Triple AAA the following year, and when I flew home to Canada for the off-season, my heart was already set on going to spring training as a Triple AAA pitcher. I also believed my stint at Syracuse would be brief, and I would undoubtedly pitch well enough to be promoted to the big leagues sometime during the season, or at least make the Blue Jays' forty-man roster by the end of the year. In my mind, all my chickens had been counted and hatched. I believed I was headed for the big leagues.

I arrived in Canada fired up. I couldn't wait to spread the news about my incredible successes and how every hitter I faced couldn't handle the Wiener's best stuff. I even struck up several conversations in the

262 • Now I Know Who I Am

airports and during flights with other passengers and stewardesses just so I could manipulate the dialogue around to what I did for a living. I was a professional baseball player in Triple AAA on my way to the big leagues. Although I didn't brag about it outright, I was still excited about letting everyone know who I was. I got an awful lot of attention that way, and I was having a ball with the whole thing.

However, back home, it seemed very few people even understood in the slightest the enormous magnitude of my baseball achievements and future opportunities, especially financially. My mom or dad still hadn't visited me, watched me play, or kept up a regular communication of any kind. They didn't phone, write letters, rent a carrier pigeon, steal a hot air balloon, or find any other way to contact me. It was like they were in a state of oblivion, and nothing outside their minuscule circle of life registered in their brains.

I was totally flabbergasted that they just didn't get it. To me, it was all so clear. It was a no-brainer. All of my family was supposed to call me every day to see how well I pitched. They were supposed to ask if I needed anything, like money for example. I had told them many times how poorly minor league players were paid, and that I struggled every month to make ends meet. I couldn't even afford a car; I rode a bike to the field every day. I was in Triple AAA of professional baseball, I was one little, tiny step away from the big leagues, and I was driving a bike! But, I could have driven a motorized wheelbarrow to the ballpark, and they still wouldn't have grabbed a clue.

I was embarrassed to even show my face anywhere near the park when I rode my old rattletrap to the park. All the other players had brand new 4X4's, new Caddies, brand-spanking new Porsches, or something else just as flashy. But, no! Randy Roy Wiens rode a bike. I felt like killing everyone who even looked like they were eyeballing me or making fun of my ride. I felt totally humiliated, and that made my contempt for my mom and dad even more horrible.

I believed in my heart my family knew the only real money was in the big leagues, because I told them all a hundred times. I never asked or begged for money, but I made it clear I was hurting financially. Also, I sincerely believed they were all supposed to write letters and be incredibly excited at the fact they had a family member headed for the big time. In my mind, it was so, so simple. They take care of me; I take care of them a hundred fold. They show me their love and support and loyalty; I rescue them from their lifetime of toil and poverty and depression and give them everything they ever dreamed of. In the majors, money flowed like oil and liquid gold, and there would be plenty of dough to satisfy all my family's needs, and then some. But, no! They just didn't get it. And, I just didn't get it. My mind couldn't comprehend the ignorance of it all.

My main problem though was my selfish attitude. It was all me, me, me. I didn't realize that Dad was working like a fool to make ends meet in face of the overload of debt Mom left him with. He worked so hard; the long hours and daily toil wore him down physically and emotionally. He hadn't anything left to give anybody. In Mom's case, her man Kane was a bum. He never worked long enough anywhere to get a full paycheck. Mostly, he sat. Mom worked like a fool to compensate for his laziness. She also had nothing left for me or anyone else, but Darryl and Kane. I should have figured it out all along, but I was living like royalty compared to them. Later in life, I figured that was my mom and dad's mindset back then. I was doing okay. They were the ones really struggling to survive.

I ended up driving a freight truck that fall when I went home to British Columbia. I worked long hours mostly six days a week, but I made awesome money. I was able to save a lot more that year, because I lived with my mom and my overall expenses were minimal. However, the relationship between my mom and me didn't improve in the slightest. I didn't forgive her blasphemic past behavior, and she hid in a morbid state of denial. It was obvious Mom was always depressed and mournful, but she never offered to talk about it. She only changed the subject whenever we approached a sensitive issue. Actually, it took us both several years to finally spill our guts and begin the healing process. I suppose that is what maturity does for you.

CHAPTER 14

Family Secrets

About a week before Christmas, I made the 500-mile winter trip south to Kamloops to visit Connie, the Sturgeons, Larry and his family, and Hank and Babe. The plan was to spend Christmas with them, and then head back to Prince George and my mom's place to work until the middle of January. At that point, I was going to quit my job and go back to California. Spring training started in February in Florida, and California provided the perfect weather for getting back into baseball playing shape. Canada still had several feet of snow on the ground in January, and about the only thing I could throw up there were snowballs.

I seemed to miss Connie every time I tried to get a hold of her, but I had an awesome time with my dear friends and my Auntie Babe and Uncle Hank. We all had fun discussing my travels, but at 5 A.M. on New Year's Eve morning, I headed north again. I had to make more cash, so I wouldn't have to stress about money so much in Triple AAA that year. And, logging back in the bush was the fastest cash I could think of. Toronto did give me a raise to $750 a month, but only for the months I actually played during the five-month season though. And, I wasn't satisfied with those slave wages. It wasn't enough to pay the bills, buy food, buy clothes, or purchase the other essentials for day-to-day living during the season. Mostly though, I couldn't afford some real wheels for baseball. I had a decent truck, but New York was thousands of miles away. Not only would it take too long to drive the old girl that far, I wasn't sure Betsy would make it.

I didn't care if my baseball car in Syracuse was an old four-door clunker with only one door that could only open with the Jaws of Life. The bike thing simply wouldn't cut the mustard. It was my second stint in Triple AAA, and no way was I going to show up at the park on a dumb old rattletrap bike again. I would cut my own throat first, I thought.

Anyway, I had kept a close eye on the weather reports. I knew I was in for some nasty weather for my 500-mile, twelve-hour wintry trek up to Mom's in Prince George, British Columbia. The weeklong zero degree temperatures had fostered a constant snowfall. A thick six-inch layer of the fluffy white stuff blanketed the road. That caused me some problems. It seemed like every dozen miles or so, I would come across another tow-truck yanking another car or truck out of the mountainous snow banks. The treacherous and deceptive black ice under the innocent cover of snow had sucked some of the drivers into letting their guards down. Many vehicles ended up skidding out of control because of their complacency and neglectful driving. I didn't see any ambulances by that stage of my travel though, so I assumed the accidents were minor. From the past experience of winter driving myself, I knew the huge snow banks cushioned most of the impact when vehicles lost control. I also knew it was more of an inconvenience for the drivers to wait for a tow truck to get them back on the road than it was anything else.

The snowplows had been working 24/7 just to keep up on the roads enough to permit pokey vehicle travel. About a hundred miles into my snow-cruise, I caught up to a massive load of logs being pulled by a new Kenworth. It had been trudging about five miles per hour slower than I was, and it threw surging avalanches of snow back up on my hood and window as I snuck up behind it. It completely blocked my view. So, I backed off. I was totally content to follow the big rig as far as it was going in my direction though. Basically, I knew there was no place to go. I couldn't pass the gargantuan truck because I couldn't even see the back of the log load, let alone past the truck far enough to get by him safely. The situation forced me to allow the slow-moving monster ahead to break trail. I had no choice. Between the massive blast of snow and ice the truck threw at me, plus the heavy snow falling from the loaded black sky, common sense told me to stay put.

I played follow the leader willingly for a good hour. A half dozen other vehicles had lined up behind me, but they were all dressed up and had nowhere to go either. Suddenly, some brights reflected brilliantly in my side mirror like someone was trying to pass. But, just as quickly, they disappeared back behind me. I could see other headlights further back through the blizzard, but then, the brights flashed again. This time though, they were almost parallel with my rear end. Irrationally, it seemed the half-ton 4x4 was unwilling to ride the slow boat to China. The maniac continued to dart out into the middle of the road every few minutes to check his visibility and to see if he had enough room to pass me and the front-runner Kenworth ahead. His moves were aggressive. They scared me to death. Why would this idiot even be thinking about trying to get by, I thought? It was common sense that he couldn't. If he did, it would be like a blind bull in a china shop. Something bad would happen for sure. The Kenworth's huge tires were throwing whiteout conditions in our faces, and nothing sane was getting passed him.

Illogically however, the guy behind me decided to make a run for it anyway. When he pulled out this time, I cringed. Instinctively, I backed off my accelerator in case he had to dive into the opening between the rig and me. But, by that time, it was already too late. He was already past me. A few seconds later, he was running parallel to the rear end of the log load ahead.

I had backed off and was decelerating under control by the time his taillights disappeared somewhere up by the rig's fifth wheel and tandem axle combination. Just then, the devil struck with furious anger. Suddenly, out of the blinding snow, I saw the semi's bright red brake lights flash hard. The instantaneousness of the reds signaled my brain that he was forced to hit the binders unnaturally. At the same time, I noticed the rear of the log load start to skate mysteriously to the left before my eyes like a monstrous ocean liner plowing sideways through water. The out of control load blocked my view of the passer completely. That is when

I heard it. A heavy, dull-like thud stunned my senses. It came from somewhere ahead of the Kenworth.

By the time I came to a sliding stop with the caravan halted safely behind me, the semi was just completing its full jackknife about a hundred feet ahead of the rest of us. The rear of the log load disintegrated the snow bank as it plowed through it. The tractor still faced north and was stopped in the right lane where it was supposed to be, but the load had slid across the road at right angles. Through the falling snow, it appeared to be a solid impenetrable wall of wood.

Instinctively, I grabbed the six flares my Uncle Hank had given me for emergencies from under the seat, and my thick hockey jacket off the seat, and I dove out of my truck. I ran towards the car immediately behind me, and I started barking orders to the big guy trying to hoist himself out of it hastily. He had a dumb-as-a-doornail look on his face, but I knew I needed him anyway.

"There's a bad crash up ahead. Light these three flares about five hundred yards back to warn traffic comin'. Tell everyone else on the way to engage their four-way flashers," I yelled at the guy brusquely through the snow.

He nodded somewhat hesitantly, but I guess he realized I meant business. He hustled off to do his job like I told him to do. Then, I flipped around and started running towards the wreck. When I reached the jack-knifed load, I dove under the logs. My hands were already freezing from the cold, and when I shuffled on all fours to get to the other side, the icy snow sent stabbing pains shooting through the tips of my sensitive fingers. I felt like slapping myself for forgetting my thick, warm gloves under my coat. But, I wasn't about to go back and get them.

As I emerged on the other side, the carnage was spread before me like a gruesome Red Asphalt movie. The grisly scene froze me in my tracks for a split second. But, to my right up by the rig's fuel tank, I saw the truck driver hunched over in the snow. His truck hadn't been involved in the head-on crash of the two 4x4 pick-ups. They were rolled up like a pair of busted accordions a few feet in front of his truck; it was obvious he was in some pain.

"Hey! You okay?" I hollered at the guy uneasily, as I shuffled through the unplowed snow to reach him.

"Yeah. I think so. I slipped getting out and kneed myself in the gut," the guy responded awkwardly between his efforts to suck some air into his deflated lungs.

"You got a CB?" I asked the guy hurriedly as I surveyed the crash site more closely.

"Yeah. But, I don't know if it's gonna work in this storm," he said more clearly this time. He was recovering from his fall.

"Radio the cops to get a coupla ambulances here pronto. Tell 'em there's a bad one here. We're only a coupla miles south of Williams Lake. Two vehicles head-on with massive injuries," I instructed the driver.

As he nodded, I began walking towards the wreckage in search of an opening to the other side of it. The road seemed to be completely blocked in the semi-darkness, and the rig's lights offered little illumination on the scene. I knew it was absolutely vital to spark and place the other flares on the other side so other approaching vehicles wouldn't crash into the field of dead already reddening the snow.

I moved tentatively around a woman's body lying lifeless in the middle of the slippery road. She had been ejected from one of the trucks when they collided. Strangely though, as I passed her, one of her eyes seemed to stare at me coldly, like she was angry with me. Her other eye was there too, still attached to half of her head plopped in a small heap of brunette hair, and brains, and gristle, and a lot of blood about twelve inches away from the rest of her lifeless body. I kept going, but my eyes seemed to stay glued to the eye still attached to the separated skull. A dark shiver shot through me right then, and I had to avert my eyes. It was sick.

As I approached the main wreckage, I saw an opening off to my left. I could faintly see the grayish-white snow bank through it, and I made a beeline through the twisted metal and steaming radiators as fast as I could. I didn't see any more bodies when I reached the other side. So, I ran. I ran as fast as my slow wheels would carry me. I didn't see any more lights approaching the crash through the snowy darkness, but when I noticed there was a corner less than a hundred yards from the wreck, the accident made more sense.

I reasoned that the rig must have just been coming up on the right corner when the 4x4 started his pass. And, it was impossible for the maniacal driver to see the on-coming truck's lights until it was too late. He was going too fast to stop. By the time he emerged in front of the rig, and the tandem wheels stopped their blinding onslaught of snow on his windshield, the oncoming truck was in his face. Simultaneously, when the approaching truck came out of his left turn towards the rig, it was too late for him to abort too. He saw lights emerging suddenly from the side of the rig running hard towards him in his lane, and he had no-where to go. The passer was a sitting duck!

I was out of wind by the time I got to an appropriate place past the corner to spot my flares. I was a good 500 yards from the blood and guts. Just as I lit my last one though, I heard a faint siren howling some-where through the dark blizzard. I stopped in my tracks. I couldn't be-lieve the good luck. It couldn't have been more than five minutes since the accident and already the cavalry was coming.

When a veteran Canadian Mountie pulled his patrol car up beside me, I didn't wait for his questions.

"There's a bad head-on about 500 yards ahead. Both ends are al-ready flared. You're gonna need some ambulances. I don't know how many are hurt. There's one dead for sure," I told the cop candidly, and waited for his response.

"We're you involved in it?" he asked me in a business-as-usual tone.

"No. I know what happened. I was behind it all," I told him quickly.

"Can you stay here for awhile? I need you to stop all vehicles right here, but wave the emergency ones through," he asked politely, but sternly. Then, he was gone.

I did what the RCMP guy told me to do willingly. The tow-trucks cleared a lane big enough to wave the traffic through an hour later. I was frozen half to death by then, and a different cop picked me up and drove me back to old Betsy.

However, before they cut me loose, a Mountie climbed into my pas-senger seat to interrogate me regarding the accident. He milked me for info for a good half hour. As I answered his questions, he scribbled a bunch of notes for his reports later. I finally finished spilling all the ugly details, including the part about the two dead eyes on the icy road. But by then, I was curious about a few things too.

"How many got hurt?" I asked the cop casually.

"Are you sure you wanna know? It's not good," he asked me apprehensively.

"Yeah. I wanna know about the crazy guy fer sure," I told the cop probingly.

"He's dead. His gearshift snapped off on impact and speared 'im through the solar plexus. He was alone. There were a lotta empty bottles in his cab, so he was probably drunk too. The autopsy will show it if he was. A lady and man are dead too, but there were two kids strapped in the back seat of the extended cab that don't seem to be hurt bad. Scared more than anything. They were prob'ly sleepin' when they crashed," the cop told me matter-of-factly.

"You've got my number in Prince George if ya need me for anything else. But, if ya need me to go to court, I won't be here long. I'm headin' back to California soon," I informed the cop honestly.

"Thanks for the heads up. By the way, thanks for your help too. There's not too many guys who take charge like that. You might've even saved some more lives by gettin' the flares out so fast," the cop told me respectfully.

I was proud of myself too, but as I drove, a state of melancholy overwhelmed me. Those kids would be without their momma and poppa now, I thought. The drunk driver should have been hung, gassed, and shot before he died. He deserved much worse than what he got.

The further north I got, the more nature released her humbling fury. Also, the more snow that fell, the more treacherous the roads became. The snowplows couldn't keep up. I drove slowly and cautiously, and in that winter wonderland, my mind slowly began to relax. I turned my expensive eight-track stereo up as loud as it could handle without blowing up my cheapo speakers, and I slapped in some Boston. I alternated every hour or so with my Deep Purple tape, and that got me to Mom's safe and sound.

When I pulled old Betsy up in my mom's driveway, I was excited. Connie was supposed to have ridden the bus the 500 miles from

Kamloops to Prince George a few days earlier, and I hadn't seen her yet. I was also anxious to see Brandon, my new nephew. Connie had given birth to him four years earlier, but I hadn't seen either of them in person since he was a baby. My gypsy-like life always seemed to interfere with us getting together. We had talked on the phone occasionally, but that was about it. Basically, we were both foreigners to each other's lives. We had our own to worry about.

Connie had bussed to meet me like she promised on the phone a week earlier, but Mom ended up seeing me drive up through the window first. She came crashing out of the house and down the wooden porch stairs like a wild banshee. She screamed and yelled and cried. She sobbed her gratefulness that I made it okay through the worst blizzard in thirty years. I didn't know the storm was that bad, because I was in La-La Land eight-trackin' it. But, I hugged her hard anyway. She shook like a bumped almond tree in harvest time, and I could tell she was desperate for my forgiveness. Her sad eyes gave her apology away clearly.

I almost broke down myself right then too. I wanted my mom back. I missed her so much. I wanted to hug and kiss her to pieces and cry our love to each other. I wanted it to be like it was before when we were still a real family. Sadly though, my thoughts never turned into actions. I was too hard. Within a few short minutes, my mind retreated back into an unforgiving despair. My heart broke once again when I remembered that Mom had left me stranded many years ago. I seemed to have forgotten her terrible deed for a while. But, it all rushed back into my brain like a raging river. I blamed her for my loneliness and deprivation. No way could I forgive her. My pride had created a steel, impenetrable wall that killed any possibility of forgiveness.

Mom ended up struggling to show me her love during my entire visit, but I rebuked her efforts. My admonishing actions were usually subtle. But, they turned mean and malicious every time Kane came into my sight. I despised the man. To me, he was worthless scum who had dishonored my mom. And, every time my eyes gave my real feelings away, they gnashed at my mom's soul. It was plain from her actions that she was begging for mercy and my forgiveness, but she couldn't say the words. And, I just couldn't understand it. She had told me countless times that she left me for my own good. But, to me, that was just a copout.

When Darryl came rushing outside to greet me with Connie carrying Brandon on his heels, I was able to banish my bad feelings to the back of my cognitive closet for a full hour. We all smiled at each other from ear to ear. We hugged and kissed our love and affections openly, and we flapped our gums like a gaggle of geese fighting over the last handful of grain. We hadn't seen each other in a long time, and we all had our own war stories to spill. Mom tried to wiggle into our conversation, but I ignored her as much as I could get away with. I was insensitive to her feelings, affections, and efforts to achieve my forgiveness. And, even though I knew I was hurting her by denying her attempts, I didn't care. To me, Connie and Brandon and Darryl were more important.

I replayed the accident scene and experience after we all settled down from our emotional greetings. Darryl was all bug-eyed while I retold the story. Connie and Mom listened with their mouths gaping. And, fat-boy Kane watched TV without batting an eyelash at the blood and guts.

Mom never gave up on me though. She valiantly continued her endeavors at reconciliation by going all out for a homemade New Year's Eve feast. She had worked many years as a gang-cook in logging, lumber, and railroad camps, and to me, she was the best cook in the whole world, bar none. She whipped up an incredibly awesome home-cooked meal of moose steaks, mashed potatoes, thick brown gravy, and a mountain of thick chunks of scrumptious homemade bread.

When I finished inhaling my second heaping plate, I was stuffed to the gills. I had craved Mom's food, and I took supreme advantage of the magnificent spread she made just for me. Before I pushed my plate away though, I remembered it was dessert time. So, I buttered up two more massive slabs of bread and flooded it with all of the leftover moose gravy. My mouth told the pleasure center in my brain that I was truly in heaven. I had come home to Mom's cooking, and for a short time, I felt contented.

While the rest of the crew expressed their amazement at the enormous amount of food I had put away already, I finished gorging myself by sopping up the last drippings of gravy from my plate with another piece of mom's mouthwatering homemade bread. Then, I hoisted myself off my chair somehow. As I struggled to walk to the front room and park for a while to digest the whole moose I had just eaten, I was also struggling to breathe without throwing up.

While I sat, Darryl started to do the dishes without being told. He was ten years old by that time, and the dishes were one of his daily chores. Kane and Mom had gone somewhere down the hall for a few minutes, and that left Connie and me alone for a few brief moments.

However, the instant Connie and I made eye contact, she started to bawl like a motherless calf. She sobbed uncontrollably. Her crying jag continued for a minute or so before she could gather her emotions enough to speak to me without gasping for air. I had no idea what had distressed her so much, but it didn't take long before I realized she had been living in a raging hell since Mom took off with Kane six years earlier.

"Rand. I have to talk to you about somethin'," she said to me sadly, as she swiped at her tears.

"What, Con. Whatsa matter?" I replied concernedly, while I heaved my overloaded gorged gut up to the edge of the old couch I had been sitting on.

"It's about Kane," she spluttered sullenly.

"What about 'im?" I hissed back at Connie resentfully.

I had hated the sight of Kane ever since he tracked, trailed, roped, and manipulated my mom into leaving Dad and me. Since that day, I had visited my mom, brother, and sister on a few occasions, and Kane always proved to be a worthless piece of scum. While Mom slaved day and night to put grub on the table and pay the bills, Kane would sit on his fat duff at home. He would watch television and eat, and he was useless when it came to helping Mom around the house. Mom had tried to convince me for years that he was a master heavy-duty mechanic who made enormous wages. He could magically fix anything on a car or truck that needed fixing with his superpowers. He was a valiant military medic and a war hero too. She said he treated her like a queen. But to me, he was a bum and a fraud. He sat, he ate, and he ordered Mom, Darryl, and Connie to cater to his every whim. Darryl was too young to make a move, but I was overjoyed when I heard Connie had moved away from him a few years earlier to Kamloops.

Since I first met Kane, I had always wanted to destroy his slimy face with my fists. I wanted to play hockey against him and crush his skull against the boards and the ice until his brains oozed out in a red river. I judged him as a dishonorable and degenerate lowlife, because he had never taken care of my mom like he promised he would.

Over the years, I had visited them a few times only, but it was obvious Kane was a loser. Mom suffered because of it. It made me cry sometimes when I thought about her, and my heart ached when she had to toil endlessly because of his laziness. She would come home from working fifteen-hour shifts cooking for a crew of men in a camp somewhere out in the bush, and she would still have to cook, clean up after, and bow down to the master whenever he ordered it so. The whole situation disgusted me. Even though I still felt she had wronged me, she was still my mom. And, I truly cared about what happened to her. I wasn't mature enough to tell her at the time, but mostly, I hadn't learned the merciful gift of forgiveness yet. I lived in my own arrogant world, and other people's feelings were secondary most of the time.

Consequently, I held myself back from pulverizing the jerk for two reasons. One was out of respect for Mom. She had abandoned me, but I still loved her desperately. I didn't show it much, but I did. I may have snubbed her affections and love, but that was only because I had become so hardened. I was incapable of letting anyone in, including my mom. But, that never hindered my love for her in the slightest. She was my mommy. The second reason was that I didn't want to go to jail for the rest of my life for killing a piece of scum. It wasn't worth the price. I had too much going for me in baseball, and I wasn't about to throw my future away when I was so close to the dance.

"Come into Darryl's room. No one can hear what I'm gonna tell you," Connie told me hesitantly, as she peeked warily down the hallway to see if Mom and Kane had heard her crying and talking to me. They hadn't.

As we walked towards Darryl's bedroom though, Mom and Kane came out of their bedroom and saw me on Connie's tail.

"Where ya goin'?" Mom asked us suspiciously.

"We're just gonna talk in here for a couple minutes," Connie told Mom cautiously without looking at her.

Connie tried to hide her swollen and teary face with one of her hands when they entered the hall, but Mom noticed her distressed appearance right away. She eyeballed both of us for a second. Then suddenly, I noticed my mom's face turn from her normal complexion to a darkly morose expression. She realized what was up. It had dawned on her in the blink of an eye why Connie had been so eager to bus the long trek.

"I hope you're not gonna be long. I wanna visit too," Mom responded dejectedly, and with her tail between her legs, she continued to walk into the front room with Kane to wait for us to finish our little talk. I had no clue what all the suspense was all about, but I did know that Connie was extremely upset about something. And, I wanted to help her if I could.

After Connie made sure the door was closed tightly, she sat against the headboard of Darryl's bed despondently. I reclined onto one arm at the foot of the bed. I felt so sorry for my sister. I remembered right then how we used to fight so viciously before Mom and Dad split up, but since then, we had grown very close. We had little contact with each other, but we had welded an unbreakable, steel-like emotional bond. It seemed we were always in tune to each other's feelings whether they were ones of misery or bliss or anything in between.

"Tell me what's goin' on, Con," I ordered her impatiently.

"Kane is Brandon's father," she blurted out. At the same time, Connie's eyes hit the deck. She couldn't look at me in her utter embarrassment.

I sat up on the edge of Darryl's bed starkly a short second after Connie's words registered. A million thoughts rampaged through my brain. All I could do was just stare blankly at nothing in my confusion. Seconds turned into minutes.

Suddenly, I felt my face turn white. I put two and two together. Connie was twenty-one. Brandon was four. It takes nine months to build a kid. All of it added up to the sordid fact that Connie was only sixteen when Kane got her pregnant. And, Mom was still living with this disgusting man.

Out of nowhere, a switch flipped in my brain. My first thought was to run out to the front room and kill Kane with my bare hands. I saw a blood-red hue flash into my mind's eye right then, and I felt the wild bliss of seeing his body squirming violently in his last death throes between my legs beneath me, his eyes bugging out of his head like two big zits being popped, and his mouth gasping for air while I choked him to death.

Just then, Connie looked back up at me. I hadn't responded to her true confession.

"Don't don't do nothin' dumb, Rand!" They're not worth it!" she managed to squeeze out between her tears and phlegmed-up throat. She saw the obvious crazed look in my face, and she knew what I was capable of.

"Don't worry, Con. I won't do nothing, 'cept get you and Brandon outta here," I told Connie calmly, even though I wanted to scream against the injustice. I am sure she could see great plumes of smoke coming out of ears as my blood began to boil with hatred for Kane and a mounting disgust for our mother.

"Whattaya mean, you're getting me outta here?" Connie asked me squeamishly. She was scared at what I might do, and she studied my face intently to try to get an idea what I was up to. She was trying to decipher whether I was really planning to go kill Kane like she suspected, or I really meant what I said about leaving right then.

"Go pack. We're leavin' now," I instructed Connie firmly. I couldn't stay in that house for one more minute, whether it was dark and in the middle of bad weather with treacherous roads or not. I knew if I did stay, I would end up behind bars before the sun came up again. And, I knew I would probably be there for the rest of my life.

In about five minutes, I had chucked my belongings into my base-ball bag and Connie had tossed her and Brandon's stuff in her suitcase. While Mom and Kane watched television in the front room waiting for us to emerge from the back bedroom, finally, we did. Only, the scene wasn't what they had expected. When we filed down the hall, I was carrying Brandon under one arm like a football and my baseball bag with the other. Connie was carrying her stuff, and she stayed on my heels silently as I led the pack by the front room doorway leading outside.

As I came into Mom's view by the door as she sat in her recliner beside Kane, she jumped up with a panicked look on her face.

"Where ya goin'?" she demanded pathetically, although it was all pretty clear to everyone that the cat was out of the bag.

"We're leavin'," I blurted back at her as callously and abrasively as I could muster. In that moment, there wasn't anything nice or feathery or soft in my brain. It was all unbendable steel.

I couldn't look her in the eye. I couldn't look at Kane either. I knew I would kill him right then and there if he even opened his yap and looked like he might say something. Apparently though, he had sensed my fury. And, it was obvious he was smart enough to keep his lips shut, because peripherally, I noticed he didn't budge his fat rear an inch.

"Why, Rand? What happened?" Mom whimpered, as she searched my angry face to see if there was any way at all to salvage our relationship.

"You know better than I do!" I snarled at Mom as sarcastically as I could manage out of the corner of my mouth.

I didn't even break stride as I opened the door and walked out.

"Connie! Let's roll!" I snapped at Connie, as I descended the few porch stairs leading to my truck. I didn't ever want to look at either of them again.

In about two shakes, we were gone. As I drove down the long driveway though, I glanced back towards the house. Mom was standing at the front room window sobbing. She was staring at us with such a pathetic chagrin, and I felt really sorry for her. But, just as quickly, I remembered that I once stood at our front room window bawling too. I, too, stared after my mom in utter disbelief as she destroyed my whole world.

Connie, Brandon, and I drove all night. I was honed in on delivering Connie and Brandon to Dad's place, and then, I was heading south to California. I immediately formulated my plan to call my logging boss and quit my job, to get back to Merced as fast as I could, start my baseball conditioning earlier than I originally planned, and fly east for spring training camp in Florida when it was time. I figured once I delivered Connie, I could escape the madness all around me.

During our long ride, Connie and I talked non-stop. The roads were extremely dangerous at night, but the miles flew by smoothly. Old Betsy purred along, and for background music while we yacked, I slapped in an eight-track of the Eagles. Their mellow style seemed to calm us both down, and we were able to open up to each other minus the previous hysteria.

I matured that fateful night. Before that time, I only allowed someone or something into my world if I could benefit from it or them. I didn't think of anyone but myself. I was Randy Wiens. I was going to play in the big leagues. I was going to be rich and famous. No one cared about me, so why should I care about anyone else, I thought before that night.

However, my life changed drastically as Connie explained in graphic detail how her life had been since she agreed to leave with Mom six years earlier. As she spoke, I wanted to take her in my arms and just hug the sadness out of her. I wanted to tell my sister that she never had to worry about that animal again. I was going to take care of her. As soon as I made it to the big leagues, all of her wants and desires would be met. I would buy a nice home for her and Brandon, and she would know she was loved and respected. She was my sister, and no one would ever hurt her again if I had anything to do about it.

Connie began her enlightenment cautiously with a little small talk about my baseball excursions. She didn't know how I would handle the horrible reality of what she was forced to endure. But, I was impatient as usual. I wanted to get to it. So, I just started asking her point blank questions based upon what she had told me years before regarding Brandon and what I believed until then.

"Con. I thought you told me you got pregnant when you fooled around at a party one time," I asked Connie calmly as we drove carefully through the wintry blackness. I wanted Connie to feel comfortable and tell me all the details, and I knew she would stay clammed up if she sensed that I was still too mad to listen to her story.

"That's the story I had to tell. Kane said he'd kill me if I told anyone. And, I knew you or Dad would kill him and go to jail forever if I told you the truth. So, I just lived with it until now. I knew you were comin' up this fall after your ball was over, and I planned to tell you as soon as you came. But, I kept missin' you. Ridin' the bus up here was the only way I could tell you before you went south again. And, I couldn't wait another year. It's all been killin' me. I was almost ready for the nuthouse because I couldn't tell anyone," Connie explained excitedly. She was opening up freely, and I kept digging.

"What really happened then?" I asked her quietly.

"He raped me," Connie blurted willingly.

"What!?" I exclaimed, as I jerked my eyes from the icy road in front of me to eyeball Connie's face. I couldn't believe what I had just heard.

"Kane raped me. He started about three months after we left you. I was fifteen," she said eerily, as if she was conjuring up a ghastly ghost from her closet of skeletons.

"You're kidding," I said unbelievingly. I was shocked, to say the least, and another sudden rage started to consume my brain again. I was totally dumfounded that my mom stayed with this creep. Didn't she know the guy had molested her daughter, I thought?

At the same time though, I didn't want my sister to stop talking. I knew she needed to get it all off her chest, and I wanted to know the whole grisly truth too. So, in my impatience, I began grilling her like an old army drill sergeant. About my fifth rapid-fire question later, Connie got irritated with me and grabbed the bull by the horns. She had waited six long years to spill her guts, and I was rudely interrupting her with my incessant questioning tactics.

"Rand. Can you just listen, please!? I'll tell you everything, but if you keep pushin' me so hard, I'm gonna lose it. This is hard enough without all your pressure," Connie pleaded with me, and of course, I conquered my over-enthusiasm immediately.

"Sorry, sis. I know this is tough for you. I'll shut up now," I apologized calmly and zipped my lips.

Connie filled my ear with her darkly disturbing revelations for the next several hours while I drove carefully through the dangerous night. Brandon slept between us quietly, and my brain reeled as she talked.

"We were livin' in Golden at the time. It's a couple hundred miles from Kamloops. Mom had just took off for work one morning on a Saturday, and Kane came into my room. Of course, he wasn't workin'. He was too lazy. I was still in bed and he only had a robe on. He walked right over to my bed and pulled the covers back and climbed on top of me. I started to cry and scream at him to get off me, but he just grunted his disapproval of the idea. Darryl must have heard me yellin' at him, because he came runnin' into the room to see what was happenin'. When Kane noticed Darryl watchin', he screamed at Darryl to get the hell out. All I could feel was a stabbing pain down there, but he just kept going as I screamed in panic. I was a virgin, and he was hurting me. I was so scared; I didn't know what to do. It was obvious he didn't care in the least though. He just kept pounding on me. Thank God he didn't take long, and then, he just climbed off and put his robe back on without sayin' anything.

"As he walked out, he turned around. In an evil tone, he ordered me to never tell anyone about what happened. He stared right through me as I covered up, and I was deathly afraid of him even more than I was already. In the three months since we left you and Dad, he had blown up about twenty times. It seemed every time Mom confronted him about getting fired from his job, or quitting his job, or just not going to work because he was a lazy, worthless bum, he would become violent instantly. He never hit Mom or me or Darryl that I know, but he threw a TV through the wall one time, he smashed all the dishes another time, or he would just destroy the closest piece of furniture he could reach. He would look at us with his devil-eyes, and swear and curse a blue streak about how no one appreciated him. I believed he was a crazy man from the beginning, but Mom seemed hell bent on stayin' with him no matter what. So, I just hid whenever I sensed he was about to go ballistic. Darryl would run and hide, and he told me often he was always scared to be around Kane too. I knew Darryl was only six, but he knew Kane was nuts like I did.

"After it happened the first time, little miss naive me never believed in a million years he would come after me again. So, I just kept my mouth shut. In my naivety, I thought I wasn't really hurt at all, so I just tried to forget what happened. Three or four days later, he came in again though. Mom was gone to work again, Darryl was on the school bus somewhere comin' home, and I was doing my homework. Kane wasn't home when I got there, and I remember being really happy because he wasn't. But, when I heard him drive up, I got a bad feeling. I was right too. He came directly into my room and ordered me to take my clothes off immediately. I told him no, I don't wanna do that, but he wasn't going to take no for an answer. Oh sure you do, he said to me. It's fun.

"Well, it wasn't fun. His breath stunk and his armpits reeked as he grunted over me. I didn't move, and he got done in a minute or two. This time though, he said he would kill me if I ever told anyone about this. 'I'll kill all of ya,' he said. Right then and there, I knew my life would never be the same. I was terrified. I believed what he said. I knew I would die and everyone else would too if I told. So, I kept my mouth shut.

"He came after me almost daily after that. It usually happened when Mom was at work, but When Mom was home, Kane would make excuses to her that he was going to get wood, or go fishin', or run an errand. Of course, that was all just a ploy. He would always take me and he would park in secluded areas in the bush around where we lived. As soon as the truck stopped, he would climb on me like an animal.

"It got to the point where it became a duty for me. I figured I had nowhere to run to, and I couldn't tell anyone. I felt helpless. So, I just put up with it. It never took long and it didn't really hurt, so I just lived with it. He didn't care if Darryl was around or not. He scared him like he did me and he didn't talk either." Connie told her story excitedly. I noticed the Rocky Mountains were slowly lifting off her shoulders as she spoke.

She had been talking for quite awhile, but I had a burning question burrowing through my mind I just had to ask.

"Sorry to interrupt sis, but didn't Mom know about all this even though you didn't tell her? She had to know something. She's not that stupid," I asked Connie in my perturbation.

"She had to have known. One day, Mom was at work, Darryl was at school, and I was home because we had in-service. By that time, I just expected Kane to have his way with me, and I had gotten to the point to just follow his orders willingly and quickly. That way, I could just get it over with fast. So, when he called me into the bathroom, I knew why. He told me to hike my skirt up and sit on the sink. Just as he finished, we heard Mom come in. She walked directly down the hall to the bathroom, but the door was closed. She must have seen the light on under the door, because she yelled out, 'What's goin' on in there?' Kane had his pants belted up by then, but his shirt was off. I jumped off the sink, put my skirt down, and sat on the closed toilet. Kane opened the door, and Mom stood there with a mad look on her face. She demanded to know what was going on, but Kane dismissed it all by tellin' her I was just pickin' zits off his back. Kane couldn't look her in the eye, and he just walked past her to the kitchen. I went to my room, and I heard them screaming at each other for hours. I heard Kane throwing stuff all over the house like usual, but I stayed in my room. When Darryl came home, he was ordered to his room too.

"So, yes. The answer to your question is: she must have known. But, she never said anything to me or did anything about it. I just assumed he threatened to kill me and Darryl if she did anything stupid, so I just figured nothing was going to change," Connie continued calmly.

"I can't believe any human, let alone our mother, could ever let that happen. If it was me, I'd either cut the animal's throat while he slept, or I'd call the cops, or I'd be gone with my kids the first chance I got," I told Connie frankly. I was stunned and mortified at what she was spilling.

"I can't believe it either. But, that's nothin'. Wait'll you hear the next part. The more Kane messed with me, the more I hated Mom. I thought moms were supposed to save their kids from the animals, not feed their kids to them. So, I started lippin' her off regularly. When Mom told me to watch Darryl, I'd say no obstinately. She would smack me around when I talked back to her, but I still didn't do what she told me to. Besides being Kane's sex toy, I was also tired of being Mom's slave. Yeah, she worked long hours every day, but I had no life either. I went to school, got good grades even though I was being molested at home every day, and I cleaned the house, cooked, and watched Darryl seven days a week. I was more of a mother to Darryl than Mom was. I was sick and tired of the whole mess, and I let Mom know about how mad I was every time she came home. I never told her about Kane, but I complained about everything else. She'd whack me, but I simply didn't care.

"One Friday night, Mom had left for work, and I had some friends over for a sleepover. I rarely had that opportunity, but Mom happened to be in one of her rare good moods, and she let me have a party this one night. I still was responsible to watch Darryl, but I didn't care.

"When my friends came over, we were having a great time. I didn't even think about Kane, but about midnight, he hollered at me from the top of the stairs to come upstairs for a minute. I couldn't believe my ears, but I knew I had no choice. When I got up to Kane and Mom's bedroom, he was already naked. He said he would only take a minute and I could get back to my party. But, there was another problem too. Since Kane started fooling around with me, I had problems with my period regularity. Kane told me to go on the pill when I was sixteen so I wouldn't get pregnant, but when Mom took me to the doctor to find out about the pill, she didn't let me get it because she said it would promote promiscuity. So, I didn't go on the pill.

"The night of the party, I had a bad feeling that it was a bad time for messin' around. I told Kane, but he wasn't interested. Usually, when I told him it was a bad time, he'd wear a condom. But, this time, he didn't. While he grunted and groaned grossly on me, the bad feeling kept getting worse. I knew I was in trouble the next day when I started throwing up. When Mom saw I was sick, I told her I just had the flu. She asked me if I was pregnant one day a few weeks later, and when I told her yes, she asked me who did it. I was scared of Kane, and I knew he'd kill me if I told her the truth, so I told her I got pregnant at a party.

"When the doctor confirmed it all, Kane stopped messin' with me. But three weeks after Brandon was born, Kane came after me again. This time though, I told him I'd scream if he ever touched me again. I didn't care if he killed me or not. He left me alone that day and took off somewhere.

"Later the same day, the cops came to the door. They asked where Kane was. They explained they were investigating him for check fraud. I was scared of the cops and I shook in my shoes, but I didn't know where Kane was. An hour later, Mom came home early from her job and told me Kane was arrested for forging checks. I said, "Oh goodie!" Of course, Mom bailed him out. His sentence was suspended, and they just put him on probation. The reason they let him slide with probation only was because Mom said she'd pay back all Kane's debts.

When Mom came home from her waitressing job the next night, I told her I was leaving on the bus the next day for Kamloops. Mom didn't know at that point that Brandon was Kane's kid. Mom raised holy hell, but I took off to Kamloops anyway. I figured it was about time she hired a new slave, and she didn't have any more to say about it anyway, because I was eighteen. I could do what I wanted.

I got on welfare right away in Kamloops, and I had rare contact with Mom, Darryl, or Kane. Two years later when I was twenty, you had just headed to California to play college ball, I got a knock on the door. It turned out to be Kane's probation officer. He still had a couple years to go before they cut him lose. Anyway, he was a nice man. He told me Mom was about to marry Kane, but he needed to talk to me first before he would give Kane permission. Kane had confided in him that he was Brandon's father, and he wanted to make sure Mom knew what she was getting into.

"He suggested that I tell her about Brandon right away. So, I did. When she came to town one day shortly after the probation guy came by, I told her Kane was Brandon's father. Immediately, she saw red. She swore up and down and flatly denied the facts. In fact, she told me I was just jealous, and I wanted him for myself. Well, I have ta say that really blew me away. It completely destroyed the few feelings I had left for Mom. I was devastated emotionally, and my self-esteem vanished altogether. She married the animal anyway," Connie continued to describe her life.

By the time we got to the part where Mom and Kane planned to marry, we were approaching my dad's house. There was no way I wanted to talk to him about anything, because since he left me in the lurch, I went out of my way to avoid him whenever possible. So, I pulled old Betsy up at Cache Creek, a small town about six miles from Dad's house and sixty miles from Kamloops. I told Connie to drop a dime on him and tell him to pick her up forthwith. When he confirmed he was on his way, I knew we still had about twenty minutes before Dad would show up, so I waited for a few minutes and talked to my sister.

"Sis, I am so sorry for what happened to you. I know your life has been a livin' hell forever, but you need to know you no longer have to bear it alone. I'll keep you abreast of what's happenin' at my end, so you can call me collect anytime. That's not much help, but that's about all I can do for now. When I make it to the bigs, I can take care of you properly," I explained to Connie sadly. My heart was wrenched in agony for her.

"Rand. I'm so proud of you for takin' me outta there. But, more than that, I'm glad you're the first one I told. I should have confided in you earlier. From now on, things will be different. And, I will call you. I love you little brother. I'm proud to be your sister. Give 'em hell in baseball. Me and Darryl will be rootin' for you. We may not be there, but you need to know we'll be thinkin' of you always. Drive safe," she told me lovingly, as she leaned over in the truck seat and affectionately stroked the side of my face with tears in her eyes.

Of course, the hardened, tough, non-sensitive Randolph started weeping softly too. My tears just came, and I didn't have anything to say or do about it. I thanked sis for her love, and then she was gone. She grabbed Brandon and her suitcase, and I watched her walk away and disappear into a small café a few yards down the block from the pay phone to wait for Dad. And for me, I definitely didn't want to hang around. I had just experienced all the negativity in my life I could handle for awhile. The continuation of Dad's and my feud would have to wait for another day.

CHAPTER 15

Trading Dreams

The trip to California that year was pretty morbid. The slashing swords of disappointment gutted me slowly as I drove. I was sad that I couldn't help Connie more than I had done, especially during the sickening nature surrounding Kane's rapes and molestations. Plus, the whole fiasco regarding my mom and what she allowed to happen to my sister was beyond my comprehension. I just couldn't believe it. What could Mom have been thinking, I thought? How could she marry the creep after everything had happened, then accuse her daughter of vile misdeeds to top it off. The whole ugly mess all the way to Merced tortured my mind. I even started to wish Lorena Bobbitt were around back then. I thought callously that, maybe she could have given my mom some of her courage to go Medieval on Kane's business.

Although my return to California was two weeks earlier than I had planned initially, I decided to make the most of it. I tried to think positively in spite of the horrendous news back home about my sister. And, I was successful in doing so. I treated the extra two weeks as a blessing in disguise rather than diving back into a negative emotional funk and allowing it to disrupt my focus on preparing for spring training. Better yet, I chucked my baggage and skeletons back into the deepest reaches of my emotional and psychological closet. I denied the monsters entirely, and I became utterly impassioned to go all the way in baseball. I worked like a fool to attain a peak physical fitness. I was 1,000 percent determined to go back to Syracuse and show them all why they shouldn't have bothered purchasing my Triple AAA plane ticket. I knew I belonged in the big leagues, and I thought, Toronto Blue Jays, here I come. In my mind, major league baseball was my chance to provide a real life for me and everyone I cared about.

A few days after I arrived back in Merced, Coach invited me to speak at the Hot Stove League dinner he had promoted to raise money for the local Little League organization. It was an annual event where Coach recruited his ex-college players—who went on to play professional baseball—to speak and inspire the young kids to stay in school and pursue sports with respect and honor. However, Coach's invitation turned out to be a life-altering experience for me instead of just a social function to raise money.

Before the dinner, Coach hosted a gathering at his home for his pro baseball speakers plus a few friends. That is where I met Sheryl. She was a friend of Coach's family and a fellow teacher. She was also an avid baseball fan, and overall, she was highly renowned and respected as an extraordinarily gifted athlete. Naturally, I was always on the hunt, so when I introduced myself to her by the hors d'oeuvre table, I had more on my mind than pigs in a blanket. We shot the bull for an hour or so, and I decided I really liked her a lot. She was about twelve years older than I, but that didn't seem to matter. We hit it off right away, and I even offered to drive her to the Hot Stove dinner.

I was elated when Sheryl accepted my invitation. She seemed different from the other women I had dated, and predictably, I started prodding her for personal information. I apologized to her for being so plainspoken, but when I explained that I had to leave for spring training in about five weeks and I didn't want to beat around the bush, she told me she wasn't offended at all. In fact, she even said she admired my straightforward style. However, Sheryl made it crystal clear that there were limits.

In the next five weeks, Sheryl and I became very, very close. We were almost inseparable. When she wasn't at school and I wasn't working out, she was at my rental shack. Or, I was at her house. We cooked each other dinner every night, and afterwards, we would usually curl up on the couch and talk and listen to music. In turn, I spilled my guts about my sordid life. I also expressed my determination to play in the big leagues. And, I talked about the kind of family I needed and wanted to have some day. Sheryl talked about her family too. She professed her religious lifestyle and her supreme passion for it. She told me of her love of sports. And she agreed with my desire to create a loving family.

Sheryl made it very clear that I wasn't going to be able to seduce her though. She was saving all of it for marriage, and that was just the way it was. And, for me, her rejection of my sexual advances was different than I had usually experienced. I believe that is why I began to fall in love with her so quickly. She was pure and good in every respect. She was beautiful with impeccable character and personality. And, she was a star athlete. She was one of the best women's athletes anywhere. Everyone respected her for her high moral standards, character, and her competitive nature. And, she was tough as nails. When we wrestled around playfully, I had to defend myself strongly, otherwise she would pin my 6'4" and 210 pound frame at the drop of a hat. Sheryl was definitely no pushover. But, she was soft and gentle at the same time, and to me, she had it all. I was so happy. I couldn't remember when I had experienced so much love and loyalty so freely. The other women I had been intimate with seemed to only want me for my baseball status and what potential financial rewards it offered. But, not Sheryl.

Consequently, I felt excited about life, which had been a rare commodity, and I worked even harder to get in shape. Being around Sheryl inspired me about everything, and I even started thinking that marrying her was even possible somewhere down the road. She already had a house, a car, and a great teaching job with an exorbitant amount of time off in the summer during baseball season. I figured that, if we did hook up, I could go play ball for a couple of months in the spring, then she could join me in the summer during her vacation. With my first major league contract, I knew I could support her totally. She could quit her job and stay home with the kids, because we would have it made by then. We could buy a home in Toronto, and we would be financially secure to do all of it comfortably. Sheryl was on the same page too.

However, I didn't formally ask Sheryl to marry me yet. I thought it was too soon. We had only known each other for a few weeks, and I thought dropping the bomb on her parents that quickly had potential for disaster. Sheryl agreed. So, when I headed to spring training, we decided to just write each other and call regularly. When Sheryl finished school, the plan was for her to fly to Syracuse or Toronto, wherever I was playing. Then, it would be more appropriate to pursue the next step.

I flew to spring training in Florida on schedule and in great shape. I was also greatly inspired because of what looked like to be a rosy future in baseball and with Sheryl. I was living large in my mind, and memories of my childhood and parents seemed to disappear. I was going places, and my thoughts of a real family of my own seemed to be at my fingertips. Those fantastical feelings were so succulent, when I licked them, my taste buds rejoiced. They also craved that the delicacies and tantalizing morsels would never end.

When I touched down in Tampa, I didn't hit the road running. I hit it sprinting. My foot-speed was always mediocre at best, but when I stepped onto the field the first day of spring training, I made up my mind that it would take a full brigade and a dozen heavily armed tanks to keep me from dominating on the hill. I believed there was no person or thing that could stop my run to the end zone. I was in great shape, I was throwing bullets, my slider was unhittable, and I had a real woman waiting for me back home in California.

However, my state of immeasurable bliss didn't last long. About two weeks, fourteen phone calls to Sheryl, one phone call from Connie, and a meeting with the Toronto Blue Jays' head office administrators later, my whole world disintegrated horrifically once again.

The gruesome dismantlement began on a warm Florida sunshiny Friday. I had just finished dealing a three-inning hitless, walkless, and brilliant masterpiece on the mound against the Boston Red Sox's triple AAA spring training team, when one of Toronto's head scouts hailed me from the bleachers as I jogged off the mound towards the dugout.

"Hey Wiens! Come to the front office after you get a drink!" the scout yelled to me affably, as he stood up from his perch in the stands.

I acknowledged his request with a slight nod, and immediately, my mind was bombarded with a myriad of thoughts. I had proven to be one of the top three pitchers in spring training, in my opinion, and I started to believe that there could only be one reason why I was being called in to the office. The Toronto brass was going to promote me to the big league team. What else could it be, I thought? My mind reeled. I forgot about how thirsty I was, and I gathered my gear as fast as I could move my hands. I hardly even acknowledged my teammates' slaps on the back, their high fives, or their shouts of encouragement and respect for shutting down the Red Sox so handily.

As I took long, loping strides to the office, I tried not to run. All I could think about was a big league contract and the financial security it would offer. I thought about how wonderful my life would be if I had a worthy financial position so I could propose to Sheryl and provide her with a magnificent lifestyle. I also yearned to be able to take care of Connie and Darryl. And, I hungered for the day when I could take care of all my friends who had taken care of me when I was abandoned and down for the count. The possibility that it all just might happen in the next few minutes was mind-boggling.

Sadly though, those fantasies were crushed instead of realized when I entered the office.

"Have a seat," the scout offered in a business-like manner and pointed at a vacant seat by a huge oak desk at the same time. Three other suits were standing or sitting at various locations scattered about the large office, but the head scout did the talking.

"Thanks," I responded coolly, as I parked my rear in an over-stuffed chair.

"I'll get right to the point Randy. We've decided to send you down. We have been watching your performance very carefully, and we all appreciate your incredible work ethic, your competitiveness, and your huge heart. However, we don't feel you belong in Triple AAA quite yet. You can see the trainer when you go shower. He has your itinerary and plane ticket," the scout spit out at me, all in one breath.

All I could do was stare at the scout in disbelief for several seconds. I couldn't say anything or debate the specific reasons the Toronto bosses felt I wasn't good enough to stick in Triple AAA, and suddenly, I hated all of them right then. I hated the Blue Jays. I hated baseball. And, I hated life. How could they do that to me, I thought? How could they not see that I belonged in the big leagues, not in some lower-level minor league somewhere in Timbuktu? Didn't they just witness a dominating performance? Didn't they see how the frozen ropes, the pee-rods, the smashes, and the big flies were extremely rare when I was on the Triple AAA mound? Why, Lord? Why? I thought, as I walked out of the monsters' office with my butt dragging. What was I going to do, I thought?

I did pick up my ticket from the trainer a little while later. Then, after I showered and cleaned out my locker, I took a taxi back to my hotel room to sulk. My plane wasn't leaving for the boonies until early the next morning. On the way, I told the taxi driver to find a liquor store. I wanted to grab a cold six-pack. I needed some company in my misery, and Sheryl, nor anyone else for that matter, was there to cry with me.

My mind was blown from the scout's ugly revelation. I didn't know what to do except mope about the injustice. I listened to music to try to take my mind off my complete failure.

An hour later, I had just cracked my fourth beer when the phone rang. I had Alice Cooper's, *Dead Babies* blasting on the radio when I decided to pick up on the seventh ring.

"Hello," I managed to mumble into the talking end.

"Hi, Rand. How's my little brother?" Connie mimicked my somber tone on her end.

"Hi, Sis. How'd you get this number?" I asked Connie sullenly. I was curious as to how she found me in Florida. The only one who knew my number was Sheryl.

"I called Merced College for Coach's number. He gave me Sheryl's number. She gave me your number. I called you," she stated matter-of-factly, like it was easy to find someone on the other end of the continent with no problem.

"I'm glad you could find me, but it's too bad you caught me on such a rotten day though. I wanted to talk to you when I had some great news instead of bad news," I kind of whined at Connie.

"Whattaya mean? What happened?" she asked worriedly.

"They sent me down. I won't be in Triple AAA this year. Maybe never," I informed Connie in a completely dejected tone.

"Awww, Rand. I'm so sorry that had to happen. Maybe it's just for a short time though. Maybe they'll bring you back up right away?" she told me encouragingly.

"It doesn't sound like it. They really didn't tell me anything, except that I wasn't good enough to play Triple AAA. And, I can't understand why for the life of me. I pitched good last year at this level, and I've been unhittable all spring training," I continued my sob story.

"I wanted to call you and offer my support and tell you how proud of you I am. Sheryl told me you were doing so good. I also wanted to keep you up to date on what's been happening at this end. But, maybe I'd better leave that till another time," Connie explained, and then I cut her off.

"No. I wanna hear what's goin' on. Tell me what's happenin'," I replied impatiently.

"Well, okay. But, it's pretty ugly. Are you sure you wanna hear it now? It can wait," she asked me apologetically.

"I do wanna hear it, Con. You've got a lot more problems than I have, and I wanna help any way I can," I told her reassuringly.

"Don't be too shocked when I tell you all this, 'cause it's pretty revolting," Connie warned me again.

"Don't worry about it. Just tell me," I ordered her more firmly this time.

"Okay. But, you gotta promise me you won't talk till I'm done. I wanna get it all out before I break down. Okay?" she stipulated frankly.

"Okay. I'll shut up now," I promised her.

"When you dropped me off at Dad's and went south, a lotta things started to happen real fast. First, you need ta be really proud of Dad for handlin' it the way he did. He didn't fly off the handle and go kill Kane right away either. And, he sat and heard me out without getting mad at me. It surprised me, but he took it well. I forgot to tell you, but it was Dad and Della's anniversary, and they were on their way out the door to celebrate when I called them from the restaurant. But, they came right away anyways. I'm proud of both of them for helpin' me the way they did.

"Anyway, the welfare kicked in some support right away, and they found me a decent apartment in Kamloops. Then, they asked me who Brandon's father was so they could go after him for child support. I told them I didn't wanna have to go to court, because I didn't wanna ever have ta face Kane or Mom ever again. But, they said I would probably have ta if I was going to be able to get any money. I hesitated about pursuing anything then, but then I decided I wanted Kane to publicly admit what he did to me and to take responsibility for all of it. But, at the same time, I didn't want him to have visiting rights. Besides that, I had no job and no money. I had no choice.

"When I told the welfare lady, she put me onto their lawyer. When I talked to him, he told me I probably wouldn't be able to charge Kane with rape, but I should take a paternity test to prove to the court that Kane really is Brandon's father. So, I did. And, they made Kane take one too. And, a week ago, it all came to a head. I went to court and they put me on the stand. Kane and Mom sat on the other side. Mom tried to get my attention, but I ignored her. I wouldn't look at either one of them. I ended up spillin' the whole thing in front of God and everybody. When I got done, Kane's probation officer got up on the stand and told the judge that Kane had confided in him that he was Brandon's father.

"You won't believe what happened then when they put Mom on the stand. That was the first time that I was able to look at her, and when she sat down, we locked eyes. But, when she swore on the Bible she would tell the truth, and then she started talkin', my mouth dropped to the floor. She stared right at me and told the whole room that I wasn't nothin' but a nasty little whore. She said I ran around and slept with anything in pants. I partied and got drunk all the time and that's how I got pregnant. Randy, our mother did that. When she got off, they put Kane up there. But, I guess the judge had heard enough, because he started to beat on Kane like a bongo drum. The first thing he revealed was Kane's positive paternity test results. Then, the judge let 'im have it with both barrels and ended by apologizing to me. He said he was sorry that the six-year statute of limitations had expired, and he couldn't award me any paternity compensation because of it. However, he did say, in his heart, he believed my story and not his. And, I was really happy

Mom and Kane had to take responsibility even though I didn't get any monetary support.

"When we all left the courtroom, it turned out we were both parked in the alleyway behind the courthouse. I had my friend's car cranked up going down the alley when Mom and Kane came around the corner. I was really tempted for a minute to run 'em both over and leave 'em as road kill, but I just smiled and waved to them instead.

"Well. Wattaya think about all that?" Connie asked me inquisitively.

"None of it really surprises me at all, Con. After she left me at the winda, and then she didn't do nothin' about Kane rapin' and molestin' you, then she married that animal anyway, nothin' would surprise me. I wouldn't blame ya if ya never saw or spoke to her again. I prob'ly won't after all this on top of everything else," I told Connie brusquely.

Connie and I talked for a while longer, and after she tried to offer some words of encouragement to me about my baseball, we hung up. I perceived she was happy to able to talk to me and share her terrible experience, but the news drove me deeper into my funk. The world seemed to be ganging up on me again, and the only thing I could think of was to call Sheryl. Maybe she could take my pain away, I thought, as I drained the rest of my beer.

"Hi, Sheryl," I said, without my usual enthusiasm when she picked up.

"Hi, Randy. I was hopin' you'd call," she responded affectionately.

"I couldn't wait to talk to you either. But, I have some bad news," I told her openly.

I needed a loving shoulder to cry on. There was no one else I felt I could call or talk to. Sheryl was it. I knew if I called any of my people back home, they wouldn't understand the magnitude of my misery for sure. They had to get up every morning around three or four or five and toil physically in their logging world and harsh Canadian elements of nature. My life was definitely more lenient, and me whining to them about being sent down to a lower level of professional baseball would be totally inappropriate, to say the least. Anything professional carried an incredibly higher social status in their eyes, so calling them was taboo. I was considered successful and blessed and privileged. So, there was no consolation for me with any of them.

My friends would have willingly lent me an ear or a shoulder to cry on. But ultimately, I was expected to suck it up. I was expected to battle back in the face of adversity like they and I had always done throughout our lives and stop bleating like a lost sheep. Getting back on the bucking bronco and riding that sucker was the only way to handle life's disappointments.

"What happened? Are you alright?" Sheryl asked me compassionately.

"Yeah. I'm okay. I'm just depressed. They're sending me down. I can't believe it. I've been pitchin' awesome. My numbers show I'm the third best on the team throughout all of spring training," I explained confusedly.

"Randy. I know it must be hard for you, but you are only twenty-two, and you've only played as a pro for a short time. You'll get your chance. You just can't give up," she told me encouragingly.

In fact, just those few words turned me around. Sheryl's bit of wisdom made me see the forest for the trees. To make a long story short, I talked to Sheryl for a little while longer and continued to get re-fired the longer we talked. And, her support ultimately caused me to find my confidence all over again. In fact, I willingly accepted my demotion, and I dominated whenever I pitched for my new team for the next two months solid.

Tragically though, my coaches or Toronto's suits or scouts would never talk to me about their plans for me. My coaches always said they didn't know what the head office had in mind for me. Their job was only to write their reports and recommendations to their superiors. They didn't make the decisions for Toronto's organization. When the big shots blessed us with their royal presence, they were clammed tighter than a welded hull plate in a United States military destroyer. They would hardly talk to me at all, and when they did, it was only when I hunted them down on the field or at the hotel. All they said was to keep working hard. That's it.

Consequently, I snapped. I made up my mind to quit. No questions. No advise. No nothing. I just quit.

However, I first proceeded to throw three innings of shutout ball with six strikeouts, one soft dinker hit, and no walks in front of about 5,000 fans that night. Then, I taxied back to the hotel after the game and packed. I flew back to California the next morning. I didn't say goodbye. I didn't tell anyone. I didn't care. I was going home to start a real life, and I was hoping it was going to be with Sheryl. I was going to become a cop, and I was going to apply the same passion I had for baseball and hockey to my police work. And, I was going to be a great father, husband, and provider for my family. Toronto, baseball, and fame and fortune could kiss my rosy red rear. They could keep their money. They could keep their royal lifestyle. They could keep their suits. They could keep their lips zipped when some impassioned, hard-working young man asked or needed just a little communication and respect to save him. Randy Wiens was going home.

I didn't call Sheryl to tell her of my decision to quit. It was the first day I didn't call her since I left for spring training, and I knew she would be worrying and wondering why. But, I wanted to surprise her. I wanted to show up on her doorstep and ask her to marry me. I wanted to tell her that she wouldn't be marrying a pro baseball player, but she would be getting the hardest working, affectionate, and loving man she could ever imagine. I would take care of her and our future kids forever, and I would protect all of them from life's monsters. I would always be faithful and true, and no one would ever hurt her if I had anything to do about it.

Well, my surprise and proposal speech didn't work like I planned. Sheryl was totally shocked to see me waiting at her house on her doorstep after school for one thing. And, after I finished my passionate and tender request for her hand, she wanted the floor.

"Of course I'll marry you, but I wasn't planning to do it now. I was gonna spend the summer with you, then I was hopin' we could get married in the fall after baseball," she told me in a disappointed tone. It was obvious she was stunned about me quitting so abruptly and showing up on her doorstep out of the blue like I did.

"Sheryl. I want you to be my wife. Everything will work out. Baseball isn't the only thing in the world," I said encouragingly, trying to convince Sheryl I was doing the right thing.

"But, Randy. You are so good. And, everybody knows it. You just can't throw your chance away like this," she pleaded with me.

"But, they don't think I'm a big league prospect. If they did, I'd still be playin' Triple AAA. And, they'd talk to me about it. All they do is snub me when I try ta talk ta them about my future,' I complained to Sheryl, as she listened patiently and empathetically. She hugged me hard in her support. It was obvious she sensed my frustration and disillusioned spirit about my baseball.

"I don't believe that. Why would they promote you to Triple AAA from Single A last year to begin with if they didn't think you were a major league prospect? Plus, you are only twenty-two. Most guys don't get to the Majors till they're twenty-five or older. I bet they do have plans for you, but it's their policy to not talk to you about it till they feel you are ready," she continued, trying to reason with my dejected will.

"I wanna life now Sheryl. I can't play games like that. I've worked too hard to still be in limbo. I've been a gypsy all my life, and I still don't know what's happenin', I vented, as Sheryl listened intently. However, it was pretty clear she wasn't going to give up without a fight.

"Look. Randy. I love you very, very much. I want to be your wife. I want kids. I want to be happy with you forever. But, I also know you well enough that you just can't quit like that and be happy. It'll haunt you for the rest of your life," Sheryl continued to debate my irrational behavior and mindset.

Regrettably, I had my mind made up. It didn't matter what she said. I refused to go back.

"No. It won't. I can go to the police academy and be a cop. That's what I always wanted to do if I didn't make it in baseball or hockey anyway. I just don't wanna fight it anymore. I need you in my life now. I wanna have a real family and a new life now. Not down the road somewhere in fantasyland. It's time for me to accept that I'm just a regular guy. I'll work hard for my family and we'll all have a good life," I told Sheryl stubbornly.

"But, you can still have it all, Randy. I'll support you 100 percent. You don't have ta worry about money or me or anything. If you go back now, we'll talk morning and night, I'll love you and encourage you and show my unconditional support, and I'll be by your side in a month when I'm done with school for the summer. We can get married in the fall, and we can start a family. I'm ready for a real family and a real life too. I want it all as much as you do. But, don't throw your chance away. It's a once-in-a-lifetime opportunity. You're too good to give up so soon. If you don't make it, say in three more years, then quit. But, now you have too much to lose. Besides all that, I know being a cop won't hold you. You need more than that," Sheryl spoke unrelentingly.

Sadly, I knew she was probably right. Plus, I really began to understand Sheryl's true character in the process. She barely knew me, but she was willing to sell her soul for me and support me unconditionally on a whim. And, that made me yearn for her hand, and marriage, and a family, and a real life even more.

Simultaneously though, I despised the frightening and contemptible thought of flying off into the wild blue yonder alone again. Loneliness, and a lack of a sense of belonging anywhere, had haunted me since I was a kid. I just couldn't muster the courage or emotional strength to do it. Sheryl was there in California. I believed my only real future was with her—right there—right then—forever. Everyone, and everything else, could take a long walk off a short pier, I thought.

"Sheryl. That's not what I want anymore. I don't wanna wait for happiness anymore. I need it now. I hope you will still love me and you won't be disappointed, but I made up my mind I'm not goin' back. I will give you all I got right here, and then some, if you give me the chance," I pleaded, and I hugged her affectionately and kissed her softly to show her my love.

CHAPTER 16

Tainted

Sheryl and I were married two months later. We went on our two-night, three-day honeymoon, and Sheryl got pregnant with Ranger, our first child, during that short time. I entered the police academy to become a cop a few weeks later, but she never gave up her case about me going back to professional baseball the whole time. She wouldn't hound me about it. But every time I would perform athletically in the community in baseball, or hockey, or tennis, or basketball, or any other sport we got involved in, she would lovingly whisper in my ear that I could still be a big league baseball player any time I wanted to be. On top of all that, if I ever decided to quit my job to go back to baseball, she assured me that she would support my decision 100 percent, no questions asked. That was Sheryl for you.

My mule-headed brain wouldn't be convinced though, so we continued on. We had three kids in the next five years with two miscarriages in between. We coached, watched, and supported our kids, who all played in three sports each year. And we provided a pretty good lifestyle for them. We were both excellent athletes and strong competitors ourselves, and we battled each other in tennis, ping-pong, racquetball, basketball, golf, roller hockey, and most other sports every waking moment. However, that was only when we could squeeze time from chasing, delivering, picking up, or following our kids for some sport or church or school activity.

I got involved with her church for a while, but I decided it wasn't for me after about six months. To my disliking, church had too many rules, too many regulations, and too much control over my life. On Sunday, hunting, fishing, cutting wood, or playing with my kids in the ways I wanted weren't allowed. Sunday was time for church, and that stuck in my craw.

Church also demanded too much accountability. And for me, I liked to drink and party. I liked to cuss when I felt like it. I like to share off-color jokes with my friends. I wanted to do things other than church on Sunday. And above all, I didn't want anyone to bug me about it. There was no way I needed God in my life anyway. I felt I had survived a few hundred pretty horrible experiences in my life without him. Accordingly, in my mind, religion was simply a crutch for those who weren't mentally tough enough to make it on their own. They needed someone or something to lean on in times of trouble. My nurturing taught me that I had to be mentally and physically tough enough to handle life's monsters on my own without help from others. That was mainly because I learned repeatedly from countless personal experiences that I couldn't count on others to help me when I needed it most, like my childhood abandonment, and the moral and financial support I was desperate for during my college and professional baseball careers, for example. Unfortunately, that is what I believed. Sure, I was always fascinated by the stories I learned in Sunday school when I was a kid about Jonah and the Whale, David and Goliath, and the parting of the Red Sea. But they were just cool stories to me. Religion and God never fit in to my mind as important or necessary entities.

You see? I was tainted meat by the time I got to Sheryl. My head wasn't right psychologically. Being on my own for so long had perverted my mind. I had been able to do whatever I wanted to do, whenever I wanted to do it. I had no chains, no rules, and I was sure not interested in violating my own interests. I liked my independence too much, and I didn't want to relinquish it to anyone or anything. Sure. I wanted and needed Sheryl and a family desperately. But, I had no clue that my marriage would demand a radical change in every way I thought and acted. So I threw my nose up at Sheryl and almost every decent thing she believed in. I did my own thing no matter what she said or did. No one could make me realize and understand my dysfunctional behavior and mindset.

As a sad result, Sheryl and I began to argue about everything. For example, I wanted to keep drinking beer and blow off church. I didn't drink a lot when we first got married, but I enjoyed a cold sud after a game, to celebrate, at a social function, or just because. But Sheryl hated any part of alcohol, and she despised my participation in drinking because it symbolized the fact that I broke my promise to her about living clean and righteously when we got married. Because of Sheryl's inflexibility in the matter, I became more obstinate about almost everything in our relationship too. I even started to think she was just trying to control my life completely. So I demanded that she allow me to keep the fridge stocked with cold ones to drink whenever I wanted to, or to offer our company when they came around. But Sheryl wouldn't stand for it. Every time I imbibed, she would climb my frame with all guns blazing. If I bought alcohol and brought it home, she would dump it down the sink when I wasn't looking. Of course, that riled me. I fought back by drinking more and more often.

The same kind of fracas occurred when I wanted Sheryl, the kids, or all of them to skip church on Sunday, or a church function during the week, to do something fun with me like go hunting, fishing, camping, traveling, or just playing in the cul-de-sac in front of our house. But, no. Sheryl demanded that Sunday was for church, and everything had to be altered to attend church functions.

However, the reality was that my blame game was totally erroneous. In other words, Sheryl's religious beliefs were not to blame in the slightest. I was. I was angry constantly. I blamed everyone and everything for my childhood and my failure in baseball, and it seemed that nothing besides playing in the Bigs could ever quell the rage and injustice in my mind because I didn't make it in baseball all the way. Although I always had great jobs with above-average pay and benefits, and always rose to the top of the food chain in them at warp speed, I was never satisfied. I

304 • Now I Know Who I Am

always wanted more. But I could never put my finger on the buttons of wisdom and understanding in order to find out what it was until it was too late. Sheryl had the intelligence and wisdom the whole time, but I was too prideful and egotistical to let her guide and direct me. She should have been able to communicate her wisdom to me like a harmoniously yoked mate is supposed to be able to do peacefully without constant ridicule or reproach. But, I was too isolated in my irrational thinking. No one knew anything important but me.

Consequently, my emotional peace was simply out of the question. It was forever lost in some remote orbit somewhere, and I had no idea how to capture its illusiveness. Sheryl tried constantly to make me realize that God and his son, Jesus Christ were the only painters of the path to righteousness and internal peace, but I ridiculed that idea whenever she brought it up. And I blamed it on her weakness.

In the midst of the doom and gloom that I mostly only imagined in my marriage, Sheryl and I vacationed to Canada when Ranger was nine, Kodi was seven, and Logan was three. During that trip, we had a great time. It was during the winter break from school, and because Canada offers some of the best winter wonderland sports activities known to mankind anywhere in the world, we rejoiced in the great outdoors. We played ice hockey on a makeshift rink we scraped off, we snowmobiled with some of my old friends, and we tobogganed the days away in laughter and merriment. We ice-fished, had snowball fights, and we built raging bonfires outside to warm our frozen toes and hands whenever we felt like it. I was truly in heaven, and I even started to feel like it was the beginning to the fantasy life I had always only dreamed about. Sheryl was loving and affectionate, and Ranger and Kodi seemed like they couldn't get enough of the world I had left behind thirteen years earlier to start my baseball career in college.

I was truly in hog heaven during the first part of that trip. I am sad to say that my elation, as well as Sheryl's, was short-lived though. About a week or so into our fantasy vacation, Darryl, my brother, drove the few hundred miles from where he lived up in northern British Columbia to visit with my tribe and me. He had never seen Logan, and it had been several years since he had seen Ranger and Kodi. So, he decided to make the trip down to Kamloops where we were all staying with Connie, our sister. To make a long story short, Darryl didn't really come for a pleasure cruise just to visit. He came to spill his guts all over the floor of Connie's front room.

"I have something I have to tell you guys," he stated hesitantly, after about a minute of hugs and greetings.

Darryl was obviously gravely concerned about something on his mind, because the tormented look on his face was out of character for him. Usually, he was happy and jovial and always ready with a crack-me-up joke of some sort. But, not this time.

"What are ya talkin' about?" I asked Darryl questioningly, as Connie and Sheryl's ears perked up concernedly at the same time as we all lounged and yacked on Connie's couches.

"I gotta get somethin' off my chest," he kind of stammered, as his eyes hit the deck forlornly. He was totally embarrassed, and I knew right away it was something very serious. Darryl was never a drama queen, and when he turned solemn about anything, it was usually grave.

"Whatever it is, we're here for ya Darryl," Connie chirped in lovingly just then.

"Good. Cause I really need your support right now," he said pitifully.

"Connie's right. We're behind you. And whatever it is, we'll help you through it," Sheryl agreed with Connie's understanding, while I nodded my approval at the same time.

"Before I start, I need you guys to hear me out without interruptin'. This'll be hard enough as it is without comments from the peanut gallery. OK?" Darryl requested, pleadingly.

Connie, Sheryl, and I all nodded our willingness to let Darryl talk until he was done. And, it didn't take long for us all to learn why he was being so dramatic either.

"Well, I guess I'll start by saying that my life has been a livin' hell since you moved out, Connie. The day you took off, Kane came after me every day for sex. I was only seven," Darryl said matter-of-factly, as his eyes stayed glued to the carpet and the awful words spilled forth.

Darryl no sooner finished his second sentence when Connie and Sheryl gasped their horror, and I cut him off.

"What? You gotta be kiddin'!" I blurted out angrily.

At that precise moment, I wanted to rip Kane's head off. But he had already died from a heart attack several years before. All I could think of then was to get on the horn to blast Mom for letting Kane get to Darryl. Connie's deal was horrible enough.

"Look. I told you I needed some space to get this out. Can you hold your horses till I'm done? Please?" Darryl pleaded again, and I obliged him, even though I could feel and smell the smoke billowing from my ears while Connie and Sheryl cringed in their seats.

"It all started one day while Mom was workin' like usual. And as usual, Kane was at home and not workin'. When I came home on the bus from school this one day, he ordered me to come into his bedroom when he heard me slam the side door to the fifth-wheel trailer we were livin' in at the time. I didn't think he was home, but when I heard him yell at me when I came in, I thought he was just going to scream at me for slammin' the door, or somethin' stupid like that, like he always did. Anyways, when I got down the short hall to his room, he immediately ordered me to take my pants off. I couldn't figure out what he meant right away, and when I just stood there without movin', he got up from the bed impatiently. I was scared, because he had this strange look on his face, a look I never saw on 'im before. When he stood up, he hesitated for a split second while he studied the confused look on my face, then he took the two steps toward me really fast and bent over in front of me. For a split second, I thought he was just pickin' somethin' up off the carpet. But, I was wrong. He grabbed onto my pants from the sides and half ripped them off me. I yelled at him to stop, but he manhandled me into a doggy-style position over the bed while he dropped his drawers in the same move. I hadn't grown up to defend myself, so basically, he had his way with me without too much of a struggle at all. I couldn't move under his power, and all I could do was to grunt and sob every time he penetrated me.

"It seemed to be over with in a few seconds, but by that time, I thought I was about to die from the pain. I never felt anything that excruciating ever before. Anyways, when he finished, he pulled his pants back up and walked outside. He never said anything at all, and all I could do was lie on the bed in pain and totally confused about what had just happened and why.

"Kane was gone somewhere when Mom got home from work a little later, and right away, she saw that I was distressed about somethin'. When she asked me what my problem was, I told her that Kane put his do-do in my bum. When Mom heard my words, she just sat stupefied for several minutes without saying anything. She blew the whole thing off a little later by saying something like it didn't really happen, or it was only my imagination, or something that sounded really stupid to me. Of course to me, it was all true. But, I couldn't figure out why Mom wouldn't come to my rescue. I needed her to save me from the animal. But, she didn't.

"I heard them scream at each other from their room half the night till I finally fell asleep completely exhausted from all the trauma. The next thing I knew, it was morning. Mom woke me up for school like nothin' happened, and life went on. I figured Kane's daily attack on my back end, and his constant orders to give him oral sex, were all part of life for several years after that first episode. Mom didn't do anything about it, and I wasn't old enough to know the difference. After awhile, Kane started to get worried about me snitchin' him off at school. I could tell he was stressin' because he threatened to kill me and Mom if I ever told anybody about what he made me do. By that time, I was old enough to know what he did every day was wrong, but I was too scared to tell anyone. Besides all that, he would knock me around like a beach ball almost daily. He ordered me around like I was his private slave. I hated him more every second.

"By the time I was twelve, I had murder on my mind. I tried to figure how I could kill him when nobody was around. I thought I could hit him over the head with his own ball-peen hammer while he napped in the afternoon like he always did. When he stopped kickin', I thought I could drag him outside and bury him out in the neighbor's cow pasture that ran close to where the trailer was parked. There were no houses or people or roads within screaming distance or view from the trailer, so I started to figure I might be able to pull it off. But, I didn't. I just put up with his abuse for a couple more years.

"For seven years, I was his sex slave. In the meantime, we moved a dozen times. It seemed Kane worked a few days here and there, but he would always be fired or quit, and we'd move again. We were gypsies, and I could never seem to make any friends. Every time I would find a buddy, we would move again. If we did happen to be in one place long enough, I still would be too scared to bring my friend home. I was afraid Kane would come after me in front of my friend, or he would go after my friend and make me watch. So, if I did invite a buddy over, I made sure the animal was gone.

"When I was about 14, we finally moved into a nice house with a few acres of property, and I started to think about killin' Kane again. We were a long way from our nearest neighbor, and I figured I had plenty of land to bury him on. This time though, I had a different idea on how I was gonna do it. I thought I'd just give him a good whack with the hammer and just stun him. While he was dazed, I'd tie him up real good and drag him out to the big hangin' tree in the huge back yard we had by the small pond. I'd throw a rope over the largest branch about eight feet off the ground, tie a noose around his neck, and hoist him up so his feet just barely touched the ground enough so he wouldn't suffocate too fast. Then, I would go to work on 'im with my friend's moose-guttin' knife that he forgot at my house when we were whittlin a few days before.

"To my great surprise, just when I was about to make him pay for what he did to me, he stopped comin' after me. I was stunned at first, then I began to think that maybe he finally wised up and he realized I was getting too big and strong for him to manhandle anymore. However, I didn't care at that point. I was so happy. I ran everywhere. I bounced around laughing and giggling, and I jumped up and down for joy every five minutes. For obvious reasons though, I only celebrated when he wasn't looking.

"A month later, Kane died. He croaked. He ceased to exist. His fat disgusting whale body had a massive heart attack one day when Mom had gone to camp for a two-week stint in the bush to cook for her railroad crew. I found his stinkin' dead carcass when I came home from school one day deader than a doornail. Naturally, I felt cheated by the injustice of it all, but he was dead all the same. I was so happy about the prospect of livin' life without that animal around that I couldn't wait to call Mom at work and tell her the good—er—the bad news. When I tracked her down through the complicated CB and portable radio systems the railroad had to reach the deep bush area Mom was working in, she only cried briefly. The next thing I knew, she was home.

"We lived pretty happily till I moved out at eighteen. Then, she pulled up stakes and moved to Kamloops. And, basically, that's my story. It's been eatin' at me for years, and I couldn't keep it a secret anymore," Darryl finally finished his repulsive story, while all of our mouths seemed to hang open in mid air.

We were all stupefied at his entire experience. Connie, Sheryl, and I looked back and forth at each other without saying anything for quite some time before I took the bull by the horns. I got up from my couch position and went to sit by my brother. I put my arm around him. I just started talking to him encouragingly. I tried to make him understand that whatever monsters ever came his way again for the rest of his life, we would be there to save him. Connie and Sheryl all gathered around and offered their tears and hugs and support too, and we all cried together with Darryl for several minutes. Then, it was done. We never talked about again. What could be said anyway? The monster had struck. The monster was dead. All we could do was to vow to love and care for each other unconditionally from that point on forever. That's it.

Sheryl, the kids and I hit the road back to California a few days later. My anger grew dramatically the more I thought about Darryl and how Mom had violated his trust so appallingly. But mostly, I worried about the atrocities Darryl and Connie had to endure for so long. I was deeply troubled as to how their minds were really able to endure those horrible memories. I knew for sure they were haunting them daily. I could see it in their eyes, and I understood their pain.

It was all so mind-boggling. As I continued to drive, I began to feel guilty that I was spared the brutality, the rapings, and the vile molestations. I figured that, if Mom didn't leave me there at the window that fateful day, I would have been able to save my brother and sister from Kane, the monster. I would have gutted him for sure if he ever touched any of us. Jail or no jail, I would have fixed him good. I wouldn't have endured one second of his lustcapades.

My anger about everything in general didn't wane for the rest of the twenty-two years Sheryl and I were married. Consequently, we were only able to function as a strong and happy family was supposed to for short periods. My deformed mind seemed to always drive our boat back onto the rocks and ruin our peaceful times.

One of the disgusting consequences of my anger took a great toll on my relationship with my kids. I constantly put too much pressure on them to always be the best. I loved them and supported them in everything they endeavored to do, but I always had my size thirteen on their necks. I would rarely let them up for air, and I would take my frustration and disgust with my own life out on them. I never beat them or physically abused them like my dad had done to me, but my angry demeanor always kept them at a distance.

At the time though, I thought I was teaching them all how to be tough and hard like I had become. I believed that life was tough and then you die. Because of that misguided philosophy, I felt my kids had to be hardened like me to survive out in the real world after their silver spoon was tarnished. But, I couldn't have been more wrong. My way drove my kids away. Sure, they all loved me and cared for me. But, my gnarly attitude kept them from seeking me out for advice, or love, or just a hug because they felt like it. But, I couldn't see it. Sheryl tried to explain it to me a million times, but I always told her she was full of nonsense.

Consequently, it was natural that they never seemed to feel or know my real love for them. I was always too intense. I rarely provided them with a feeling of peace. I rarely offered them a safe haven where they could come and plop their little heads on my lap and feel secure. Simply, they didn't perceive me as being approachable enough even to just yack about their day or their everyday troubles. Why? Because I was too wrapped up in my own selfishness. I didn't realize my gruff nature drove them away, instead of my mercy and grace drawing them to my breast in unconditional love.

As far as my social behavior, I always burned with a short fuse. In other words, I would fight at the drop of a hat, and I didn't care who or how many of them there were. I just didn't care. I learned early in life that, if I showed any physical or emotional weakness at all, there was always a pack of wolves ready to chomp on my fresh meat. So, I stayed on guard and rarely allowed anyone to gain the upper hand.

Unfortunately though, for the first time in my life, I got too drunk to defend myself appropriately in a bar one night. A busted bridge and a shattered nose later, I woke up bleeding profusely from several areas of my face. In my drunken stupor, I didn't even remember what had happened. The real story was that I was playing pool in the bar like I usually did the last few years of my marriage. I started yapping to a young bull about how he cheated on a shot he failed to call. He challenged me. I accepted. He beat me to a pulp. I don't remember any of it.

That was a huge wake up call for me. That is when I realized I had a drinking problem. Never before had I gotten to the point where I couldn't take care of business in the bar, in hockey, or anywhere else for that matter. But, not that time. The bar beating made me realize that I better start making some changes in my lifestyle and find my pleasure and entertainment somewhere other than in a drinking establishment. Sadly, it never dawned on me until it was too late that my pleasure was always waiting patiently at home, loyal and faithful as always. That's right. Sheryl was at home. My kids were at home. I was out—out to lunch.

A few years before my thorough thrashing in the bar, I got the brilliant idea to become a teacher like Sheryl had been for over twenty years already. I figured that if I became a teacher too, our family could enjoy more time together and maybe travel to Canada more often and spend more time with my family and friends up there during summers off. At the same time, I felt that we all lived in a concrete jungle in California, and I blamed a lot of my anger on the fact that all of my family was missing out on a real life that only Canada could provide.

So, I did become a teacher. And, Sheryl willingly and enthusiastically supported me when I quit my job. She encouraged me constantly, and she told me daily she was proud of me for all of my hard work and my determination to become a teacher.

With Sheryl backing that move, I tore into my studies like a mad tornado. All I did was read, write, eat, and sleep for a year and a half. I averaged a book and a paper a day earning my English degree during that time. But, I couldn't have accomplished any of it without Sheryl's undying devotion and hard work too. She worked full-time at her job. She took care of the kids and all their transportation needs to their sports and activities. She took care of the house. She took care of me and helped me by typing all of my papers.

You see? I am a hen-pecker. And, in order for me to finish typing anything, I need a month of Sundays. I ended up earning a BA degree in English, and I became a very good teacher in a very short time. But, there was no chance in a million years that I would have accomplished my goal without Sheryl's efforts, love, and support.

Sickeningly though, the teaching profession couldn't hold me either. I was still angry, and teaching also offered me more time to reflect about everything due to the easier working conditions than I was accustomed to. Before teaching came along, I worked nights and weekends and all hours of the day and night to bring home the bacon. Those working conditions added even more fuel to my fire of frustration and anger. Teaching provided daytime working hours for the first time since baseball, as well as shorter working days, all the holidays off, and the long summer vacations. Consequently, I had too much time on my hands. And sadly, I made all the wrong choices in utilizing my new abundance of time. Stupidly, I became infatuated with the bar scene and spent my afternoons and evenings in them instead of being home with my family. And, I chased women, even though I was married.

Sadly, I didn't respect Sheryl, my kids, or my job like I should have. And, I didn't respect myself. Instead of taking advantage of my cushy job and the time off it provided to repair and build a strong home life, I ran to Canada for several summers and blamed Sheryl for destroying our marriage because she didn't love me enough to spend two or three months at a time up in Canada with me. The reality was that all the kids had summer all-star teams they wanted to play on. Sheryl was willing to come to Canada for a few weeks, but not for the entire summer and take the kids away from their obligations to their sports teams. And, like all mothers, her argument was always that they needed her at home. Home was where I belonged too, but I was too selfish to see any of it. All I could see was the next bar I could find and the next pool game to conquer.

The next thing I knew, I was going to Canada alone with my dog, Rascal, for the summers, while Sheryl stayed home with the kids. Naturally, I continued to blame our marital and family dysfunction on Sheryl, her religion, and everything else I could conjure up in my stupid brain in order to justify my solo treks to the great white north. Eventually, divorce was all that was left. The next thing I knew, we split the sheets for good. I moved into the proverbial apartment.

However, filing for divorce from Sheryl after twenty-two years of marriage failed to bring me the peace or happiness I felt I had been missing my whole life. It didn't wake me up from my forty-four-year sleep of ignorance, selfishness, and arrogance. It didn't keep me out of the bar. Meeting Karyn was a turning point, but I still wallowed in the same boiling soup. The headlights of reality only switched on when I held Sheryl's dying head in my hands, helpless to save her from her life's only monster. Me.

Before the accident, nothing Sheryl did or said had helped me or convinced me to change my ways, my thoughts, or my mindset. I was too stubborn. I was too selfish. And, I still blamed others for everything. I took responsibility for my actions and willingly accepted the consequences for the decisions I made, but I didn't understand that my actions and choices were mostly wrong and often hurt people. I thought my ways were the right ways, and I believed everyone else was screwed up and misled.

Sheryl had talked to me a zillion times. She had some church people talk to me. She had members of her family talk to me. She even had my own friends talk to me. Her main purpose in all of it was to try to make me understand that no human can deal with life's stresses and horrors on his own, including me. Every human needs help from someone or something for emotional survival. For Sheryl, that savior was God. She believed with her mind, body, heart, and soul that, only by accepting God into my heart unconditionally, could I find inner peace. But, I never listened. I denied him, again and again.

It naturally followed that I continued down that bad road of pernicious thinking and behavior. It ended in the filing of our divorce after twenty-two years of Sheryl's efforts to break through my thick skull.

When I made the final decision to divorce Sheryl, I tried to convince her that there was no way in the world it was ever going to work between us. She had too many problems that I could no longer deal with. But, in reality, I was the one with the problems. Sheryl wasn't perfect, but I was the one who caused the turmoil and stress in our home. I forced issues upon every member of my family. I was the one who had poor behavior and the miscreant character. But, I still blamed it all on her. I couldn't see the forest for the trees. My way was the right way only.

When I forced the divorce issue and moved out, Sheryl still tried to make me understand that if we could just get back together and try it again, she would make the changes I wanted. Out of her love for me, she was willing to compromise her standards. After twenty-two years, she realized that was the only way she could hold me, or even get me back at all. But, I was too stubborn. It was too late to fix what I thought was too broken for any mending to work. In my mind, we were just too different.

Several months after the filing, it was getting close to the actual finalizing date for the divorce. Sheryl called me one day and pleaded with me to go away with her for a long weekend coming up. She told me she was going to prove to me that she could be the woman that I always wanted her to be. But, I was stubborn. I said no. I said no for days and days. The next thing I knew though, I began to capitulate. I did have a conscience, and I began to feel an utter respect for her love and loyalty during all the years of sadness I had caused her. I figured if I just went away with her for one last weekend, she would finally realize that I couldn't provide her with the happiness she craved and deserved.

Consequently, I reasoned that I would go with Sheryl one last time under the cloak of a three-fold purpose. The first was out of respect for Sheryl for all that she had given me for so long. The second was closure for me. But, the third was a little more malicious. I felt I had to force the closure so Sheryl wouldn't want to be with me anymore. I conspired to be cold, uncaring, and unemotional to her throughout our trip. I never planned to ever hurt her physically, but verbally, I planned to snub her advances, to communicate sarcastically when we talked, and basically, to try to make her understand that I had nothing good left for her. I wanted closure. It was time to split the sheets once and for all. Finally, we agreed on the whole concept towards the end of our trip, a few minutes before we crashed.

We were in the truck in the middle of the night coming home. Earlier that night, I took Sheryl to a bar so I could drink and play pool. I drank too much to drive legally or safely. I ended up holding Sheryl's head in my hands while the rest of her slowly crushed to death. The cops came. She died. I went to jail. I got bailed out. I went to court. I got sentenced. I went to prison. Only then did I start realizing and understanding how badly I miscalculated, how badly I misjudged, how horrible my behavior, thoughts, and mindsets really were. I was one sick puppy. That was when I started making changes. That is when my transformation began.

Going to prison was the first baby step down the road to that mental reconstruction. This is difficult to admit, but I had to go to prison. I needed to go to prison. The horrifying nature of prison was my only salvation. God knew that. He knew I could never begin my climb back into the acceptable behavioral realms of society and humanity without first experiencing the hideousness of prison. Only by doing so could I ever truly understand how tainted my mind really was. Only when I lived with those animals and other miscreants of humanity could I understand that I had become one of them on the outside. Only by living with them, eating with them, sleeping a few feet away from them, and sharing their daily lives with them, could I ever begin to figure that maybe, just maybe, I was the jerk and the idiot and the fool, and not everyone else in humanity. Well, God was right. He nailed it. Then he nailed me. And there I sat. I was in prison with nothing but wicked memories to churn in my mind. It was like a bad broken record that no human could pull the plug on to stop it.

CHAPTER 17

Back to Reality

Thinking about my mom and dad, Connie and Darryl, baseball, hockey, Sheryl and the kids, and all the rest so pro-foundly, I had to escape back to prison from time to time. My mind couldn't take the abuse. I relived all of it over and over and over. But, returning from my past wasn't always caused by my slaughtered brain and bad memories either. Sometimes, it was due to the ongoing bloodshed and the harsh realities that were traditional in prison life. For example, I was deep in thought one day while I walked to the shower at the end of my tier at Folsom. Even though I noticed the shower curtain was closed, I couldn't hear the water running. So, I assumed it was all a go for me.

However, when I reached the shower and pulled the plastic curtain back, the butchery I witnessed snapped me back to my prison reality. It was extraordinarily grisly too. A naked white supremacist guy was lying in a crumpled, bloody heap in one corner of the four-man shower area. I didn't recognize him personally, but I could tell immediately with whom he was affiliated. He was a Nazi Low Rider just like Ironman was. He was covered in blue and black tattoos depicting the NLR logo. He sported several swastikas of various sizes. And, the three-inch lettered white power insignia was centered on his stomach about belly button high.

His body was flopped lifelessly in one corner of the shower. He was positioned in a half-sitting and half-lying mode on his right side with his chin hanging limp down on his chest area with his head leaning against the wet wall. He was bleeding profusely from his entire left forearm area, and the stream of blood flowed like rich lava out of a freshly blown artery. It poured off his arm down between his legs and disappeared momentarily. It re-emerged from under his left leg and formed into a thick rivulet that finally vanished down the shower drain a few feet away from his obviously dead or dying body.

To me, it looked like the racist guy's entire inside forearm area was chain-sawed. It was mangled that badly. But, as I took a few more steps more towards him and felt his left carotid for a pulse, I noticed that an empty refried bean can, with its decapitated lid lying next to it, was partially hidden behind his back. The edge of the lid had obviously been sharpened into a razor-like slashing tool. It was pretty clear it was the weapon that had carved his arm up; there was a lot of blood and bits of skin and flesh still stuck on it. I knew the can was part of the commissary supplies all inmates had access to. But, I couldn't decipher whether he used the sharpened lid to kick his own bucket, or an enemy of his was trying to make it look like suicide.

Whatever the reason, I didn't hang around worrying about it. I stepped out of the shower area fast-like, and I proceeded to punch the COM button on the wall outside the shower. When the correctional officer answered from his gun tower, I calmly told him that there was a man down in the shower, and he was cut up pretty badly. The cop acknowledged my call by ordering me to hit the deck immediately. He pressed the emergency horn button on his wall simultaneously. And, in seconds, every con on the tier, inside or outside their cells, dove to the cement or onto their bunks in unison. A few more seconds later, a dozen fully armored members of the goon squad poured into our tier from various security doors.

The first goon to reach me lying prone on the floor didn't stop. He continued on into the shower to check out the situation. I didn't hear him call for an EMT, because another goon was barking orders at me as if I had something to do with the hacking. When I told him I found him that way, he seemed to believe me. About a minute later, he confirmed my story. The tower guard radioed him that the cameras revealed no foul play. The white supremacist had tried to kill himself. And, by the looks of things at the time, I figured he just might have pulled it off. I could feel no pulse when I checked him earlier.

When the EMT's exited with the bald supremacist guy, the goons basically cut the rest of us loose. The guards dispatched the inmate designated to handle our tier's janitorial duties to clean the shower right away. Only then was I allowed to shower somewhat peacefully. As I engaged the water though, I wondered if my mind would ever blow to that degree. I wondered if my mind would ever be sick enough to recognize suicide as the only way to a peaceful emotional existence.

Speaking of staying healthy in prison, staying alive is the most pressing concern for a convicted criminal. However, it isn't the only physically frightening aggravation an inmate has to deal with daily. Physical illness runs a very close second. It is dangerous too, because the medical care and treatment is barbaric at best. In other words, if a con isn't in current cardiac arrest, or he doesn't have full-blown AIDS or TB, or he isn't presently experiencing some other death-is-apparent-if-not-treated-immediately condition, the con is left to rot until he is on his deathbed.

I experienced the horrid prison health care system first hand. On top of everything else prison had to offer, I acquired jock itch during my sentence. Under normal conditions back on the street, jock itch was a minor physical irritation that could be taken care of quite simply with a little powder or cream appropriate to the task. And for me, jock itch was routine. It was a regular physical blasphemy on my body every time summer rolled around. I caught it regularly from working out and sweating so much in the blasting heat of the summer. It was only natural that the fungus' curse hunted me down in prison too.

Anyway, when it first hit me, I filled out the appropriate medical-visit form hanging by the base of the gun tower. I commented on it quite strongly to the nurse that the irritating rash the jock itch gave me kept me awake at night. I also stated that I experienced jock itch regularly, and that I just needed him to give me some stuff to take care of it. Then, I dropped it in the little slot by the stack of forms and under the label that read: "If you have a medical concern, fill out the appropriate form correctly and submit it. The nurse is available on Mondays, Wednesdays, and Fridays from 1–4 P.M."

To my utter dismay, it all turned ugly in a week. My jock itch became unbearable. I scratched and rubbed my groin flesh raw with my fingernails. I rubbed it with the course towel I was issued. And, I even tried to pour cold water over it to relieve the burning and itching. But, to no avail. Nothing helped. By the time I filled out the fifth form, and no call came to see the nurse, it was two weeks later. And I was mad. I felt I could have killed all the guards, the nurse, and the doctor right then and there. I couldn't think straight. I couldn't focus on my teaching job. And, the harder I worked out, the more tenacious the fungi attacked my groin and genitals. It felt like a million bugs had taken up roost, and they definitely weren't going down without a huge fight.

Finally, the cops beckoned me to sick call over the loudspeaker one afternoon. Of course, I couldn't take a single step without ravaging my problem with my fingers through my prison getup. My fingers moved automatically too as if they had been hypnotized to perform their normal repetitive function. I probably looked like a pervert to everyone with whom I came in contact, but it didn't really matter much at the time. I was hexed, and my involuntary scratching was out of my hands, and out of my control.

I reached the nurse's office just in time to have to wait another two hours in line. About two-dozen other sickos were sitting and standing in the hallway waiting to see the nurse about their own ailments. I didn't talk to anyone. I couldn't, even if I wanted to. It took all my power just to keep my hands from digging through my clothes, through my outer layers of skin and flesh, and down to the pubic bone. My mind was tricking me into thinking that, if I reached bone, the menacing itch would somehow go away.

When it was my turn finally, I had to face another monster I hadn't anticipated. The Wicked Witch of the West was the medical technician in charge.

"Sit down over there," the nurse hissed at me when I walked into her office. As she growled her order, she motioned me over to a plastic chair by her massive desk littered with inmates' medical records.

"Thank you so much for seeing me. I thought I was going to end up in an insane asylum," I told the nurse affably, trying to break her ice.

"Don't speak unless I ask you a question. I'm not here to make small talk," she snapped at me, as her eyes bolted up at my face from her paperwork.

The oversized female ogre was writing something furiously on a form of some kind, and I figured I had better keep my big fat yap shut. Patience had never been a virtue of mine, but I had no choice under the circumstances. Actually, I was prepared to do anything to get me some stuff for my crotch rot.

"What's your problem?" the gargantuan lady demanded rudely.

"I have a very serious case of jock itch," I said almost pleadingly. In my mind though, I wanted to tear the place apart, snag some powder or cream, and whip my prison drawers down right then and there to apply it. I was that desperate.

"Are you itchy throughout the groin area?" she continued her inquisition without looking at me. Her eyes were pasted on the five forms I had filled out and sent to her over the previous two weeks. I guessed that she had stockpiled them hoping I would give up and quit sending them.

"Yes. From my waist down to my thighs, and underneath all through the crack of my butt. It's unbearable. It's the worst case I've ever had," I continued to inform her quickly to expedite my treatment.

"Well. I can already tell you it isn't jock itch. It's scabies. The outbreak started last week, and you're the fourth person in a row to complain of it," she said a little more calmly this time, but her eyeballs bolted up to mine rather strangely as she finished presenting me her diagnosis.

Just then, I got really, really scared. I noticed a terrible sudden meanness engulf her face and eyes. It seemed she was looking at me cruelly just for the pure enjoyment of making me squirm a little with her medical revelation. At that instant, to me, she became a lady with malicious intent. And, I knew I was in for it good because of it.

"I'm really sorry ta have ta disagree with your diagnosis ma'am, but I just have jock itch. Not scabies. I get it often because I work out and sweat a lot. All I need is some cortisone cream or anti-fungal powder, and I'll be okay in a few days," I explained to the nurse lady in desperation.

"Look. I'm not here for you cons to tell me what is or what isn't. I'm tellin' ya, you have scabies. You will be quarantined and treated like the rest of 'em," she scolded me scathingly, as if I didn't have the right to voice my opinion or knowledge of my own medical history. Basically, I was at the ogre's mercy, and I was powerless to do anything about it. I was Scabies Man. There wasn't nothing else to ask what happens next. I felt like I was being beaten to death, and I had to endure the blows without retaliation.

"You'll folla the cops and do whatever they tell you," she finished with her sinister tone. As she spoke, she punched a button on her phone to raise a guard.

I never spoke to the Wicked Witch of the West again after that moment. A familiar cop escorted me back to my cell, and he barked more orders at me when we got there. He told me to gather all my prison clothing and bedding issue and follow him with it. Ben asked me where I was going, and when I told him the scoop, he grimaced. I tried to make a dumb joke about being the Folsom Prison Scabies Man, but it didn't conjure up any smile or humorous response. Ben had a lot of respect for people that way.

The cop led me like I had a thick, steel bullring in my nose to the hole. The hole reared its ugly head as I rounded another cement corner at one end of Folsom. The hole was where the system stored all the cons who didn't play by the rules, or where us quarantined convicts were segregated from the main prison population.

When the guard opened the windowless metal cell door next to several others in the long row of holes, another bolt of depression lightning lashed at my mind. It looked cold and dark inside my new quarters, and there was no bunk like my home away from home cell with Ben. There was a toilet, a sink, and a six by eight feet room entombed by cement. That was it.

"Drop all yer bedding and strip before you go in. You hafta stay in here for twenty-four hours naked," the cop ordered me before I stepped into my hole.

"Whattya mean, naked?" I asked the cop concernedly. I thought the whole deal was already way over the top of the concept of reasonable treatment, let alone the naked part.

"I gotta mattress comin' for ya in a minute, and a blanket. But, that's it. You hafta put this stuff all over every inch of your body, including your hair. And, you can't have any clothes. They'll wipe the stuff off. You hafta stay isolated so it'll have time to kill all the bugs," the cop explained in a business-like tone, as he tossed me a large tube of toxic bug killer.

Meanwhile, my mind had frozen up solid. I caught the cop's pass instinctively, but I just stood there in shock for a few seconds, listening to him in horrified disbelief.

"What about chow? I don't eat either?" I snapped out of my funk to ask the cop sarcastically. It seemed as if I was expected to go hungry on top of everything else. Of course, it really didn't matter if I ate anyway though. The hog slop they served in prison wasn't fit for a scavenger bird, an animal, or a human anyway.

"You don't hafta get smart with me, Teacher. I'm just doin' my job. You'll get fed at the regular chow times like everyone else," he yapped at me just as rudely.

Then, he slammed the steel door in my face. I had to move my naked toe so it wasn't crushed. And, as I yanked it out of the way, a thunderous echo bashed against my eardrums. When it finally subsided, I began to feel like I had just been locked away in a far off cave somewhere. There was no bench. There was no bed. There was hardly any light. There was only a stark loneliness hovering over my heart, and the guilt monsters began their charge once again. All I could seem to think about was Sheryl being crushed mercilessly under the truck and me trying in vain to dig her out.

In a valiant effort to escape my own thoughts, I sat my bare cheeks down on the icy cement and leaned tentatively against the cold cement wall. I forced my mind to redirect its focus to the tube of bug killer and the necessary task at hand. It didn't take long to develop a great contempt for it either.

However, as I smothered the diagnosed bug infestation with the slime, the nasty smelling white stuff seemed to offer an immediate relief from the relentless itch in my groin area. It felt cool, and I even began to think I had misdiagnosed my problem and the Wicked Witch of the West was right after all. The good feeling down below even convinced me to smear the slime all over my body and into my skin and hair. I figured I may as well kill any of the critters that had climbed up or down my frame somewhere.

An hour later, the door opened briefly and a janitorial con threw a mattress and a blanket inside my cell. The guard slammed the door without saying anything, and I was left to my own thoughts. While I made my own bed and laid down in it, the good feelings about the scabies stuff disappeared instantly. I started to think that the scabies, and the hole, was my real punishment. Regular prison wasn't grotesque enough. And, my arrogance and selfishness was what banished me to the hole. It was as far away from the rest of the prison population and humanity as possible.

The whole deal was another mental and physical torture test, and I tried to sleep as much as possible. I urinated when I had to. I got a drink from the filthy sink when I needed one. And, I ate when the chow cons delivered the food trays through the tiny slit in the cell door. I ate what was served, and then, I slept some more. Sleep was the only reprieve from the guilt monsters.

The cops released me from the hole about twenty-eight hours later and escorted me to the shower. I cleaned up nicely, and they issued me a new batch of prison clothes and bedding. Then, I returned to my own cell and described my experience to Ben. He was empathetic, and when I finished, he told me he had disinfected our entire cell with some stuff the guards gave him. But, he also said that no one else on our tier had contracted scabies or anything else like it.

When Ben told me his story, it made me more than a little suspicious, especially because I began to get the same peculiar feeling of jock itch in my groin area again almost as he finished talking. An hour later, the horrible itch was worse than ever. And, by that time, I was ready to dive into my cellie's locker and steal his refried beans can he had stashed for dinner. For a second, I thought the sharpened lid might be able to help me out and relieve all my pain like it did the Nazi Low Rider earlier. But, it passed quickly. All I could do was suck it up like I was raised to do.

Luckily, I was called to see the nurse right after morning chow the next day. Apparently, it was a routine check to see how the quarantine treatment worked out. But of course, in prison, nothing turns out the way you think.

"How'd it work?" a male nurse asked me affably as I walked into his office. I had anticipated the ogre again, and besides not having to wait in line this time, I was grateful that she wasn't there. I even hoped she had gotten canned. She was a mean lady.

"Not worth a hoot. It's as bad as it was before," I told the guy bluntly.

"Well then. We're gonna have ta do it all again. If you're still bein' bothered, then it didn't take," the guy told me just as straight.

"You gotta be kiddin' me! First off, I don't even have scabies. I have jock itch. That's it. I've had it a thousand times. I know what it is when I get it. The other nurse didn't even look at me. She just said I have scabies because I told her I itched down there and she just had three other scabies cases before I came in to see her," I explained to the nurse a little excitedly. I was trying really hard not to snap and stab him with one of his own pencils lying on his desk.

"Look. I'm not a doctor. Plus, I'm new here. This is my first day. The doctor told me to re-treat everyone who I wasn't positive was absolutely clear. It's too risky for the rest of the population, and it would be disastrous if it spread throughout the prison," the guy told me apologetically, but handed me another tube of bug killer and punched the buzzer for a cop as he finished.

"I can't even believe this is happenin'," I complained, as I turned to face an escort cop walking in to escort me back to the hole for another scabies treatment.

Naturally, the process was repeated precisely as before. I stripped, smeared, fumed, and slept. There wasn't anything else to do. I couldn't kill them—the bugs either.

The next day, I showered, dressed, gathered another batch of bedding, and headed back to my cell again. An hour later, the itch returned. The next morning, I wrote a letter. I wrote a letter to the warden telling him that, if I didn't get some immediate and appropriate health care, from a real honest-to-goodness doctor of some kind, I didn't even care if he or she was a veterinarian, any doctor would do, I was going to call my attorney immediately and slap the biggest lawsuit on his precious Folsom prison that he had ever seen before. It worked too, in about an hour after I handed it to the gun tower guard.

A real doctor called me into his office this time. I never did see another stinking nurse. Anyway, when I told the doctor about my dilemma, he told me to drop 'em. I did. He looked. He saw. He saw that I had a bad case of jock itch. He gave me some cortisone cream. My jock itch was gone a few days later.

In addition to the seemingly infinite indignities prison offered, and the constant threat of death, rape, or other physical danger hanging like a ghostly mist around all of us convicts, the time and deportation monsters hovered endlessly as well. I always tried to dive deep into the rivers of reflection whenever my mind allowed me to in order to escape them. And, I dove deep as often as possible, because when my escape was successful, I was able to learn more priceless information about myself. But, I couldn't always control the monsters' demands to be heard.

As a consequence, when the monsters did force their way back into my psyche, the ponderings regarding my childhood and past life experiences were always forced to the back burner. My reflections had to wait patiently for the monsters to have their way with me before I could return to my subterranean thought processes, and ultimately, the insight I needed to become a better person.

Much of my sadness at that stage of my prison term was derived from the ramifications surrounding my deportation. I had moved from Canada to the States about twenty-six years earlier, and I had built a quality life in California. I had been married with three awesome kids, and their lives in Merced were all they had ever known. Even though I knew Sheryl was gone, my kids' family and friends were in Merced, and they had sunk their roots deep into the culture and lifestyle Merced offered them. They were happy and contented there, and the thought of any them having to uproot everything they had ever known because of my stupidity was highly disturbing to me. It was like my cement head was wrapped in the same razor wire that engulfed the walls around me, and some mysterious fiend was tightening it slowly to maximize my emotional torture. It was like a herd of great steeds competing in a heart-stomping contest on my heart.

Prison was an ocean of misery because of the guilt I could never seem to escape. I felt like I was always drowning in my own shame; my gasps for precious, life-giving oxygen were always too far away to suck a full breath. In the big picture the short time I lived in that hell may not sound like much to some. But to me it was a brutal eternity.

However, many miracles occurred at the beginning of the ninth month of my incarceration. I happened to be lying on my bunk and reading my Bible just after my teaching session was over one day when a guard appeared at my cell door. His crusty tone signaled he wasn't a happy little camper when he started to speak, but when he finished his orders for me to march on down to my counselor's office, I forgot about his rudeness instantly. I had been waiting for news from my counselor for months regarding my deportation status, and I prayed right then and there that "today was the day" to find out the scoop regarding my banishment out of the country.

I walked to the consultant's office as quickly as I could without running in my anticipation. It was a long walk down and through several prison corridors of cons, and cells, and madness. And, when I got there, I hesitated briefly before I knocked my arrival. I wondered whether the man or woman on the other side of the door in charge of my future would harpoon me a few more times, or they would finally dish me some good news for a change.

"Come in and sit down," the petite lady beckoned me softly, as I stepped into her office.

The kindness in her voice gave me a good feeling right then. It was a rare thing in that awful place, but her friendly demeanor didn't carry the typical arrogance and meanness like everyone else in the system had mastered. It even looked to me like she didn't belong there. She wasn't one of them.

"Thank you so much for seeing me. I've wanted to talk to you for a long time," I returned with the same gentleness.

"I'll get right to the point of our meeting, Mr. Wiens. You won't be deported after all. In a nutshell, because your mother was born in Wisconsin, you have derivative citizenship rights. Simply put, you have United States citizenship as well as Canadian. And, because of your U.S. citizenship, you can't be deported," the lady revealed pleasantly, with a little smile on her face.

Well, I have to say, I almost fainted straight away. I was in total shock, and the cat definitely snagged my tongue for several seconds.

"Please tell me this is for real. Please tell me this isn't a bad joke," I said excitedly, as I stiffened in the hard chair, suspicious of the hidden hammer hovering somewhere.

"It's for real. Your mom called the immigration officer in charge of your case and faxed him all the appropriate paperwork. It's a done deal. But, that's not all. You also have a new release date. You will be getting out in about three weeks," she continued her magical revelation, with a broader smile than before.

"I can't believe this is happenin'. I just can't believe it! Are you sure you're lookin' at the right case, and it's not a mistake?" I almost yelled at the lady in utter astonishment.

"There's no mistake. When you arrived here from Tracy prison, you began to earn good time-work time. Every inmate gets it for good behavior and doing well in his job. In your case, it calculates out to about four-and-a-half months. You had eighty-five percent of sixteen months to do to begin with which is about thirteen-and-a-half months. With four-and-a-half months off, that means you'll end up doin' a little more than half of your sentence, about nine months total," she went on in her friendly manner.

My first reaction was a great concern and worry. The courts had ruled that I serve a mandatory eighty-five percent of my sentence due to the violent felony I was convicted of. And, because of the violent conviction, I had been ordered deported forthwith upon my release. The judge said there was no reprieve. But, I kept my yap shut tighter than a two-foot thick steel safe with millions in it. Who was I to argue with the powers that be, even though it was all very suspicious?

It seemed that all I could do was to stutter and stammer my gratefulness to the lady for the unbelievable news she laid on me. Then, I walked back to my cell in a fog. My mind raced from thought to thought like a bunch of wild banshees flipping from tree to tree chasing each other. I had gone through so many hateful emotions; the happiness I felt suddenly seemed strange and foreign. It was also quite breathtaking and wonderful. It was glorious, and God was suddenly my hero. I had prayed for forgiveness a few thousand times over the last eight months. I didn't know it until then, but he had been listening to me the whole time. He also must have seen my new heart too. Because, he forgave me. He showered me with his mercy after that. He granted me unbelievable miracles. And, I was so touched by his infinite kindness, I dropped many a tear as I entered my empty cell. No one was around to see them, so I let them fly without inhibition.

The new possibilities hit me like a ton of bricks falling on a Toyota. I wouldn't be deported. I would get out of that horrible place four-and-a-half months sooner than I had expected. I didn't have to uproot Logan. Kodi and Carlie and Ranger didn't have to travel the 1500 miles just to visit me. I still had a chance with Karyn. I could still teach school in California. And, I had a new life and opportunity to start over as a better person.

In all the initial excitement, I tried to think of how I could contact my people the quickest way possible. My good news dam was overflowing like crazy, and I was busting at the seams to tell my kids, my mom, Karyn, and the hundred other people who had written me regularly, the same people who had supported me through the entire judicial nightmare.

However, my mind suddenly turned heavy and dark once again. The cynical monster came at me with all talons poised for its strike.

And, I dove back into the thoughts of doubt and negativity and distrust. How could I really believe the counselor lady, I thought? I had so many seemingly wonderful things happen to me in my life before, only to have them dashed in a single heartbeat. My lawyers told me I would have to do the thirteen-and-a-half months, and I would be deported for sure when I got out. The judge said the same thing. And since my sentencing, I believed the ruling was set in stone. Even though I was just told differently by the prison authority in charge of my case, I just couldn't believe what she told me.

From that second on, the two horses of good and evil stole the show in my brain. It was like they competed in a tug-of-war to the death on my psyche. For one brief instant, the gallant white steed would gain ground and I would believe and rejoice in the counselor's revelation. But, in the next one, the mad and contemptuous big black daddy of them all would drag the white one backwards like he was an ant on ice. Ugliness would take over, and I just knew the lady was full of it. No sweet, young, and friendly thing like her could ever know what she was talking about, I thought, especially in that barbaric city of uncouth and inhumane men. She must be a rookie, and she had my case mixed up with someone else's. That was really it. The black horse was right all along. There was no other possibility. But then, whitey would gain ground again. It was all like a pendulum of torture. I thought I was going to finally snap from its perpetual motion.

On top of all that, I was totally confused. I didn't know if I should tell my people about the possibility of me getting out early, and the news about the deportation. I had so many wonderful people, family, and friends pulling for me, I felt that I would let them all down if it all didn't materialize the way the counselor said. On the other hand, I knew I had to tell someone. Otherwise, I didn't have a ride home if I was sprung soon like the lady said.

So, I decided to call my mom, Mark, and Karyn after several hours of torturous deliberation. I didn't want to give any of them hope. But, I also knew they had earned the right to know. They had stayed totally loyal and loving and supportive through the whole mess. I owed them that respect. Besides, I knew they could keep the possible good news under their hats until I actually did get out, and my kids would be happily surprised if my early release really happened.

When I finally decided to call, the time monster snarled at me again. It was Thursday. That meant us whites didn't get phone privileges until Saturday. That was because the blacks and Mexicans got their kick at the phone cat Thursdays and Fridays respectively. And, that made the next two days unbearable. The two horses maintained their endless battle in my head, and I became an anxious wreck. All I could think of to do was to work out harder and longer and search the Bible for passages of faith, and trust, and hope to keep my brain from unraveling altogether.

I finally had my turn on the horn the following Saturday morning about 7 A.M. I called my mom and told her the news. She confirmed that she had talked to the immigration people like my counselor had said, and that she had faxed them all of her birth certificate and citizenship paperwork. Mom was confident that what the counselor had told me, and what the immigration had told her, was accurate. She also told me she would be there when I did get out. And, when she did, I broke down on the phone. We cried together for several minutes before I got a hold of myself enough to explain I was only permitted a short time on the phone, and I had other calls to make before the guards booted me off.

The next few weeks were horrible like I anticipated. They were far from glorious, because I didn't know what was going to happen for sure. Was I going to get out in a few weeks? Was I not going to be deported? Or was it all a terrible mistake? Although the unknowable kept up its lingering cruelty, I no longer cared about the blood and guts splattering all around me. I didn't care about the slop they served. I didn't dwell on the gross indignities in every facet of my life. After the meeting with my counselor, it seemed my brain had a limited capacity to hurt, and the ugliness all the prison madness offered suddenly became old hat. It had become the norm, and I wasn't concerned about all the dirty deeds around me anymore. I had grown used to it. Only the early release and deportation mattered.

However, when it came time for bed, that was another horror story. I was still haunted by Sheryl's face contorting, and her body being slowly crushed under the massive weight of our truck every time I closed my eyes. I wasn't able to sleep like a peaceful human being. It was possible that I was going home soon, but Sheryl still visited. She was reminding me that I should never, ever forget what I did. As I lay in bed, and as Sheryl passed inside my eyelids, my head would shake involuntarily every time in absolute shame.

I was released from Folsom prison early like the lady counselor told me. I wasn't deported either. But, until the moment I walked out of that concertina-wire-bonneted hell, I didn't know for sure if it was really going to happen or not. I kept waiting for that fateful tap on my shoulder by one of the guards as I walked down the last cement and steel prison corridor to freedom. I even looked over my shoulder to see if he was on my tail raising his arm yet. Why did I think like that? Because, the-big-black-grand-daddy-horse-of-them-all was dominating the white horse at the time. Real freedom was the only weapon left in my arsenal to conquer the monster's evil whinny.

CHAPTER 18

The Ex-Convict

Before the accident, I was rarely happy or joyful about anything. I was mad at all the injustices in the world. I was totally blind to the boundless joy my wife and kids provided inches away. I had contempt for most people, because I judged them as weaklings and inexperienced in life in general. I thought, "There is no one else in the world who has experienced the grotesqueness in life like I have. There is no way they can understand me and my ways. So, to heck with them all. I will live my own life the way I want to. I will follow the rules of society I choose to. I will walk the fence line when I have to. I will flaunt the natural laws and morals and common rules and laws of societal decency whenever I can get away with it, or it feels good to do so." That was Randy Wiens before he crashed and killed his wife in the dark. I never once set out on a malicious mission to be flawed in character like that. But, that is the person I became.

When I was cast from society into that prison hell of a human existence, the hardness I had engulfed and perfected in my life came in handy too. I was able to fool the Ironmen, the Psychos, and all the other prison castaways, because I was big and strong and I didn't back down from any of their despicable intimidation and attitude. I gave them all the infamous I-am-Randy-Wiens-you-will-have-to-kill-me-first routine, and that made them all believe it was better for them to step on. For all of them, there were easier little chickens to pluck than the big, bad baseball and hockey player and teacher from Canada.

However, all that nonsense was the game I had to play to physically survive in prison. Sure, it was true that I could take care of business when I had to. And, I was never afraid to "get down" when trouble hit the fan. But emotionally, after Sheryl said, "Get me out of here. I don't want to die here," I was no longer afraid of the soft little teddy bear inside me that had always screamed to get out. I was still afraid to let it out of its cage whenever a fellow con was hovering, because my weakness equaled injury or death in that place. But, in my own space and time, I was finally able to cry.

Before the accident, I rarely shed a tear even when I felt safe by myself. I wouldn't let my guard down even in private time, because I believed I couldn't take the chance of getting soft. So, I never allowed myself to yield to the dainty thoughts and pleasantries that others could. I kept it all together, tightly wrapped in the barbed wire of false bravado. I thought there were too many monsters in life, and hardness was their only equal. The Wiens' culture hammered that into me my whole life. So, that is what I knew. And, that is what I exhibited to most. Some of my family and close friends knew the depth of my true sensitivity, but the majority of the world saw a hardened, in-control man's man who would rather die than be perceived as a pansy.

Strangely though, something very profound happened when I was released from the Big House: I wasn't angry anymore. I found myself living and breathing a new ability to express my deepest inner feelings without inhibition. I was no longer mad at the world. I didn't hate each step, or every breath I took, like I did before. I no longer hated the people who horned in on my line at the store or cut me off in traffic. I no longer believed in my heart, mind, body, and soul that I had to be hard and tough to survive life's treacherous highways, or die trying. All of that nonsense seemed like it was cast off somewhere out into the infinite galaxy.

While I pondered my new lack of inner rage at the world in sheer amazement, I found something else had miraculously taken its place. God had softened my heart. Instead of anger, the golden eagle of humble appreciation spread its mighty wings in my mind. Simply put, I appreciated every minuscule thing life put in front of me. Now, when I say, "every minuscule thing," I mean exactly that. The following examples illustrate some peculiar things when it comes to appreciation in general, but to me, they really symbolize every tiny, insignificant aspect of life the normal person has taken for granted for his or her entire life.

For example, when I got out of prison, I was eternally grateful for the invention of the almighty roll of toilet paper. No, make it the three cases of toilet paper from the local supermarket. What is he talking about, you might ask? Well, let me break it down for you.

One of the first things I purchased upon my release was toilet paper. No! Make that three, twenty-four-pack cases of toilet paper. Why? Because I never ever wanted to run out again. In prison, the anxiety in general, and the nasty food they served, were like perpetual laxatives. They both played Taps on my constitution. And, to remedy the runny situation, the prison administration saw fit to issue us their gracious gift of a single roll of toilet paper to take care of things. What I mean is, they gave me one roll of toilet paper a week. No more, no less. If I ran out of the precious treasure, their motto was—tough beans. And, then, I had to use my finger or whatever to take care of business. Now, I know the finger thing sounds pretty gross, but that is what a man is left with when he kills his wife and is dumped down the disposal of human society for doing it.

There were only two ways to combat the gross indignity too. One of them was to only use a few squares of the valuable commodity for each non-urinating toilet adventure. That way, I could spread out the bounty to last the week. The other way was to purchase more rolls from the prison system's black market. In other words, the various gang members robbed toilet paper rolls from the weaklings as a side business; in which case, a single roll of paper gold cost me fifty stamps. Now, we all know that is a very expensive price. So, as one might imagine, I was pretty chinsy with each wipe.

While I shopped the first time as a free man again, I bought about a hundred disposable razors, eight tubes of toothpaste, six toothbrushes, ten containers of deodorant, five tubes of jock-itch cream, five bottles of foot powder, ten bars of soap, three of the largest bottles of shampoo, three hair brushes, four nail clippers, twenty pairs of underwear, twenty pairs of socks, and seven pairs of jogging shorts. I know it was overkill, but I never wanted to run out of life's little pleasantries ever again.

Although my new appreciation for the little things in life would create a list a mile long, one other incredible phenomenon in life I took for granted, before I had to search desperately for Sheryl in the total blackness because of my ignorance, was the daily shower. Before, it wasn't anything special. I could shower anytime I wanted to and stay in there for an hour if I felt like it. During my time behind the razor-wired cement walls, the five minutes they gave us to hustle to the shower, finish showering, and slip and slide back to our cells, was like winning the lottery twice a week or once a month, depending on if we were locked down or not. After they cut me loose, it was like winning the lottery every day. And now, every time, I savor every drop of the precious liquid as it beats on my body. I revel in its mystical fingers of pleasure and its awesome cleansing powers. And, I respect the privilege of its simple nature—every single glorious time.

I still remember the first shower I took when I got back home too. It even included an interesting little twist to the special occasion. Now, one might say that I am overdoing it a little when I said the shower was a special occasion. Well, all I can really tell you is don't ever drink and drive, kill your wife or husband or child or friend or another human being, then have to go to prison because of it, to really find out what I mean.

As I dove under that glorious hot liquid, trying desperately to wash off the gross incarceration scales stuck to my body and mind, my first order of business was to take my underwear off in the shower, soap it up really well with the bar soap on the wall, and proceed to wash and scrub it cleaner than a whistle. I didn't catch myself doing the deed until I started to wring them out after the rinse. It had become habit to wash my underwear during every shower. Showers were few and far between, and I only had a couple of pairs of underwear from prison issue. Actually, when I reached up to hang them on the shower curtain rod I snapped out of my daze. I had been so caught up in the gloriousness of being free in my own shower, that I failed to realize I didn't have to wash my underwear in the shower anymore.

Speaking of conveniences and the privilege of having and being able to use them at will, I was ecstatic to finally be able to wash all my clothes in my own washer. Who would think a mountainous pile of stinky laundry stacked by the washer on the floor would look so marvelous. Well, it brought many a smile to my face when I got out of the can. It still does. In prison, if a convict sent his laundry in through the prison laundry system in his designated laundry bag once a week as allowed, ninety-nine times out of a hundred, the inmate laundry workers would steal some or all of the con's laundry and sell it. A pair of socks brought twenty stamps, a white T-shirt earned twenty-five, and a pair of clean underwear with no holes in it garnered thirty, for example.

Unfortunately though, for the unfortunate con who lost some of his issue, the theft caused some real problems when it came time for the weekly inspection of our cells and personal prison issue. If a con lost any part of his issue, he was verbally warned the first time. The second time, he was written up and the complaint was placed in the con's disciplinary file. The third time, the con was banished to the hole to straighten out his misbegotten ways and lack of responsibility to take care of his prison issue. To top it off, any and all verbal, written, and physical disciplinary actions in prison greatly affected the cons' good-time work-time status. In other words, for something as simple as losing a pair of socks, or getting them stolen, less time was deducted from the cons' over-all sentences for good behavior. Stupid? Yes. But, that was just another hammerhead shark that always lurked in my swimming area. That is the way it was.

Besides the simple pleasures of life I began to enjoy when I finished my prison term, there were many major and joyous ones as well. One of them occurred soon after my first free shower. I found myself rummaging through a stack of boxes in search of more of my own clothes to wear one morning, when I heard a faint knock on the door. When I opened it, a bolt of lightning-joy struck my heart.

"Hi son!" Mom said gleefully, with a magnificent smile plastered all over her face.

"Hi, Rand!" Connie grinned, standing by Mom's right shoulder with the same jubilance.

As for me, all I could do was to stare at them in disbelief as my tears began to flow like free rain. I had no idea they were coming down from Canada all that way to visit me right then, and all I could think to do was to hug them like a big silly.

At the same time, I had a flash of *déjà vu*. I remembered when Mom, Connie, and Darryl showed up the day after the accident at the county jail when my brain felt like freshly ground hamburger. They had heard about the accident, that I was in jail for vehicular manslaughter, and Sheryl was the one killed. They dropped the phone, came running, and voila, they appeared in the visiting room.

So, it was instinctive when I looked down the cement walkway to see if Darryl was bringing up the rear somewhere. But, he wasn't. He was still home in Canuck-land. He couldn't make it that trip because of his bad back. I have to say though that Mom and Connie's visit was like a burst of heaven. I felt so loved and cared for, that the dark horse seemed like he was languishing a million miles away ready to hit the glue factory.

When Mom and Connie took off again, Darryl showed up a few days later just as unexpectedly as Mom and Connie had done.

"Hey, Rand! Bad back or not, I had to see my bro. Besides, I couldn't let the women hog all the glory," Darryl yelled at me, lovingly and play-fully from about thirty feet away as he deplaned at the airport. And, like Mom's famous gravy smothering my heaping plate of mashed spuds, I was in hog heaven during his entire visit too.

As a matter of fact, when my family came down to visit me and celebrate my release from prison, a great deal of healing took place. And, like many other profound and wonderful magical experiences when I stepped clear of Folsom's walls, I no longer felt alone or abandoned. I felt loved and cared for more than I had ever felt before. And strangely, in my newfound softness, I cried my love back at them. As I cried, they hugged me and told me it was all going to be okay. We were family. Family sticks together through thick and thin and battles all the mon-sters together.

Although many pleasing and wonderful and joyous blessings crossed my trail after prison, the Big Black Daddy came back to visit from time to time. However, he was never invincible like he had been after the accident and in prison. He was much weaker and frail, because the White Horse of positiveness and faith was slowly building a great barn of his own in my head. And, he wasn't about to let the bad guy bully him either. When the Black did come calling, it didn't take long for the White Horse to chase him down, kick him in the teeth, and drive him back to his outdoor corral in the rain.

Even so, in my human frailty, the Black was still able to flank me once in awhile in his guerrilla-like custom. And, from time to time, he would bring some monsters as back up. One of the nasty beasts was the parole python.

I was placed on parole for the three years following my release date from prison. Simply put, parole is similar to prison, but the walls are a lot wider apart. I check in with my parole officer once in awhile or whenever he tells me to. I pee in a plastic cup for him to test for alcohol consumption, and I wait for him to come to my house to check on my actions, travel, behavior, and with whom I hang around. I can never be in the remote vicinity of a firearm or weapon of any kind, and I fret whenever I step on a crack because I never know if it will be the one to break my back, violate me, and send me back to prison in leg irons and cuffs again.

So, I just wait. In my newfound softness and virgin patience, I wait for the three years to pass. I wait for the succulent delicacy of freedom to whet my taste buds with its glorious nectar.

In the meantime, I am no longer compelled to look over my shoulder. Why? Because I have nothing to hide anymore. Before, I was like a lowly sneak. I skulked around like a thief in the night. But now, I am no longer an ostrich with its head in the sand. I practice a fresh and sanitary existence with my entire mind and might. Although I know I am not perfect or completely unsoiled by any stretch of the imagination, the real fact of the matter is, holding my wife's dying head in the dark washed a lot of my filthy laundry. It scared me straight. Besides, I would rather die first than go back to prison. It isn't safe there.

340 • Now I Know Who I Am

Another time the dark horse sneaks through the cracks and triggers a brief ugliness has to do with my teaching profession. In prison, I believed I was going to be deported for sure, so I wrote off teaching ever again from the moment I was sentenced. I knew that Canada honored the status of my California credentials, in that my credentials became invalid when I was convicted of the felony. Moral turpitude was their justification to yank them. So, I knew Canada wouldn't let me teach there either. It was a detestable blow on my pride and my psyche too, because I had worked like a madman to obtain my English degree and teaching credential and find a good teaching job. But, for the most part, whitey always seems to prevail now. He keeps reminding me that I have many other talents to offer.

Speaking of blessings, I received a major shocker as I sat perusing the television movie options one evening a few months after the prison guards closed the door behind me for the last time. It was a strange phone call actually, and it raised the hair on the back of my head when the bomb was first dropped. I guess what I am really saying is that I am a brand new father. I am forty-six years old, all my other kids are grown, and I am a new papa. But, it isn't like you might be thinking though. You see, I have a brand spankin' new twenty-four-year-old son I knew nothing about until the phone rang that night.

When the phone rang, the lady on the other end reminded me that we had dated during the fall after my first year in professional baseball. She was eighteen and I was twenty at the time. She said she got pregnant, but she didn't want to tell me about it. And, in her grand unselfishness, she thought the news might distract me from my baseball career. Instead, she gave the baby up for adoption when he was born, and she never saw him again until he came looking for his natural birth parents a short time ago. At twenty-four, he found his mom. His mom helped him find his dad in California. She told me about our son and that his name was Ryan. I called him. He flew down to see me.

To say Ryan and I hit it off right away wouldn't be giving the situation real justice. In fact, it was like Ryan had been my kid, living in my home, his entire life. We have the same likes and talents, and especially, we share the same abilities to annoy others with our frankness and humor. First, he is 6' 6". He is a star basketball player, and he has his teaching credential. He loves all sports, family, and is very, very ambitious like the rest of the Wiens' clan. Although his last name isn't Wiens, he is definitely a Wiens. There is no doubt in my mind. As for where we are personally, our relationship has only just begun. We e-mail each other regularly and talk about our lives and future relationship. We talk about how cool it is to have found each other and how wonderful it is that we can share the rest of our lives getting to know each other.

After Ryan blasted on to my scene and into my life, it was reaffirmed once again that every human's life was filled with countless blessings and challenges. The two horses are always around in the same vicinity and sharing the same air. That is how God made the world way back when. He gave us all challenges so he could test our mettle and faith in Him. He knew what he was doing, and he knew the faithful ones would always survive the evil horse's periodic rampages.

The bottom line is that for me, like everyone, life is still hard to stomach at times. There have always been difficulties, and there will always be difficulties, no matter how hard I ride the white horse. That little fact has not changed since the beginning of time. It won't change until the end of time. For example, not long after prison was in my rear view mirror, the monster of death called once again. He came a knocking one spring day when I came home from watching my son play college baseball.

In other words, my mother was killed in a car wreck up in Canada. My mom and aunt were on their way to a church meeting when their car spun out of control on the icy winter highway they were traveling on. They slid broadside into an oncoming motor home that couldn't maneuver out of the way in time to avoid the collision. My mother was the passenger. She was killed instantly. My aunt was torn up pretty badly, but she is on the mend. It will take a long time for her to heal up, but she should be okay down the road.

About my mom, and my feelings about her when my sister and brother called me with the tragic news, I didn't cry at first. There were a lot of people around at the time, and my old act of not showing how I really felt because I was tough, kicked in momentarily. But, as soon as I was alone, I broke into a zillion little bits of sadness all over the kitchen tile. I cried and remembered my mom's love and loyalty and kindness and graciousness and mercy she had bombarded me with since Kane died fifteen years earlier. She had made up for lost time countless times over, and to me, my mom was the best mom in the world. I had forgiven her and because of it, our relationship blossomed into a magnificent splendor of love and loyalty and friendship that will never be rivaled. She was my mom.

After Kane croaked, and before she died, Mom did it all for us kids. She was there when we needed her, and she called all of us at least weekly just to shoot the breeze or catch up on her grandkids' activities. She was the best cook, the best friend, and she became the best mom any kid could ever hope for. She was the greatest, and I will miss her dearly. Whenever I am in nature now, I think of her, because she found peace and solace in nature's awesome healing powers. She loved the mountains and trees and rivers and lakes and streams, and all the creatures that roamed the wilds of Canada. And, whenever I asked her why she reveled in nature so heartily, she would always say, "I am able to contemplate my navel when I am alone in nature. It gives me a chance to appreciate all of my children and all the rest of God's blessings."

Whenever I cook, I think of my mom, because her cooking was incredible. She would be the first person to tell you she was no gourmet queen of any kind. However, my mom could make a tasty meal out of nothing, and it would stick to your ribs too. In a nutshell, you definitely would never go hungry if Mom had anything to say about it. And, besides the heavenly tastes she always conjured up to tickle your mind's pleasure center, her cooking chased all the bad meanies away at least for a while. I don't know how she did it, but sitting at her supper table, or breakfast table, or whatever table, she was the earth's cooking goddess. And she never allowed negative feelings or comments to ruin one of God's greatest blessings, the family supper table, if she had anything to say about it.

Whenever I am in church, I think of Mom, because she found God had always been watching her like the King of all hawks—like I did. We just never knew it before. She found the God just waiting for her like he was always waiting for me, waiting for me to wake up and smell the spiritual coffee of forgiveness and salvation and the only path to inner peace. He was waiting for Mom. He was waiting for me. He is waiting for all of us to grab onto His Word for all we're worth. He knows our lives depend on it.

When my mother died in that horrible wreck, I know she died forgiven. And I know she knew it too. She died with a peaceful heart and mind, because she knew God had forgiven her. She also knew her kids had forgiven her long ago. That's why I know in my heart that Mom is happy in heaven with God. She is basking in his glory. She sought him out. She found him. She accepted him into her heart. And because of his infinite mercy and grace, she was able to turn back the evil horse and all his mighty kin that plagued her life for so long.

Mom died loved and forgiven, and she will always live in my mind side by side with Sheryl. They were both true warriors and wonderful women, and I am learning to welcome their visits at night with a smile as well as a tear.

CHAPTER 19

Now I Know Who I Am

Like many people, I have experienced some pretty horrible things in my life. And, like many people, I have ugly psychological and emotional baggage because of them. Unfortunately though, until my prison experience, I didn't know where my skeletons originated. When I finally figured it out, I realized my baggage was perpetuated by an uncontrollable, anger and frustration within me, which was caused by some bad childhood experiences. In turn, that baggage fuelled my cynical attitude. Eventually, it tainted my mind completely by disabling my ability to reason appropriately according to the rules of the road and society. As a natural byproduct, my failure to understand and cope with what happened to me earlier in life created a great inability in me to make sound judgments in many aspects of my life. Many times, I didn't think reasonably. My bad choices naturally followed.

In my mind, my life's monsters justified my arrogance, stubborn pride, selfishness, and hardness. It justified my inability to nurture relationships both earthly and heavenly. It justified my drinking. It justified my drinking and driving on a regular basis. As a matter of fact, the skeletons in my mind and the anger and frustration they carried with it justified most of my poor choices all around.

However, I am no victim. I want no sympathy. I only want an open ear, an open heart, and an open mind to share my story with. I want people to read and hear my story, so they can understand some of the psychology behind their bad behavior and poor choices in life like I have. That way, maybe they can learn from my mistakes as well as their own. Maybe they can learn to make some better choices in life, and consequently, to prevent a lot of their loved ones' emotional pain and suffering like I have. Maybe they can begin to learn to avoid the cruel mental torture they have caused for themselves like I have. Maybe they can finally begin to learn to enjoy God's gracious gift of inner peace like I have.

To begin with, all of us are dealt a different hand in life upon our conception. Some of us are poor monetarily, some are rich, and the rest are in between somewhere. All of us, no matter who we are, no matter how much we have materially, have problems in our individual position in life. No one is perfect. No one is invincible and indestructible. And, no one is excluded from earthly dysfunction. There are just too many nasty monsters in everyday human life.

Sadly, however, because of all the monsters that infect us every day in our world, we tend to compromise society's standards as well our own when the going gets tough. We seek the easy and convenient and comfortable road, and many times, that road pulls us into the badlands of temptation to alleviate the emotional stress and pain. Unfortunately, bad choices and bad consequences follow those compromises very closely.

For example, when something bad happens in life, or when we are faced with a crossroads that leads to both good and bad things, what do we do? Do we hold hatred and contempt in our hearts because someone has abused us physically or mentally? Do we stay angry forever at everyone because people didn't treat us humanely or with respect somewhere in our childhood or life? Do we act with a grand impulsiveness, because we feel we need to grasp the little piece of happiness in front of us before it gets away, and because it might be a long time before another one might come along? Do we lack forgiveness because we have a hard heart? Do we quit our jobs or our marriages, because the grass seems to be always greener on the other side? Do we blame others, or other things, instead of blaming ourselves for our problems? Do we have a problem with trust, and consequently, we are always suspicious of other's motives? Do we judge others for their frailties, and weaknesses, and differences, when we have as many or more of them than the next guy? Do we think the rules of society don't apply to us, and we always look to get away with something because it is more convenient, mysterious, or tantalizing? Do we engage in life with a kind and generous and humble heart, or do we engage in a selfish life where no one else is really important? Do we drink to hide our skeletons and forget the bad things that have happened to us? Do we use drugs to please our brain's pleasure center, because we can't seem to find joy or happiness anywhere else in our world? Do we eat to disguise our lack of love and affection, or our lack of a father or mother figure, or the emptiness we feel in our hearts because of something else that is eating at us? Do we literally fight anyone and everyone who steps on our fragile ego, because we don't know who we are, and fighting is the only way we think we can prove we are real men? Do we deny God, because we are men, because men are tough, because men don't need no help from nobody, because men don't want to be sissy boys, and because men don't want others to think they are soft and vulnerable and have real feelings and emotions like all humans have? Do we continue to dwell in our own confused mind and continue on the same ugly path to destruction? Do we wait until we kill our wife, our kid, our loved one, or our friend under a truck before we catch a clue about drinking and driving? Do we wait for some other horrible thing to come along before we figure out that we are wrong in how we think and act, and we make the proper changes before all is lost? Or, do we see the forest for the trees before it is too late, and we realize that only we can make the choice to become a better person.

For me, I feel I am completely unworthy of the blessings I have received in my life, especially since the accident. But, for some mysterious reason, God allowed me the precious gift of time in prison to figure out who I was and why I was so angry at the world and everyone and everything in it. In other words, the solitude God gave me gave me life. The night of the accident, he smote me bad. He plucked me from my life as I knew it. He put me in a place where I would have to deal with time and survive or succumb completely under time's invincibility. God knew that Randy Wiens needed prison, and the time it demanded, to straighten him out so he would no longer hurt his family and other people in his life.

At first though, time was a horrible curse on me during the aftermath of the accident. Time was a curse during the first four days in jail after my arrest when I found out Sheryl had died. Time was a curse during the three months after the accident leading up to my prison sentencing. Time was a curse on me during all those times because I had to stand face to face with responsibility and go toe to toe with it, or die altogether mentally. The guilt monster took over when the other one got tired, and then, they both traded off until I was banished to the penitentiary. Until that fateful prison experience, I thought I would be insane forever.

Time in prison was a curse for a while, but it was also a great and wondrous miracle. The time in prison allowed me to contemplate my navel like my mom used to like to do in nature. It permitted me the grand opportunity to reflect upon my life and my behavior. I reflected, and I finally learned who I really was. I learned who I was and what and who I had become. It also taught me who I wanted to be. It taught me that I had to change my ways—or else—or else the cookie jar of happiness and inner peace would be unreachable goodies forever.

Before the accident, I didn't care about much of anything like a lot of people. I lived selfishly for me only. If things were convenient for me, I would go along with the desires of my family or the others I came in contact with in daily life. If things weren't convenient, I would blow them off like insignificant little bugs, and I would proceed to make myself happy. My family members and friends and other loved ones were expendable, and I sought out immediate gratification. Wrongly, I thought the pleasure those things gave me would make me happy. But, I was wrong. Now, I know that love, patience, mercy, grace, humility, and faith in God's Word are the only tools to build true happiness, in life and in all relationships.

In prison, living with and breathing the same air as the rest of the outcasts from society, I chose to begin my transformation. And now, time has become a grand luxury to me, a luxury most people don't have to really be able to figure out who they really are, to realize how badly they have been hurting others without knowing they had been doing it, or knowing they were doing it but not caring enough to change.

Time has allowed Karyn's and my relationship to blossom as well. Our interests and values meshed beautifully, and now we are happily married. Our combined families are thriving, and we have faith in the blessed future ahead of us. We cherish our time together. We cherish the simple pleasures in life. It is truly miraculous that I have a second chance at a happy life. And, I know now that only God has made it all possible.

Speaking of my new perspective on marriage in general, I learned a lot about marriage in prison. I learned in my prison reflections that marriage has rules of engagement like all other human relationships. Before, I only thought I respected Sheryl. But, it was obvious to everyone but me that I disrespected her instead. Before, I was rarely willing to compromise about anything, and that lack of humility caused serious problems: no one else in the house felt safe or free to speak their mind, because I was so quick to judge or ridicule or badger them with my own opinions and judgments about everything. Before, I wouldn't communicate openly about sensitive issues. I thought the others in the family wouldn't understand where I was coming from anyway, so what's the use? That lack of communicational ability caused serious trust issues. My own family was always suspicious of my actions and behavior. Before, I snubbed anything to do with religion, because I thought it was a crutch and a complete waste of time. I wouldn't give my wife the time of day when it came to spirituality, even though spirituality is a vital component in completing an individual, and any relationship in general.

Now, I am just a big polluka living the marital and family systems like I should have done during the twenty-two years with Sheryl. I respect my wife always. I communicate openly and honestly. And, I am willing to compromise on just about anything that comes up. The way I think about it now is: what's the point of arguing about the little things. After the indignities of prison, I am learning that everything is a little thing. And finally, I am a Christian, just like my wife is. We look forward to going to church together and holding hands and sitting close to each other the whole time, every time. We raise our children together with the same loving nature and humble consistency, and we all laugh and giggle at my cooking and my hairy back. We are truly blessed. Love and respect, empathy and selflessness, and humility and mercy and grace are really the true golden nuggets of human life. I am now working very hard on all of them.

When it comes to choices, I am learning to process information first before I act immediately upon impulse. I learned from my reflections in prison that every human's physical and emotional survival is determined by the individual choices he or she makes daily. Good choices maneuver the individual's roller coaster of life to the magnificent heights of peace, prosperity, and exaltation. Bad choices fly the plane of life into the side of the mountain. Good, reasoned choices foster and exhibit mercy, grace, and humility. Bad, impulsive choices steal souls, ravage hearts, and crush wives under trucks.

I am now relying upon my faith when it comes to making choices. Proverbs 3:5 (NIV) says, "lean not on your own understanding." My way, my methods didn't work. I am learning to listen to God, the white horse, and the positive side of life. And I hold hope in listening to God's voice. Proverbs 3:5–6 (*The Message* Bible version) says "trust God from the bottom of your heart; don't try to figure out everything on your own. Listen for God's voice in everything you do, everywhere you go; he's the one who will keep you on track."

About the concept of the proverbial Higher Power: now I know he exists. For me, my higher power is God. He was my last resort that fateful night of the accident. He should have been my first resort all along.

And now, I know I had a God-shaped hole in my heart, a hole that only he could fill. By finally reaching out to God after the accident, I started to become whole for the first time in my life. My transformation began in that moment. I just hadn't realized or understood it yet. It continued when Coach came to my place with Philip, and along with Lloyd and Karyn and a whole passel of other friends and family, my transformation built up steam even more. By the time I got to prison and began reading and studying about God and getting to know Christ, and by the time I initiated and facilitated my prison Bible study group, my spiritual transformation had complete control over me. And, I was no longer able to pull my own strings. It was God's hand that guided me in my life at that point.

Now I know God, his son Jesus and the Holy Spirit live within me. You see, now I know I am a child of God. I always have been. He has watched over me, protected me, and prepared me to become the new Randy Wiens. God waited patiently for me to accept him. But, I denied him until the night of the accident when I was left with nothing but a flare prayer. You know, the times when you have nothing left but a prayer. Out of desperation, and sheer brokenness, you finally send up a flare to God, hoping you will catch his attention. The funny thing is, he has waited for my prayer. He always has been. He was listening. He did answer. And now, I am finally ready for my patient God to love me.

I used to think I was the only one who had real problems. Sure, I would feel sorry for the starving kids and the death and devastation caused by an earthquake in some other part of the world, because I did have a conscience, and I was sensitive to the plights of others, but I only had compassion and empathy for others when it was convenient to do so. Now, I have learned that every human has challenges in his or her life. I've also learned that every person is valuable in God's eyes. Not one of us can look into another's eyes that God has not deemed as a valuable person. His love is infinite. He can see the beauty in all of us. He only awaits our request and desire to walk with Him.

Miraculously, I can look people in the face again. I can do that, because I have experienced forgiveness from so many incredibly merciful people. For example, Sheryl's family members are the most wonderful and merciful and forgiving people I have ever met, or ever will meet. They don't harbor anger and meanness at all. In fact, their attitude towards me is the exact opposite. They are friendly and kind and gracious. They are that way because they have known the Lord a lot longer than I have. Sometimes, I wish I had their wisdom and spiritual strength when I first married Sheryl. I would have been a pretty good in-law if I had. I know that now.

As far as other people are concerned, many of them ask me questions on a daily basis like: "How ya doin'?" "How're your kids doin'?"

"What're you doin' now?" "What're you gonna to do?" "How's it all affected you?"

Well, I have to say, those are all open and dangerous questions. And each time I hear one of them, a flood of emotions rush through my mind. Every detail is triggered in my mind's eye yet one more time. I could say that I am doing great. I could say that they are doing great. I could say that I'm writing a book. I could say that I'm going to love my wife and kids. I could say that I'll never be the same. However, I realize all of those answers are too shallow. The curious people really want to hear the unclouded facts and details, because they are sincerely concerned. Or the actual blood and guts fascinates them, and somehow it relates to their own life experiences. So now, I just answer those questions openly and honestly whenever they are asked.

Question: "How ya doin'?"

Answer: I am able to stay above water mostly, but I drown sometimes like everyone does. When my mind swims, I am full of joy. I am joyful because I am happily remarried. My kids are courageous, hard-working, and loving people. I have finally accepted Christ. I am a better person now than I have ever been. And, I am working very hard to become better. It is a process I know will take a lifetime, and yet, I know I will never achieve perfection as long as I live. Only God is perfect. I can only strive to be more like him, because now, I understand my own human frailty. I am not invincible like I thought I was for most of my life.

Consequently, in my peaks and valleys of life, anger and sadness are only a quick thought away. They are lurking monsters in my mind starving to suck me into their dark crevices. I loathe myself at times, because in my mind's eye, I see Sheryl under our truck struggling to breathe. Her beautiful life is being snuffed out because of me.

I hear her telling me sternly, "Get me out of here. I don't want to die here."

I hear her ask me pleadingly, "Can you lift it off?"

I hear her say anxiously, "OK. My legs are getting numb now."

I hear her agonizing groans over and over and over. Then, she is no longer able to speak.

At the same time, in his infinite mercy, God doesn't allow me to dwell in that hell for very long when I do visit there from time to time. My new faith in him reminds me of the countless blessings he has bestowed upon me, and I appreciate every little thing in my human life because of him.

Question: "How're your kids doin'?"

Answer: Ranger is doing incredibly well. He is a star college baseball player. He was recently married to a beautiful young lady from southern California. When I watched him come out of Sheryl, I was overwhelmed with tears of joy. Our first child was born. I was scared and worried at first, because he had a huge cone-shaped head, like the place he had just come from was too narrow to squeeze through or something. But, it was gone shortly. It molded back into shape in a few hours. Now, he is a beautiful and humble young man. I am proud of who he has become as a person. I love him very much.

Kodi is happily married and working on her teaching credential like her mom and dad did. Carlie, Kodi's daughter and my granddaughter, is three years old and very precious to me. I crave the times Kodi brings Carlie to visit me. Carlie reminds me of Pinky—I mean Kodi—every time I look at her. Carlie triggers my memories of me watching as Kodi came sliding out of her mom into the world. She was so pink. I couldn't believe it. I cried as she cried her first breaths. My favorite name for Kodi today is still Pinky. I am proud of who she has become as a person. I love her very much.

Logan is a star high school baseball and basketball player. When he came out of Sheryl, all I could see was his head and his feet, nothing else. His feet were so big; I knew he would always be halfway home if he ever fell down. He is happy and ready for whatever life brings his way. I cried when he came out too. Just the thought of having another perfect child like Ranger and Kodi made me cry a river. I am proud of who he has become as a person. I love him dearly.

However, in all of the above comments, I know it is only the external side of my children that I see and that they present to me. I don't know their personal thoughts. I don't know how often they miss their mother. I don't know how often they cry at night, and wish she were there to talk to, and to hold them gently and scare away all their monsters like she always used to do. I don't know if they can really trust me or if they have really forgiven me. I don't know their innermost thoughts that they may or may not be willing to share with another living soul. I don't know the conversations they secretly hold with their mother.

However, I do know now that all I can do is love them and be there for them always like their mother was. And, maybe time and faith will be merciful and erase all their monsters regarding me and what I did to their mom. I pray daily it will be so.

Question: "What're you doin' now?"

Answer: I lost my teaching credential because I was convicted of vehicular manslaughter, a felony. It is difficult to attain a credible job due to my ex-convict status and stigma, so I have decided to write a book. It may or may not be of the right quality or genre to warrant publishing, but that really doesn't matter. Writing my book allows me to share my story with others. And by doing so, I pray it can help them deal with their monsters and begin their transformation as well.

Writing my book has also been mighty therapeutic for me. It has brought together, sorted out, and organized all the immeasurable reflections I experienced in prison. It has brought me into touch with my true feelings regarding my past thoughts, behaviors, and experiences. It has made me realize that before the accident I didn't know who I was. It has made me understand that I had to make a conscious decision to change if I wanted to have any sort of relationship at all with my kids, my wife, or any other person on the planet. Then I did make that life-changing decision. I will rejoice in God's infinite mercy, grace, and forgiveness forever now because of it.

Last but not least, although I was lost for many reasons, writing my book has forced me to acknowledge my personal faults and defects as a man and how I can change them to good things in the future.

Question: What're you going to do now?"

Answer: I am going to love and honor and respect my wife and kids. I will continue my marathon walk with God, follow his path, and try to become a better person. With God's mercy and grace, I will try to forgive myself for what I have done. I may never be able to do so completely, because I am only a man. Therefore, I am weak. I have limitations. However, if there is any chance at all, I know I must trust the Lord to show me the way. Also, I must surround myself, and my thoughts, with good and righteous people. And, I must always try to help others before I seek my own comforts. I will never be able to do all these things all the time, because I would have to be perfect like God is to accomplish that impossible human task. But, I can try to improve and grow, and get better at unselfishness.

Question: "How's it all affected you?"

Answer: In every minuscule part of my life emotionally. I praise God I will never be the same!

Question: Do you think you will ever experience true inner peace after everything that has happened in your life?

Answer: I will always know I killed my wife and my children's mother. I didn't mean to do it. But, I can't deny the truth. There is no refuting it. However, there is a good chance I can forgive myself someday if I stay close to God. I know now that he alone can save me from my monsters.

After the accident, I simply went from one prison to another. The cement-walled, concertina-wired one blessed me with the opportunity to escape the one in my mind and finally calm down. After four decades of anger and imprisonment in my own mind, the guarded prison allowed me time to think. It allowed me to reason. It allowed me to analyze. It allowed me to reflect. Before, I raced from one thought or action to other blindly and obsessively. I had zero patience for anything if it wasn't convenient. I couldn't earn or accomplish fast enough. If the reward didn't come almost immediately, I'd quit and do something else, no matter what the consequences were. It didn't matter what aspect of my life it was either. I would always seek the greener-looking pasture.

Before, I was so disgusted with myself that I even avoided mirrors. But now when I look in a mirror, I look right into my own eyes. I study my face. I analyze my facial features. I inspect my complexion. I see the weathered lines of character, and I welcome them. I welcome them because I know how far I have come. I have trekked through the sludge of my own human weakness and frailty, and I have made many mistakes along the way. But, I know now that God gave me a great human spirit.

That miracle allowed me to survive life's monsters. It gives me hope for the future. It inspires me to help others carry that hope as well.

True inner peace? I honestly don't know. But at least now I am willing to spend the rest of my life walking with the Lord and try to find it. I know it will be a lifelong marathon. But I am more than willing now to begin my quest. I am willing to walk that marathon with him because I want to continue to improve myself as a person. I used to run everywhere. I never got there fast enough. I endangered all the other relationships in my life because of it. In that tiny prison cell though, I had a chance to finally stop running from myself. In prison, I found out who I was. And now I know who I am.

I am a child of God. I am loved. I am worthy. I am not alone. I am forgiven. I am a man with a great desire to become a better person.

I am a work in progress.

After Thoughts

I sincerely believe everyone has a story tell about his or her life. I also believe everyone should share that story with as many other people as possible. Why? Because we can help each other by sharing our life experiences. We can garner valuable knowledge and information from each other's personal experience and insight. Sometimes, another person's experience is something we would like to replicate. It's a great idea. It's a splendid model of behavior and actions. Other times, we can learn from another's mistakes. We can learn what not to do, and thus, we can avoid heartache and suffering and tragedy. This great exchange of information and experience is what makes us uniquely human. We have the ability to choose to listen and to change our ways.

You have most likely read my story if you are reading this now. You know the irreversible mistakes I have made. When I killed Sheryl that night, in an instant, my life changed forever. I was judged and convicted and cast from society into prison. Before I was a teacher, and a coach, and I was well respected in the community. I thought I had it made. I made a good living. I had a lot of time off. My kids were all studs in sports and good in school. I had nothing but blessings blossoming all around me in my life. But then, in a quick blink of an eye, it all vanished before my eyes.

However, all is not lost. Even when we make mistakes, it's never too late to change. There is always hope. There is always the choice to change and make it stick. Personally, I found my hope in securing wise counsel: my heavenly Father is always first now. In desperation, I reconnected with him in jail after the accident. I also surround myself with others who lift me up rather than pull me down. Now, I go to church. I attend a men's Bible study. I socialize with men of character who encourage me in my daily walk. I am learning to listen, understand, and practice the positiveness they emanate. I am learning to ride their white horse of mercy, grace, and forgiveness. And I am learning their great humility.

You too can seek wise counsel like I finally did. For you, there is always God too. There is always a friend, a teacher, a pastor, or someone who can help you find yourself like I did. They are out there waiting for you to ask them for help. Take it from me. None of us can do it alone. I could've had help my entire life, because God was always there, waiting patiently for me to come to him. Sheryl was always there too, but sadly, my pride and ego always prevented me from asking her or anyone else for help. I'm a man. I'm a Wiens. I'm tough. I can do it myself. That's what my stupid, ignorant mindset kept telling me. Well, let me tell you something. Pride and ego were my worst monsters. They may also be yours. If they are, you must kill them before you kill someone under your truck. Why? Because there is nothing more profound than holding your wife's head in your hands as she is slowly being crushed to death.

CONTACT US

Visit Our Website at: http://www.randywiens.com
Or Write Us at Our Email Address: randy@randywiens.com

BOOK

Now I Know Who I Am – A Work In Progress.
We value your feedback. Write to us at our email address above.
Additional copies can be purchased from our website. You can purchase them online, or if you prefer, you can fill out an order form from the website and mail it with your payment.

VIDEO

Randy has developed *Monsters At The Gates*. It is a profound and honest educational video on drunk driving—Randy recreates the actual accident scene in which his wife is killed—and he is the driver. He describes in bone-chilling detail how he holds her head gingerly in his hands—while he struggles to dig her out—in the dark—in the middle of the night—as the rest of her body is slowly being crushed to death by their overturned truck. This video is a must see for every driver no matter what the age.

Visit our website for more information — or to order a copy.

SPEAKING ENGAGEMENTS

Randy conducts **motivational speaking engagements** to share his story with others first hand. He offers various speaking packages to high school and college groups, amateur and professional athletic groups, church groups, drunk driving schools, and other groups interested in his story. He is dynamic as he reveals the irreversible consequences of drinking and driving. He is inspirational as he encourages others to seek help from others instead of battling life's monsters alone. He is passionate, in that, no human is invincible.

Please visit our website for more information.

DATE DUE
